Military R&D after the Coid War

NATO ASI Series

Advanced Science Institutes Series

A Series presenting the results of activities sponsored by the NATO Science Committee, which aims at the dissemination of advanced scientific and technological knowledge, with a view to strengthening links between scientific communities.

The Series is published by an international board of publishers in conjunction with the NATO Scientific Affairs Division

A Life Sciences **B Physics**	Plenum Publishing Corporation London and New York
C Mathematical and Physical Sciences **D Behavioural and Social Sciences** **E Applied Sciences**	Kluwer Academic Publishers Dordrecht, Boston and London
F Computer and Systems Sciences **G Ecological Sciences** **H Cell Biology** **I Global Environmental Change**	Springer-Verlag Berlin, Heidelberg, New York, London, Paris and Tokyo

PARTNERSHIP SUB-SERIES

1. Disarmament Technologies	Kluwer Academic Publishers
2. Environment	Springer-Verlag / Kluwer Academic Publishers
3. High Technology	Kluwer Academic Publishers
4. Science and Technology Policy	Kluwer Academic Publishers
5. Computer Networking	Kluwer Academic Publishers

The Partnership Sub-Series incorporates activities undertaken in collaboration with NATO's Cooperation Partners, the countries of the CIS and Central and Eastern Europe, in Priority Areas of concern to those countries.

NATO-PCO-DATA BASE

The electronic index to the NATO ASI Series provides full bibliographical references (with keywords and/or abstracts) to more than 50000 contributions from international scientists published in all sections of the NATO ASI Series.
Access to the NATO-PCO-DATA BASE is possible in two ways:

– via online FILE 128 (NATO-PCO-DATA BASE) hosted by ESRIN, Via Galileo Galilei, I-00044 Frascati, Italy.

– via CD-ROM "NATO-PCO-DATA BASE" with user-friendly retrieval software in English, French and German (© WTV GmbH and DATAWARE Technologies Inc. 1989).

The CD-ROM can be ordered through any member of the Board of Publishers or through NATO-PCO, Overijse, Belgium.

Series 4: Science and Technology Policy – Vol. 6

Military R&D after the Cold War

Conversion and Technology Transfer in Eastern and Western Europe

edited by

Philip Gummett
University of Manchester,
Manchester, U.K.

Mikhail Boutoussov
UNIDO,
Vienna, Austria

Janos Farkas
Technical University of Budapest,
Budapest, Hungary

and

Arie Rip
University of Twente,
Enschede, The Netherlands

Kluwer Academic Publishers

Dordrecht / Boston / London

Published in cooperation with NATO Scientific Affairs Division

Proceedings of the NATO Advanced Research Workshop on
Military R&D after the Cold War: Conversion and Technology Transfer in
Eastern and Western Europe
Budapest, Hungary
27–31 August, 1994

A C.I.P. Catalogue record for this book is available from the Library of Congress.

ISBN-13: 978-94-010-7275-5 e-ISBN-13: 978-94-009-1730-9
DOI: 10.1007/978-94-009-1730-9

Published by Kluwer Academic Publishers,
P.O. Box 17, 3300 AA Dordrecht, The Netherlands.

Kluwer Academic Publishers incorporates the publishing programmes of
D. Reidel, Martinus Nijhoff, Dr W. Junk and MTP Press.

Sold and distributed in the U.S.A. and Canada
by Kluwer Academic Publishers,
101 Philip Drive, Norwell, MA 02061, U.S.A.

In all other countries, sold and distributed
by Kluwer Academic Publishers Group,
P.O. Box 322, 3300 AH Dordrecht, The Netherlands.

Printed on acid-free paper

Softcover reprint of the hardcover 1st edition 1996

Table of Contents

Preface

Countries establish defence industries for various reasons. Chief among these are usually a concern with national security, and a desire to be as independent as possible in the supply of the armaments which they believe they need.

But defence industries are different from most other industries. Their customer is governments. Their product is intended to safeguard the most vital interests of the state. The effectiveness of these products (in the real, rather than the experimental sense) is not normally tested at the time of purchase. If, or when, it is tested, many other factors (such as the quality of political and military leadership) enter into the equation, so complicating judgments about the quality of the armaments, and about the reliability of the promises made by the manufacturers.

All of these features make the defence sector an unusually *political* industrial sector. This has been true in both the command economies of the former Soviet Union and its satellites, and in the market or mixed economies of the west. In both cases, to speak only a little over-generally, the defence sector has been particularly privileged and particularly protected from the usual economic vicissitudes. In both cases, too, its centrality to the perceived vital interests of the state has given it an unusual degree of political access and support. The result has been the build-up, since the Second World War, of formidable capacities for the development, design and construction of armaments, closely interlocked with major political, bureaucratic and military interests. It is against that background that, loosely following former US president Eisenhower, we can speak of the build-up in a number of countries of military-industrial complexes (MIC).

The basic objective of the MIC is to serve the political goals of a country or a group of countries with particular reference to defence goals. Our concern in this book is with what happens to that complex, and particularly to its industrial and scientific and technological components, when the international environment changes radically, so altering the defence goals of the state, and hence the access to economic resources and political power of the industrial interests within the MIC. Just such a change occurred, of course, in the late 1980s and early 1990s with the end of the Cold War, the dissolution of the Warsaw Pact, and the breakup of the Soviet Union into independent republics.

Leaving aside the argument that investment in defence industries represents a wise 'insurance policy' by states, there have traditionally been three groups of arguments which have sought to establish the economic significance of military industries:

- Military industries create well-paid and highly skilled jobs, and reduce unemployment;
- Military industries originate technologies which can be used for civil applications (the 'spin-off' argument);
- Armaments exports may generate a substantial income for the exporting country.

Against this, it has often argued that the overall social value of military products is negative - that is, that they do not increase the quality of life in the broader sense of this phrase.

The first argument above has often been invoked in those political situations where the share of national wealth enjoyed by the MIC is called into question. The second, while frequently heard, has been at best problematic, it having been claimed in particular that the argument does not apply to economies in stagnation or to only slowly developing economies, which is to say, to the majority of countries in the world. And while the international arms trade may be indeed a source of income for a given country, a more complete cost-benefit analysis, taking political as well as economic dimensions into account, can identify off-setting disadvantages, such as putting at risk the availability of international economic aid, or increasing the level of political instability in that country's own region of the world.

With the end of the Cold War, coinciding with the global economic recession of the 1980s-90s, defence budgets in many countries have been sharply reduced. These budgetary cuts have transposed some of the earlier political arguments about disarmament and arms control into economic arguments about the future of defence industries. The key questions have become: what to keep (and how); and what to do about the unwanted remainder? From the latter question stems the subject of this book, namely, that special case of industrial restructuring known as defence conversion.

Conversion should be viewed as a long-term process, requiring careful policy preparation, and with implications for overall economic performance which are not straightforward to assess. At the same time, the released economic potential is huge, with military expenditures in the NATO countries, for example, falling by 15 per cent in real terms between 1985 and 1994. For the Eastern European and Commonwealth of Independent States (CIS) countries, the situation is less clear, basically due to a lack of reliable figures. Russia is overwhelmingly the major country among this group. Some estimates put military related expenditure at between 25 and 50 per cent of GNP during the final years of the USSR; other, NATO, sources put the figure at 17% at the beginning of the 1980s, falling to 12% in the early 1990s. In terms of jobs, the Soviet MIC employed over 6 million people in the mid-1980s, about 72% of whom were in Russia and 18% in Ukraine, with the corresponding figures for the USA and Western Europe being about 3 million and 1.5 million. These figures show clearly the greater magnitude of the conversion problem for the countries of the Eastern Europe and the former Soviet Union than for western countries, even if for the latter, as we shall see, the difficulties are extremely acute in certain regions. The scale of the problem, and the disparities between east and west, make the problem of conversion a major issue for the economic, political and social balance and stability of Europe in its entirety, and for the countries of North America.

WHAT IS CONVERSION?

Conversion is here understood as a set of measures enabling a country to transform its formerly military-oriented industries and R&D institutions into commercially viable, competitive and civil oriented entities. In different countries, the scope and diversity of conversion processes depend upon several factors:

- the degree of 'militarisation' of the national economy;
- the level of development and overall stability of the national economy;
- the social and political situation including relations with foreign countries;

- the indigenous experience and availability of expertise in industrial restructuring at different operational levels, viz., *policy, institutional, and enterprise levels.*

The experience of conversion activities in many countries, as we shall see, shows that strenuous but isolated efforts at each of the above operational levels rarely lead to success. For example, a realistic and cost-effective conversion program designed for a given enterprise may fail if not supported by adequate measures at higher levels. Similarly, political decisions on the de-militarisation of the national economy cannot, by themselves, initiate efficient conversion of individual enterprises and secure their success. This was clearly demonstrated in Russia in 1992 when, after a radical decision taken by Mr. Y. Gaidar's government to reduce military procurement by 80%, only a few successful conversion projects began.

In order to overcome the multiple economic, managerial, financial and technological problems that hinder conversion activities, constructive coordination of efforts is needed between the three operational levels listed above. At the *enterprise* level, it is important to relate the implementation of concrete conversion projects to dynamic changes in global and national economies (such as technology trends, markets, investment opportunities etc.). At the same time, any positive results from projects at the enterprise level should be reflected at the *policy* and *institutional* levels, as also should the lessons from any negative experiences.

OBJECTIVES AND STRUCTURE OF THE BOOK

The aim of this book is to summarise international experiences in conversion gained at the three operational levels, to offer some conceptual analyses that may help in the construction of policy frameworks, and to identify some practical possibilities and proposals for decision makers and managers of conversion projects. By these means, we hope to contribute towards increasing the effectiveness of conversion, reducing the investment risk, and, particularly in the countries of central and eastern Europe and the former Soviet Union, contributing to the overall success of the transformation of their economic circumstances.

The book arises from papers presented at a NATO Advanced Research Workshop in Budapest in August 1994, organised by the editors. It begins with two thematic chapters which address, respectively, developments in Eastern and Western countries. Four chapters then follow which further elaborate analytical approaches and empirical context relevant to our subject. Part Two of the book offers substantive empirical discussions of developments in a variety of western and eastern countries.

The editors are grateful to the NATO Scientific Committee, and the Scientific Affairs Divison, for the award of the grant that made the Workshop possible, and for their patience in awaiting the publication of this volume, itself a learning experience in East-West cooperation. We are also grateful to all the participants in the Workshop, both those whose papers are reproduced here, and those whose papers, for one reason or another, it has regrettably proved impossible to include. Special thanks are also due to Mrs Christine Brown for coming to terms so rapidly with the intricacies of camera-ready copy.

Conversion Strategies in Eastern Europe and the former USSR: a thematic overview

MIKHAIL BOUTOUSSOV

United Nations Industrial Development Organisation
Vienna, Austria

INTRODUCTION

This is the first of two thematic chapters which introduce perspectives on the subject of defence conversion from the East and the West. The plan of this chapter is as follows:

First, a systems representation of an enterprise is introduced. This helps us to analyse how conversion affects the main subsystems of a former military enterprise. The elements of the system that will be addressed are the goal setting subsystem, the technology base, the human resource base, the structure, and the management.

Second, this approach is used to analyse and compare different conversion concepts and strategies proposed in recent years.

Third, various possible ways to elaborate a sound conversion project at the enterprise level are discussed. Three specific domains in conversion project design/implementation are described. These concern the inter-relations between potential markets, necessary investments and the 'technological gap' between available military technology and its potential civil analogues.

Fourth, concrete conversion activities are described and analysed, drawing principally upon experience from Russia, but with observations from other countries. Examples are presented based upon regional policy in the conversion of military industries and institutions in St. Petersburg; conversion support infrastructures in Bratislava and St.Petersburg; and experience of German and Russian participants in conversion projects.

Finally, the role of international cooperation and foreign investment in conversion is considered, once more on the basis of concrete examples.

Source material for the chapter is taken from various papers that were presented at the NATO ARW in Budapest, some of which are reproduced in full later in this volume, others of which are not. It is convenient here, then, and also a pleasure, to acknowledge the contributions of Prof. T. Cronberg, Ms. K. Vassilopoulos, Mr. K. Karzmarczyk, Mr. H. Schmidt-Bischoffshausen, Mr. S. Naryshkin, Mr. G. Altshuler, Mr. V. Ivanov, Ms. K. Simeonova, Ms. G. Karas, Prof. M. J. De Meirleir, and Mr. H. Semerad.

P. Gummett et al. (eds.), Military R&D after the Cold War, 1–32.

HOW CONVERSION AFFECTS AN ENTERPRISE SYSTEM.

Following Kast and Rosenzweig (1985) any enterprise can be represented by five mutually overlapping and interacting subsystems:

- goal setting;
- enterprise structure;
- technology base;
- human resource base;
- management.

Conversion is a profound transformation which moves the enterprise to a completely new environment (that of the competitive market) and a new market sector (civil-oriented goods and services).

The goal-setting subsystem

Let us consider the first subsystem, which is responsible for elaboration of the enterprise's goals and values. The enterprise is immersed in a specific social, political and economic environment typical for a given country. Since the main goals of any company are defined by the requirements of this environment, changes in the basic political/economical setup, such as the transition from centrally planned to market economy, creates severe problems even for many civil enterprises. In order to re-adjust their goals to the new reality, these enterprises have had to initiate serious changes, such as divestment and privatisation.

For a military enterprise, specific problems in changing its goal setting subsystem are caused by the nature of conversion. In all countries, regardless of economic system, the ultimate goal for military products is 'performance at any cost'. All other determinants, including economic factors, are secondary. Through its goal-setting subsystem, the military company communicates with its ultimate customer, the state.

In the USA, these relations are described as involving a very strong influence from the Department of Defense (DOD) upon the structure and functioning of the defence industry (see Cronberg, this volume). A specific feature of the US military industry is its decisive relationship to this single customer. It is the most important determinant of the military industry in USA, because the DOD's power permits it not only to directly set up the specifications of the military products but also the rules under which business is transacted. This is not to argue that the private defence firms have no market power. However, they exercise their power in the context of the rules set by the government.

Contrary to pure market principles, work from the DOD is acquired not only on the basis of bidding for contracts, but also through direct allocation to firms within the MIC. Indeed, more than 65 percent of all defence contracts are awarded in this way.

In the context of Eastern Europe and the former USSR, the relations between the state and its military suppliers were even more rigid. These countries were distinguished by the top-priority status that they traditionally granted to the military sector, which enabled certain shortcuts in an otherwise over-bureaucratic system. Accordingly, the defence industry in socialist countries, as opposed to the civilian industry, enjoyed good access to the best raw materials and other supplies. Military design bureaux had access to prototype production facilities and were able to make experimental models and tests before commencing the production cycle.

Quality control also differed between the civilian and the military sectors. In the latter, designs and prototypes were carefully finished and tested. The technical documentation was checked and the personal authority of the chief engineer in the design bureau enforced. The larger R&D institutes have, in fact, been functioning like prime contractors in the United States.

In contrast, a *civil enterprise* working in market economy conditions, needs a different set of goals. Its products and services normally have to satisfy several mutually conflicting requirements: cost, quality, and delivery.

In the centrally planned economies, however, even civil-oriented industrial activities were not driven purely by market requirements. Consumer markets depended upon existing industrial capacities rather than the other way round. Such 'capacity-driven', rather than 'market-driven', relations between markets and industry were not conducive to better understanding of the enterprise goals in conditions of a real competitive market. This applies even to those top industrial managers in Eastern Europe and CIS whose military enterprises have been partly involved in civil-oriented production (in Russia, about 12 per cent of consumer goods having been produced by MIC enterprises).

Conversion in the former socialist countries hence entailed a double transformation of the goal setting subsystem - a re-orientation towards civil goods and services, within an economy which itself was changing from central planning towards a market orientation. It goes without saying that such dramatic changes in the goal-setting subsystem imply substantial transformation and re-adjustment of the other sub-systems of former military enterprises.

Enterprise structure

The second subsystem of any enterprise is its structure. This defines how tasks are divided and coordinated between different departments or units. Formally, the structure is defined by organisation charts, job descriptions, rules and procedures, and is concerned with patterns of authority, communication and work flow. In military enterprises, due to the strategic importance of their activities for the state, everything was done to assure the achievement of the ultimate goal of performance at any cost. This goal could have been attained by a strongly hierarchical, well controlled pyramidal structure. However, to secure their well-being, the managers of military enterprises created multiple departments with duplicated objectives. This led to severe overstaffing and structural rigidity, which in turn required sophisticated supervisory and controlling functions to be installed into the structural subsystem.

Needless to say, all this made the structural subsystem incapable of adjusting flexibly to dynamic changes. Those who worked in military enterprises know how reluctant they were to adopt a new style of work, new technologies, or new information systems.

Technology base

The third subsystem is the technology base of the company. This includes the techniques, equipment, processes, know-how and facilities needed to transform inputs into outputs. The development level of military technologies has always been defined by the competition with the 'potential enemy(ies)'. During the Cold War, the arms race between West and East provoked permanent technological upgrading. Both in the USA and the USSR, the military authorities not only defined strict technical specifications for military products. Their supervision also extended upstream into the technological process, defining quality control procedures, requirements for the smallest components, and so on. Every possible effort was made to keep abreast with the 'world level', the achievement of which created competitive pressures within military production.

Nevertheless, despite this emphasis, the process of technology transfer and consequent enrichment of the technology base by timely acquision of the latest achievements of the world science, has been rather uneven, for two reasons.

First, any innovation brings a certain risk. For market oriented civil enterprise, technology transfer is a matter of calculated risk, a result of cost-benefit analysis. For military industry, where even a small fault might have grave consequences, such a trade-off cannot be applicable. Hence, the well-known conservative attitude of military industries towards innovation.

The second reason was, and still remains, the immense secrecy surrounding military production, which created the 'domain' structure within the military industrial sector. The exchange of novel technologies between two military enterprises belonging to different parts of the administration was a rarity. Thus, in the USSR, the ministries responsible for the different armed forces were for a long time producing their own microchips, so rendering their computer systems incompatible. In order to dominate in the arms race despite these and other obstacles, many military industries and institutions were duplicating each other, resulting in narrow specialisations and heavy budget over-spendings.

Human resource base

The fourth subsystem is called 'psychosocial' by Kast and Rosenzweig (1985). We prefer to call it the human resource base. This subsystem comprises individual employees, their behaviour and motivation, knowledge and skills, group dynamics and influence networks. In many countries, working in the defence sector was a prestigious and well paid career, the ending of which has created grave personal problems, even tragedies. Employment opportunities within the military enterprises were reserved for the best students. In Perm, for example, the students from the Perm Polytechnic Institute selected for military employment only had to move across the street to the military R&D institutes and design bureaux. However, in addition to the career, pay and privilege motivations leading the young to work in the military, patriotic reasons seem to have played at least an equal role. Accordingly, the sharp decline of the defence sector leaves in its trail a complex pattern of demotivation and disappointment.

Enterprise management

The final, and most crucial, subsystem in any company is its managerial base. This plays a central role in fulfilling the company's goals, in design and control of the enterprise performance, and in relations between the enterprise and society. Managerial functions are vital to establish or restructure the enterprise in compliance with societal needs, to enable it to perform in the most effective way. One of the hardest problems in management of conversion is to design and implement the transition of the whole enterprise system to the 'cost, quality, delivery' approach. Conversion is a serious challenge for managers. Even if some basics of the 'cost-quality' trade-off are understood by military industrial managers, their lack of understanding of 'time-based competition' is among the hardest constraints upon conversion.

Indeed, how to achieve a compromise between low cost and fast delivery/customer gratification? Customer gratification is the prerequisite in demand-driven markets. But it strongly differs from what has been demanded before from the same enterprise by its ultimate customer of military production - the state. Customer gratification in civil markets presumes fast response to diversified needs and results in small-batch manufacturing. On the other hand, low cost is another strong prerequisite, but it implies the opposite objective - large scale manufacturing of similar goods. How to deal with this contradiction? Practical experience of working with enterprises under conversion shows that introduction of a new dimension - time, encounters severe misunderstanding and reluctance.

To sum up so far, we can observe that conversion, due to the depth of its influence on the enterprise system, is rarely a simple matter of modernisation or rehabilitation, i.e., a set of incremental steps to improve one or several production parameters. Rather, it entails a deeper impact, pulling the company into completely new market sectors and into new conditions of market competition. Like re-engineering, conversion is 'a conscious reshaping of an enterprise behind a new corporate vision, the market place and the customer' (Skinner, 1994).

CONVERSION CONCEPTS AND STRATEGIES

For Eastern Europe and the CIS, the elaboration of conversion strategies started in 1992 when it became evident that any 'peace dividend' would not emerge automatically from a peaceful political course and reduced military procurement. Like the release of nuclear energy, the 'peace dividend' requires focused and intense efforts. Before 1992, there was among politicians, industrialists and economists no consistent or realistic viewpoint on how to implement conversion. Moreover, the experience accumulated by western counterparts was not fully applicable to conditions of Eastern Europe and CIS.

Where conversion efforts in Western countries have been implemented successfully, they have been more limited in scale than those in the CIS and Eastern Europe. Thus, in the mid-1980s, Soviet military efforts represented between 15 and 17 per cent of the GNP. In comparison, military efforts in the EU countries represented 3 per cent of the GNP in 1986, and 2.4 per cent in 1992. There is a qualitatively different challenge to dropping from, say, 20 per cent to 10 per cent of GNP spent on military activity, compared with, say, 5 per cent to 3 per cent (European Parliament 1993).

In addition, Western economies did not undergo an overall economic transformation simultaneously with defence conversion. They also possessed an economic and business environment conducive to industrial restructuring - networks of consulting agencies, outplacement programmes, financial institutions, etc. Moreover, the economic wealth of Western countries allowed them to commit substantial investments to conversion programmes. The estimated investment flow from West to East Germany in 1991-1996 is

$6,000 per capita of the East German population (Czinkota, 1994). Clearly, Russia will not receive an equivalent amount of Western aid which, for a population of 150 million, would amount to $1 trillion!

Since 1992, several conversion concepts and strategies have been proposed and tested in different countries. Based on our standpoint that the target and test-field of any conversion policy is the enterprise to be converted, let us compare the validity and applicability of different concepts, using the systems representation of an enterprise.

Total conversion

During visits to the regions most affected by demilitarisation of the Soviet (and later Russian) economy, several Russian politicians proclaimed, from 1991, the idea of *total conversion* of huge enterprises, industrial regions and even of so-called 'closed military cities'. On the assumption that 90 per cent of civil production, especially consumer goods, is less sophisticated than military devices and systems, they concluded that conversion is just a matter of decision and good will - that a missile factory can easily produce household electrical appliances if it so chooses.

However, on the basis of the model of the enterprise as a system, is easy to show that this viewpoint is inconsistent. Indeed, the goal-setting subsystem changes dramatically, as we discussed earlier. The *technology base and structure* both need serious simplification, and the human resource base requires re-evaluation and reduction.

The analysis of the transformations needed in the *human resources base* shows, moreover, that not all barriers to conversion are rational. The impact of mindsets and beliefs should not be underestimated. The spiritual shock may be as great as the economic one. Soviet citizens took pride in the strength of their country, its military power and its military technology. Suddenly, in the space of a few months in 1991-1992, the country showed its readiness to replace its own achievements by Western capital and technology. But instead of Western technology, humanitarian aid was sent on a large scale with global media coverage. The question of pride was even more painful for those employed in closed cities responsible for production of nuclear weapons and warheads. As pointed out by Mr. Salo, a representative of the Russian government, at an OECD conference on Conversion in Birmingham in 1993: 'The scientists working in these cities are Russia's best graduates. How can we tell these people that they are not needed? That they are cast overboard? If we do this we do not know what would happen.'

Transformation of the *management subsystem* is equally difficult. It is increasingly appreciated that the hardest task of conversion is not the adaptation of technologies, nor even the restructuring of enterprises, but rather the alteration of the mindsets and stereotypes of the managers.

To produce commercially viable, simple but marketable products such as knives and forks or shampoo is not the kind of complex technical task the Russian military industrial managers were proud of solving. The conflict between the tasks of conversion and professionalism was clearly expressed at a trade exhibition in Birmingham, UK, in 1993. Russian military enterprises presented their most advanced conversion projects on a very high technical level in order to make contact with British and European firms interested in joint ventures. However, the Russian participants felt humiliated that only defence experts, journalists and peace activists bothered to turn up.

At a conference parallel to the exhibition, an American consultant specialising in high technology suggested that the Russians were like wax, and advised Western companies to behave well in their contacts with Russian counterparts. His position was that Russian engineers and scientists should start conversion with 'little things', rather than with ambitious high tech projects. This provoked the Russian scientists present, who emphasised that they were high level professionals who would not have to beg the West for technological aid. 'You underestimate us, do not send us biscuits. We will enter the world market as a high tech nation. We shall come into the market independent of what the Western partners think. We don't want to start with simple, little things', retorted the head of an aviation firm. This spirit was re-emphasised by Mr. Salo: 'We feel offended. We are not soft wax. The West can come with all their advice, but profit and money making are not the only thing. We are proud to be professionals. We want to demonstrate something, which the whole of our society will be proud of'.

However, the overall situation with the management sub-system is not without hope. Today's directors of the Russian MIC are heterogeneous. The interests of the older generation, who know how to work only in a bureaucratic system, differ from those of the new generation of managers interested in Western style management and independent foreign relations. The leaders of research institutes and design bureaux have different interests from the large production enterprises. Being more flexible, the former are more suited to small scale developments, contract work and pilot scale productions. The latter often comprise conglomerates of tens of thousands of workers in vast neighbourhoods with kindergartens, cultural facilities and the like. There are obviously also some branches of industry which are easier to convert than others (as we discuss below).

Changing production from 'tanks to tractors' - the familiar example - is not, therefore, an easy matter, a mere down-scaling of technological complexity. Equally complex transformations have to occur in the other sub-systems of a converted enterprise, making total conversion, in many cases, a painful and hardly realistic option.

'Hands-off' approach.

Under this approach, instead of trying to take care of everything in a converting enterprise - from keeping its hierarchical structure intact to defining its new product mix - the government leaves the enterprise alone to face its problems. This approach generates different levels of 'shock' in different countries. In East Germany, under the guidance of 'Treuhandanstalt', it was common practice to treat former military enterprises like bankrupt firms. A leading electronics firm was transferred to a trust management of a financial group for a nominal price of one DM, the only condition being that there should be no unemployment of the workforce.

In the Czech Republic and Slovakia, military plants were encouraged to present 'survival plans' to a national competition. The winners received soft loans for realisation of their plans. Similar procedures have been arranged in Russia for several sub-sectors of the MIC. In both examples, however, regardless of to whom the responsibility for the elaboration and implementation of conversion is transferred, the state eschews detailed involvement and concentrates solely on the macro-economic issues.

A typical example of a 'success story' is conversion of the tank plant in Neubrandenburg, in former East Germany. Several new companies, created on its original premises, optimally utilise existing technical and human resources. They operate in the following fields:

- scrapping heavy machinery, disposal of ammunition, large scale metal constructions;
- tailor-made closed truck bodies for different lorries;
- manufacturing of windows and facades from aluminium and steel profiles and plastic profiles;
- renovation of houses and installation of security systems;
- steel boxes and light-steel constructions;
- cranes and load-moving equipment and components;
- deep-water aeration systems;
- heat generation from gas and oil;
- assembly of machines tools and heating systems;
- project planning, project start-up services, soft- and hardware for industrial applications.

In other words, the Neubrandenburg project was a typical example of company re-engineering.

As another example, in Slovakia, neither government nor other bodies possessed adequate resources and expertise for designing and implementing sound re-engineering projects for former military enterprises. Hence, many of the 'survival plans' which received soft loans and credits did not achieve significant benefits. In fact, many conversion projects ended up as attempts to implement total conversion. At the institutional level, Slovakia also lacks many crucial components, such as consulting services capable of making diagnostic studies and performing audits, preparatory to developing feasibility studies for different restructuring options, or advising on investment/partnership opportunities, including international cooperation.

Conversion and privatisation

In Russia, the divestment of the military industrial complex began in 1993-94 with the first reorganisations of large state-owned enterprises and their re-registration as joint stock companies, with 100 percent of their equity owned by the government, and a corporate charter and board of directors. Initially, the boards comprised representatives of the Property Fund (the government selling agency), the management, and the workers, but no outsiders. The Corporatisation Decree, signed by President Yeltsin in May 1992, was correctly viewed as the first major step toward subsequent privatisation of state firms.

Parallel to incorporation, divisions of state firms acquired the right to become independent (spin-off) companies. This, however, proved to be rather difficult because of resistance from the management of the parent company and local officials. Nonetheless, such an approach can be one of the most successful in conversion (see below).

Once a firm had been incorporated, its managers and workers were able to choose between three privatisation options. In June 1994 the first, voucher, stage of privatisation was fairly successfully completed. Already by 31 December 1993, out of about 4,000 large enterprises slated for mandatory privatisation, 2,670 had actually been registered as joint stock companies. In addition, 7,812 enterprises were incorporated on a voluntary basis. The apparent enthusiasm for incorporation among many medium sized enterprises suggested that workers and managers concluded that this strategy offers more benefits and/or better opportunities to keep control over the enterprise as compared to small scale privatisation. 981 joint stock companies were formed on the basis of subdivisions of state enterprises that previously did not have the status of a juridical person. Overall, by 31 December 1993, 11,463 joint stock companies were registered.

The next phase of privatisation is to issue, distribute and sell public shares through newly created stock exchanges. In this phase, the viability of conversion projects at former military companies will be contested. The near future will, therefore, show whether the joint stock companies are able to attract the necessary resources (financial as well as consulting) in order to implement the 'hands off' concept.

Economic conversion

This concept was proposed in 1993 by some representatives of the Russian Government. With certain modifications, it has also been considered by the Governments of Ukraine, Belarus and Slovakia. The concept proposes continuing attempts to retain and even increase international arms sales in certain sectoral and geographical niches, and the subsequent allocation of part of the surplus therefrom to conversion of other, non-competitive, sub-sectors of military industries. (It should be noted that this usage of the term 'economic conversion' is completely different from that used in the western literature, which refers to the replacement of military activity in a given geographical region by radically different economic activity - e.g., replacing a military base or major arms factory by tourism) (Southwood, 1991).

The concept of economic conversion raises concerns at several levels. At the policy level, ex-socialist countries (and not only they) have previously supplied military products and services in conjunction with other agreements, all incorporated into one package. In other words, the weaponry was supplied without international competition but as a part of more general agreement. A new situation of open international competition between different suppliers should result in new policies. Are the proponents of economic conversion ready to meet this competition? Another political factor concerns the supply of armaments to countries with unpopular regimes. Such trade may invite constraints on the flow of international support for general economic restructuring, including defence conversion.

Economic conversion may also encounter problems at the institutional level. In conditions of de-centralisation of foreign trade, and of capital flight, it is not easy to provide conditions for obligatory return of revenues received from the international armament sales, and their re-allocation to conversion of other sub-sectors of the MIC. Institutionally, this concept contains multiple bottlenecks and needs additional safeguards.

Finally, at the enterprise level, economic conversion might lead managers to think that they could still avoid changes. To verify the international competitiveness of their military goods and services might take several years, time which will be lost for sound conversion efforts. However, if economic conversion is pursued by coordinated measures at all three operational levels, government may have no alternative but to execute this approach in some sub-sectors and enterprises. As indicated by Redfern (this volume), for economic reasons, politicians should refrain from substantial development even of the export-oriented sub-sectors of military industries. But if the productivity of the military sub-sector is already higher than in the rest of the economy, then it makes sense to use that sub-sector as an export driver. This does not mean, however, that economic conversion should be used to encourage too many military enterprises. As already said, the time and effort spent fostering competitive arms production may become lost for effective conversion.

Conversion from within, or company spin-off

This concept is based on the assumption that the basic assets of military industries - technology and human resources - tend to be devalued rapidly if not involved in active recycling and regeneration. This means, in turn, that not only are the resources and expertise available for conversion strictly confined as depicted above, but so also is the time that is available to it. Consequently, it might be more cost-effective to identify and efficiently convert 10-15 per cent of the existing potential *now* rather than to initiate fully-fledged conversion programmes, after delays and hesitations, and dealing by then with outdated technologies and demoralised people.

The key element of the spin-off concept is a 'potential profit centre' (PPC). A PPC is an optimal combination of innovative and commercially viable technology, inventive capacity and know-how, combined with people having entrepreneurial capabilities. 'Conversion from within' begins with identification of the PPC and continues with its development into small or medium-sized knowledge-based companies.

The distinction, often drawn in industrial societies, between the 'service' and the 'manufacturing' sectors in terms of high skill intensity in the former, and high capital intensity in the latter, is no longer valid. A characteristic feature of post-industrial society is that the life-cycles of products are becoming shorter, whereas the life-cycles of skills are becoming become longer. The upshot is a growing number of companies with high levels of both skill and capital intensity.

In knowledge-based companies, competitiveness is achieved by new ways of combining skills and capital in order to couple a technology base into products or services. This implies that it is the knowledge base rather than the technology base that defines the chances for success.

Knowledge-based companies are more flexible and dynamic than those which are capital-intensive, or than huge R & D institutions and research departments of universities. That is why they appeared in such numbers in Western Europe and the USA, and became one of the principal tools for coping with economic recession and growing competition with South East Asia and Japan.

In these companies, the phases of research, development and manufacturing are more closely fused than in classical companies. 'Scientific entrepreneurship' is the proper definition for the management of knowledge-based companies. It implies a challenging combination of individual performance and teamwork, which is not easy to achieve. For this reason, the performance and management of such a company strongly differ from similar characteristics of both large state-owned R&D institutions and 'normal' manufacturing enterprises.

In countries with economies in transition, a substantial pool of scientists and researchers became obsolete due to the decay of state-supported activities (including military-oriented ones) and to the absence of guiding principles on how to create and manage the knowledge-based company. At the same time, this entrepreneurial and intellectual potential can be extensively used as a recovery tool for these economies.

Indeed, the development of knowledge-based companies can bring multi-faceted benefits:

- improvements in the speed and efficiency of technology transfer and commercialisation due to the insertion of a 'lubricating layer' between rigid, centrally financed R&D institutions and universities, on the one hand, and a dynamic industrial sector, on the other;
- improvements in the overall economic situation due to the decrease of the non-productive military industries, the realisation of a surplus from the research-based companies, and partial re-investment of this surplus into development of other innovations. It also stimulates re-allocation of wealth, by moving capital towards sectors of economy which are able to create more value added per given investment than can traditional sectors;
- improvements in the economic/social status of scientists and researchers and decrease of the brain drain, with consequential increase of the section of the labour force capable of bringing the country to the post-industrial level of development;
- promotion of knowledge-based companies has certain specific features, from the viewpoint of management, as compared with purely manufacturing industries;
- even despite the cost of the high-tech equipment mostly used in these companies, it is knowledge, human skills, ability to receive and use information, which represent the most significant company assets. Optimal use of these assets is a managerial challenge;
- due to the compressed product development time, the R&D phases should become shorter and cheaper, whereas the new, integration phase appears as a transitional one between the research and development phases. Creation and management of teams responsible for the implementation of the integration phase is also a new challenge for the company management;
- due to the innovative nature of the products and services provided by knowledge-based companies, their marketing strategy is rather different. Marketing becomes more pro-active and inter-active, search and development of new market niches acquire a decisive role in the success of a given company;
- the role of the individual customer, and its influence on different phases of a product development, becomes much stronger.

Company re-engineering through spin-off

Creation of knowledge-based companies as spin-offs from former military large-scale enterprises or R&D institutions, results in a fundamental re-shaping of these huge and rigid entities. It may, in fact, result in the total transformation of the initial enterprise, as in re-engineering. It differs, however, from typical re-engineering due to the crucial role played by the mobilisation of internal potential (both technological and human). Conversion from within is basically a bottom-up process combined with top-down support measures. It also differs from such incremental processes as partial restructuring and total quality management applicable to total conversion projects.

Since human resources constitute one of the major assets of knowledge-based companies, proper assessment and development of the human resource sub-system is an indispensable part of conversion from within.

West European and US experience suggests two main constraints on managers at the start-up phase of knowledge-based company development:

- inadequate awareness by the managers of the start-ups about the development problems they may face after spin-off, and about weaknesses of their company to be eliminated in order to achieve a profitable performance;
- underestimation of the role of cooperation and partnership between several similar companies in the enhancement of their technological, economic, and managerial effectiveness.

We can add that privatisation of small and potentially profitable PPCs will attract more private investors, including foreign ones, than privatisation of enitre former military enterprise. Additionally to the time factor mentioned at the beginning of this section, privatisation is another positive feature of conversion from within.

ELABORATION OF A SOUND CONVERSION PROJECT

We turn now from considering the problem of restructuring military enterprises to that of designing conversion projects. These require three major components:

- a development objective (the endpoint of the planned transformation);
- a development plan (a trajectory between the initial and final stages);
- inputs required (means and tools to attain the objective).

In addition, conversion projects often require a multi-disciplinary and case-by-case approach. This is necessary to take into account such features of the problem as

- the wide range of organisational changes involved (all possibilities from incremental improvements to the total re-engineering should be kept in mind);
- possible differences of view between personnel, managers and local/national authorities;
- unclear terms of interaction between converted enterprises and their potential civil markets.

Stereotypes should therefore be avoided. Even if a conversion project succeeds in one case, its experience cannot necessarily be projected onto a similar factory in another country or region.

A further complexity arises from the often-observed reluctance of managers of military enterprises to re-orient towards civil goals because of their belief that their mission is to support their country's global, or at least, strategic objectives, rather than to concern themselves with more mundane tasks.

This characteristic was clearly confirmed during the UNIDO Conference 'Conversion and Development', St.Petersburg, 1991, where only eight out of the thirty managers of military establishments present agreed to explore conversion opportunities and to create for this purpose a new organisation, ARCTIS (see below). A similar situation has been observed in Western Europe (Brzoska and Lock, 1992), as we shall see in more detail in chapter 2.

This reluctance by military companies is not, however, necessarily a sign of a power struggle vis-à-vis a more conversion-oriented government. It may also result from basic uncertainties on the part of managers about the probability of success in re-orientating towards civil markets.

In order to structure debate on the questions which inevitably confront every conversion project designer, we propose a certain framework to be followed in discussing the different options and drafting a sound conversion scenario.

Of the five enterprise subsystems identified earlier, three seem of prime concern:

- goal setting, especially the elements relevant to potential/existing markets for the expected civil products, and to opportunities for financing the conversion project as well as the start-up activities thereafter;
- the technology base, as one of the crucial assets requiring proper assessment/utilisation;
- the human resource base, as the most essential potential for the further development.

The managerial and structural subsystems should follow and adjust themselves to transformations of the three prime subsystems.

The combination of the two main components of the goal-setting subsystem, namely, potential markets for the new products, and the scale of investments required to enter these markets on a competitive basis, yield numerous permutations

One can distinguish, in practice, three important options:

- large markets/modest investments;
- medium markets/substantial investments;
- small markets/huge investments.

Of course, these cases are illustrative and do not exclude other theoretical options which, however, hardly arise in actual practice. Indeed, the option 'large markets/huge investments' fits such projects as gas/oil industries, mining, regional development etc., which, however, relate to clusters of enterprises rather than to one particular company.

These different options correspond, roughly, to three 'technological gaps', i.e. amounts of effort (and time) needed to transform or upgrade the existing technology base of the former military enterprise (or its spin-off) to a level which allows it to enter the competitive markets of civil goods/services.

First, if the existing technology base is of limited use to future applications, then the technology gap is huge. Accordingly, the human resource base needs either total re-qualification or a social support safety net. Total conversion costs are correspondingly heavy. At the opposite extreme, if there is no need for substantial technology modifications (so called 'dual-use' technology), the bulk of the investment goes instead into market studies, human resource development, and restructuring. In this case, the necessary investments can be comparatively modest.

Analysis of conversion projects in the West and in Russia enables us to draw some correlations between the size of the technology gap and the sub-sector to which the military industry belongs.

Small technology gap (dual-use technologies).

This applies, for example, in the space and aviation industries. Here the volume of investment is comparatively modest and normally should be used to:

- define the markets for the planned civil products (which in this case do not differ greatly from their military predecessors);
- modify the technologies;
- restructure the company (moderate incremental measures are normally appropriate);

- re-train the personnel.

If these procedures are done well, returns on investment can be expected quickly, and the investment risk is comparatively small. That is why, in the aircraft and space vehicles sectors in particular, substantial foreign investment in Russia companies had already been attracted by 1993.

Common mistakes on this scenario include the following. First, there is the so-called 'capacity-driven fallacy' (e.g., 'tanks-to-tractors' conversion). One should bear in mind that:

- not all high technologies are dual-use, easily retooled for civil applications;
- the goal setting subsystem, not the technology subsystem, has priority in deriving the optimal conversion objective. It may be easier to produce tractors rather than other possible civilian products at the former tank factory, but a rigorous analysis of existing tractor markets and the level of competitors should precede any decision.

The second mistake is specific to 'dual-use' activity. Even if only a few technological modifications are required, other sub-systems of an enterprise still may require essential re-shaping. All in all, sound restructuring, human resource development and managerial upgrading are inevitable and sometimes costly measures, and should not be under-estimated.

Medium technological gap

This type of gap exists between, for example, military and civil electronics companies. Both use similar ideas and schemes but quite different designs and components due to completely different product requirements. Substantial investments are needed in this case because the conversion scenario is more complicated, and involves the need to:

- assess the markets for several product alternatives;
- define potential profit centres;
- upgrade the managerial skills of leaders of potential profit centres;
- find partners/investors interested in joint development of profit centre into profitable company;
- assist the spin-off from the 'mother' enterprise;
- support start-up companies in their development.

As we mentioned before, this scenario also represents an alternative approach to privatisation of military assets. The major privatisation obstacle here is the high book value of assets and the lack of available private capital. The value of a profit centre being much lower than that of the whole enterprise, a return on investment is more conceivable, though still not risk-free, especially in economically unstable countries.

The military sub-sectors to which this scenario appear most applicable include instrumentation/precision mechanics; new materials; communication, optics, lasers; and some sub-classes of electronics. The most promising civil applications for these projects include: medical instrumentation/materials; environmental engineering; communication systems/devices; consumer electronics; and sports goods.

This conclusion about which are the most promising civil markets for converted enterprises with a medium technology gap was reached, independently, in late 1991 by both UNIDO and the Free Economic Zone Committee of St. Petersburg. Although the Free Economic Zone itself did not materialise at that time due to the overall policy of trade liberalisation in Russia, the Committee's analysis nevertheless deserves serious attention, not least because it was derived by Dr. A. Chubais, later First Deputy Prime Minister of Russia.

For its part, UNIDO used the list of most interesting sub-sectors for the pre-selection of projects for the UNIDO Investment Forum (St. Petersburg - Novgorod, September 1994). Of more than 100 projects selected for presentation, over two-thirds cost less than $5 million apiece and about 40 per cent cost less than $1 million. About 85 per cent had expected rates of return of less than three years, and 60 per cent had rates of return of less than 18 months.

In practical terms, the following set of actions based on identification and development of 'profit centres' as core elements of future spin-off companies, is recommended:

- Secure top management commitment and agree the direction for fostering innovation from within the enterprise. The new businesses to be pursued may include new applications of existing products, product developments and new types of customer need.
- To assist in communicating a revitalised corporate culture, encourage managers to absorb the Intrapreneurship concept, and understand that it is consistent with and complementary to a technology driven business.
- Encourage 'Intrapreneurs' to emerge from within the organisation through self selection, backed up by proven assessment centres to ensure that suitable candidates are developed.
- Establish corporate Intrapreneurial teams that are willing to expend the extra energy required in translating a new product or service concept into reality. Work to initiate a process that encourages action-oriented people in an organisation to step forward with their ideas. These teams normally cross internal organisational boundaries and provide the first indications of how management structures should realign to new market conditions. As projects develop, new profit centres emerge, possibly forming the nucleus of new business units.
- Train Intrapreneurs in the additional skills they need while they develop new products, services and ventures. Teach the skills of implementing new product and service ideas through a practical business learning laboratory which links theory very closely to practical experience. Include discussion of marketing, design, investment appraisal and speed to market, all areas of weakness in a former- military enterprise.
- When appropriate, introduce foreign partners. As the long term success of new spin-off business will depend on access to Western know-how, an important element in the Intrapreneurship programme will be the ability effectively to absorb such know-how.

In terms of the international expertise that might be required by the military company, the most essential areas are as follows:

- company diagnostic study;
- identification of profit centres;
- upgrading of managers, including on-the-job training;
- formation of technology-based companies;
- identification of partnership opportunities/ subcontracting;
- coaching the company during the take-off phase as a pilot project;
- promotion of cooperation with companies from the 'Third World'.

Large technological gap

This is the typical case for some ammunition production and heavy industries. Large investments are needed to identify and spin off any potential profit centres. Where this cannot be done, then fully-fledged re-engineering is called for.

Re-engineering is a painful, capital intensive and top-down activity which can only rarely be achieved by the enterprise itself. It requires intervention by external forces (state, special foundations, acquisition partner etc.). The products manufactured by the company after re-engineering hardly resemble those before. The investment risk is large and additional guarantees are normally required.

REGIONAL CONVERSION POLICIES: CASE STUDY OF ST. PETERSBURG

Cooperation between UNIDO and the St. Petersburg region began in 1991 when the Mayor, Mr. A. Sobtchak, invited UNIDO to organise a conference on 'Conversion and Development'. It was one of the first opportunities given to international organisations to analyse the problems of military enterprises on the verge of conversion, and to make contact with the local industrial community.

Unlike many previous activities of this type whose participants had no further mutual obligations after the event, the St. Petersburg Conference not only helped to elaborate a preliminary vision of what was later called 'Conversion through Enterprise Development', but also recommended the creation of a specialised consulting agency which would incorporate national and western experience and business culture, and represent the interests and abilities of relevant military industries and R&D institutions.

The Agency for Research Commercialisation and Technical Innovation Support (ARCTIS) was created soon afterwards between the MIC and its potential civil partners/markets. ARCTIS became a necessary and timely instrument for translating business interests and opportunities of potential Western and Russian partners. Its experience is summarised in this case study.

First, we should note that St. Petersburg was encouraged to be among the earliest regions in the USSR to act on this question because conversion was critical to its economic regeneration (Naryshkin, 1994). Some features of the region emphasise this point. Thus, St. Petersburg has a very high concentration of defence industry, science and technology, comprising 17 per cent of Russian defence production. In 1993, defence enterprises produced 65 per cent of non-food consumer products, or 40 per cent of all the consumer goods, produced in St. Petersburg. About 50 per cent of all industrial employees and two thirds of the total number of employees in machine-building were defence industry employees, and a third of the city's income came from the defence industry.

The years 1990-93 also saw the following political and economical trends:

- a steep reduction in orders for military production. (Defence production in 1993 was only 20 per cent of its 1989 level);

- disruption of economic ties within the defence sector as a result of the disintegration of the Soviet Union and the incomplete approach towards market reforms at the national level;
- employees in the defence industry fell by more than 160,000;
- political and economic uncertainty unsettled military doctrine and requirements, and therefore planning of military production;
- lack of national-level financing opportunities, and difficulties in obtaining credits and loans for conversion, increased the difficulties at the regional level.

To the people practically involved in responding to these issues, the pattern of events appeared as follows (Karczmarczyk, 1994):

1991 First serious talks about conversion. A year when the government simply cut the defence industry and promoted various concepts of conversion with neither a clear economic basis nor a defined military doctrine. This was the time of conversion utopia. 'Manager' still remained a bad word, and top military industry managers had absolutely no knowledge of economics. Many were just waiting for the good old days (and money) to return.

1992 A year of absolutely no financing, when some who wanted to survive started renting their facilities and selling everything except R&D and main products. Only a few, who had reoriented fast, launched projects that are successfully running now.

1993 Autumn. Privatisation in full force. Military doctrine adopted. The situation became more certain.

1994 Only now did people related to converted enterprises start to understand the need for a certain commitment and business opportunities, though the government still pursued the short money policy which literally allowed no R&D.

To address these problems, the city authorities developed the regional conversion programme *Towards 2000* (Naryshkin, 1994). The programme was designed to assist with the following questions:

- inventory and forecast of available capacities, facilities, equipment,labour force;
- the main targets and directions of conversion;
- inventory of defence sector enterprises, with their objectives and specific details;
- necessary measures to resolve economic, social security, environmental problems;
- opportunities for inter-regional and international cooperation in conversion implementation;
- promotion of military exports.

The sectors represented in St.Petersburg, to which this programme applies, are dominated in scale by shipbuilding, followed by radio and electronics.This latter has been developing rapidly for the last 10 years and contains capacities for dual-use products and up-to-date equipment.

The priorities for civil production have been defined as follows:

- facilities to resolve environmental problems (water and air environmental protection);
- medical equipment (diagnostic, cardiological);
- technological equipment for agricultural complex, light and food industry;
- technological equipment for city services sector;

- consumer goods (TV sets, video, refrigerators, vacuum cleaners, washing machines, cameras, furniture, etc.).

The majority of these involve the medium technology gap which, in many cases, necessitates substantial restructuring of the relevant enterprise. This therefore entails large investments, from national funds (loans, grants) or financial institutions (credits, equities), or from foreign investors/partners. The acute lack of funding and the investment crisis in Russia created one of the main obstacles to conversion in St. Petersburg and forced the regional authorities to solicit support from foreign investors, on which more is said at the end of this chapter. Several international agencies, banks and consulting companies consolidated their efforts in studying the investment climate in St. Petersburg. It was found in many cases that the success in attracting finance depended upon the ownership structure of the future enterprise. In other words, the key problem became that of privatisation of the defence sector.

Enterprises where more than half of total production is military remain federal or municipal property. Those with lesser volumes of military production can be privatised, and that would develop a competitive environment in this sector. Different privatisation options are outlined in the following sections.

CONVERSION-SUPPORTING INSTITUTIONS: 'ARCTIS' IN ST. PETERSBURG AND 'JOB CREATION' IN BRATISLAVA

Let us consider in more detail two practical attempts to promote conversion.

ARCTIS

As already mentioned, the consulting agency ARCTIS was created following the 1991 UNIDO-St. Petersburg meeting. It then spent eighteen months studying the situation, and analysing the costs and benefits of defence conversion, before moving into an active phase.

The major concept of the ARCTIS programme is assistance to small and medium size businesses emerging from converted enterprises ('conversion from within'). A standard set of consulting services facilitating this concept was established, with the emphasis on deal-making, start-up phase and project monitoring. ARCTIS believes this approach to have revealed much more potential than by launching larger-scale projects, such as may have become feasible later, once governmental support of conversion has acquired a suitable framework.

ARCTIS identified the most important fields as shown below. They are fields in which Russia has traditionally been famous, plus some additional sub-fields discovered during two further studies.

- Electronics and instrumentation, where electronics is more at the level of systems than components, since Russia is still weak in components. This very weakness, however, has led engineers to original technical solutions;
- Advanced materials primarily from shipbuilding and aerospace industries;
- Medicine: again advanced materials, e.g., implants, membranes, ultrasonic diagnostics, various detectors;

- Shipbuilding: special technological solutions previously proved to be effective if applied to civilian manufacturing;
- Software resulting from the abundance of talented mathematicians and programmers.

Since 1993, ARCTIS has found it efficient and convenient to classify potential conversion projects into six major types, each with different priorities.

Type 1. 'Brain conversion': This case arises when a group of people with the right skills can simply be hired outside of their former factory. There is no need for significant initial investment. A good example is software production where the requirements are just a few computers and some work space. While this is an attractive type, it is rare for the new company to require the entire pre-existing work team. Nor is it without problems in terms of the objective of conversion. Thus, in some cases, top programmers have been hired by companies of the Russian economic 'New Wave' or Western companies for financially attractive full-time work, but at a lower skill level. The resulting loss of skills means that this cannot be considered as conversion. Alternatively, a group might be hired for a short-term project after which there is a high possibility of it turning freelance. This is closer to real conversion, though it does not lead to full time employment. It too often leads to loss of skills, since the market for freelance programmers is not very mature. So far ARCTIS has seen only one serious case of establishing a purely software company with no prior investment - a company that works on software contracts for American companies.

Type 2. 'Brain conversion' which needs significant investment: This type is more common. It involves many elements of the previous one, but requires substantial financing in order to acquire the necessary equipment, mostly from the former employer. So far these projects have proved viable if the required initial investments are less than US $ 500,000.

This is definitely more complete conversion, because it establishes a new independent business. It does, however, require substantial preparatory work not only because this is a greenfield company, but also because it will be working in a novel social and economic environment. As well as such matters as finding accommodation, and legal registration, where local support can help, one needs professional identification of the right group of researchers, identification of a project leader and longterm monitoring of the project.

This type has proved very attractive to Westerners because of its relatively low risk, while for Russian investors it is less attractive, because they are still eager to make higher profits, and more quickly. Foreign participants in such projects also claim that they feel more secure when they are sharing the risk with Russian private finance, while also retaining rights of control.

A good example of this type of conversion is Digiton Ltd, which produces soft- and hardware for digital audio signal processing. The core team comprises former staff from the local military R&D establishment, united under a team-leader and entrepreneur, and then linked by ARCTIS with Siemens of Austria. Siemens initially gave them a small test research task, and after evaluating its quality, a larger contract was given, fully utilising Digiton's skills. The resulting products are competing successfully with well known brand names. This project was described in the magazine *Business Central Europe* (November, 1994) as a conversion success story.

Type 3. Teams which are tied to unique facilities (Intrapreneurship): A much more difficult case arises over capabilities which depend on unique or very expensive equipment, owned by a big state-owned company. It is often hard to buy this equipment even if the owner no longer needs it, and even if the business plan shows a profit of millions of dollars in a few years, usually because of a lack of incentives for the management of a state-owned enterprise. In such a case, ARCTIS has, however, the capacity to rent the equipment.

A good example is Alpha Ltd which produces various cutting instruments: knives for chicken-slaughter houses, textile and leather industry, jewellery etc. Having left their shipbuilding enterprise, they rented excellent machines and space from the shipbuilding technology giant, applied their own know-how in metallurgy and started manufacturing products which are far better in quality than similar Western products, and much cheaper. The business plan was realistic but attractive: in order to build to some 250 workers, ALPHA needed only US $ 300,000 which was due to be repaid within 10 months.

In a second case, ARCTIS has promoted a Russian holography applications project, aimed at sales to the West. Part of this project concerns holographic materials: plates, films, etc. A privatised Moscow-based company, Micron Corp. readily agreed to this partnership because it helped them to utilise a large part of their capacity for a long time.

Type 4. Projects which require partial acquisition of the enterprise: This is a yet more difficult type, and one on which little experience exists so far in the region. The reasons are well-understood: unstable property rights, fickle taxes, an underdeveloped financial and legislative system. There is some hope that 1995 would, however, prove a turning point for this important type of conversion project within the Russian economy.

Type 5. Projects which require conversion of the entire enterprise: For reasons described in detail below, this type of conversion can be initiated only in the case of dual-use technologies.

Type 6. 'Bunch of small projects' case: This is a special case. R&D institutions in Russia have many commercially viable projects, which require modest financing (up to $20,000). These projects result from core activity in which they have been successfully involved for many decades. This is a typical case for a venture capitalist to take up, but such financiers are still lacking in Russia. Russian investors are not interested in venture financing, for reasons given above, while Western investors say that feasibility studies for such projects would cost more than the investment itself.

There is a way out. One could consider as a totality the pool of projects at one enterprise, and engage Russian business experts to participate in the project, making a separate business plan for each project. In the preparatory phase, local consultants could easily identify small profit-generators provided someone brought the investment capital. This particular approach has been tested in Slovakia, in the Technology Transfer Centre (TTC) in Bratislava, to which we now turn.

Technology Transfer Centre, Bratislava

The project was sponsored by Business Creation Europe (BCE)- a private company which started in 1982 and works in Europe and North America (see Semerad chapter, this volume). Initially its focus was on small business development and mobility services for large corporations, later diversifying into revitalisation of real estate and venture capital. Core in the BCE approach is the recycling of the activities, personnel and fixed assets that are redundant to civil and military companies. New opportunities for redundant employees are identified, by attracting other companies to the site, initiating and implementing spin off companies, developing outplacement programmes, and assisting promising new entrepreneurs. The redeployment of redundant employees is vitally important in winning the co-operation of the military establishment, political parties and trade unions.

The Austrian subsidiary of BCE, Job Creation Betriebsansiedlungen GmbH, was approached by UTAR, a defence engineering company, to assist with identification and realisation of new business opportunities in the civil sector. Having agreed the scope and desired focus of the assignment, Job Creation audited the client's resources, and found that UTAR was not viable and lacked the economic base to continue. UTAR's prospective market was problematic, while its management lacked marketing experience and a western orientation. A high inflation rate meant high risks for western investors, and the production facilities and infrastructure were uncompetitive. There was also a high degree of vertical integration, lack of funds and little opportunity to build on existing specialist strengths. On the other hand Job Creation found a potential of well qualified managers and employees, skills in project management and a real estate which appeared convertible. The audit also showed motivated employees, low engineering costs, knowledge of the Eastern European market and a willingness to develop new business.

Job Creation decided to develop a project based on the development of small, mainly technology oriented businesses (Conversion from within), and to present the project to the Slovakian government and later to Western investors. The main objective was to establish a joint venture company between Western investors and UTAR, centred on the development of a Technology Transfer Centre.

The project consisted of four sub-projects:

- conversion of the building to western standards, including provision of common services needed for the operation of the TTC;
- development of the existing retraining department, creating new businesses with the employees of UTAR;
- training of the local management team;
- search for business partners.

The *common services* comprised office support, including physical facilities such as reception area, conference room, canteen and telefax, as well as administrative support such as telephone answering and secretarial services. The common services also included business advice, generally of a preliminary kind, but in principle across the whole spectrum of business problems. It was also planned to provide machinery and equipment, with the purpose of enabling the budding entrepreneurs to test their product ideas and perhaps build a prototype before formally commencing commercial production.

The TTC started with the creation of 14 small businesses employing 75 people on 1840 m2 of space. The creation of businesses will be considered later on. The range of businesses included a law firm, an advertising agency, a tax consultancy, and spin-off companies from the old UTAR such as laser equipment and software development companies and workshops for small prototype development.

For the *retraining centre*, UTAR already had one British partner. This team was enlarged by an Austrian retraining expert team. The British company was teaching the use and capabilities of computers about which the local managers had neither prior knowledge nor experience. The hands-on courses and tutorial were designed so that participants could learn for themselves how to operate the hardware and software and the use of sophisticated graphics and animation. The objective was to show how information technology could be of value to would be entrepreneurs and their employees, and to instil sufficient confidence for them to make use of it. The programmes addressed a wide variety of training needs, ranging from information technology for school graduates to business skills. Together with the local job offices, an increasing priority was to establish projects which offer retraining and counselling to workers who faced redundancy in Bratislava. The UTAR retraining centre offers today a broad spectrum of courses from those geared to preparing a competent pool of secretaries, bookkeepers, and accountants to more specialised training.

The *management* of the TTC has to have a clear goal. TTC has to be seen as a business which should show a profit in the medium term. This requires a results and profit oriented leadership which in turn has to be orientated to customer demand. The start-up entrepreneur is entitled to consider himself a valued customer of the Centre. Indeed, experience has shown that a TTC requires a good customer-user mix to guarantee synergy and commercial success.. Additionally, the TTC requires an excellent location and strategies that are coherent with regional development strategies.

The identification of potential entrepreneurs is the most difficult management problem. The direct method uses advertisements in local papers seeking prospective entrepreneurs. The indirect method involves programmes at universities and high schools. Once the potential entrepreneurs have been identified, the next step is to ensure that they have a level of knowledge which is sufficient for plans. Today most Centre managers have a fair knowledge of what the ideal primary motives for entrepreneurs are, what action they like to take, and what business activities they should concentrate on. Most start up entrepreneurs put their future careers and financial security into the business, understand customer orientation and market research and are prepared to work in teams.

One of the main tasks of the Centre Management is to establish a consulting network and to ensure the success of the young entrepreneur. The performance of the management should be measured by the survival rate of businesses in the Technology Centre, which normally should exceed 80 per cent.

The *search for new businesses* begins within the region, and within state enterprises or private corporations. The focus in UTAR was upon new knowledge-based enterprises, commercialising their existing skills. The basic ingredients of any business start-up are ideas and people. Opinions differ as to which is the most important, but clearly both are necessary if a successful venture is to be established. However it is a common mistake to assume that the person with the ideas is the right person to grow the business. Experience shows that this is generally not the case.

A better methodology is to treat the idea and people as two distinct task areas and then bring them together in a joining process in a third area which could be a Technology Centre or Technology Incubator. In order to provide a regular supply of new businesses it is important that these tasks are adequately supported.

The main difficulty with business ideas is not finding them, but identifying the potential successes. In Eastern Europe this task should be undertaken by Technology Conversion Units which requires initial external assistance and foreign investment. This means that technology conversion programmes are multi-conditional. They may include more than two major partners, need more guarantees and co-ordination etc. This, however, can lead to a lack of enthusiasm by foreign partners, compared to less risky investments such as trade and tourism. At the same time, if properly arranged, conversion through spin-off companies may be quite beneficial for all partners due to the unique nature of innovation pools and business ideas in Eastern Europe.

CONVERSION AT THE ENTERPRISE LEVEL: CASE STUDIES AND PRACTICAL OBSERVATIONS

Data on disclosed conversion deals between Russian enterprises and their foreign partners for September 1992 to March 1993 shows the overwhelming domination of the joint venture as the preferred form of partnership, compared with building a greenfield company or outright acquisition. This is probably because joint ventures bring not only vital capital, but also the opportunity to acquire rapidly the missing managerial components of market oriented activities (Vassilopoulos, 1994).

This conclusion was confirmed by the discussions held during the UNIDO Investment Forum in St. Petersburg/Novgorod in 1994. The statistics of projects proposed by the Russian sponsors again showed their overwhelming preference for joint ventures, compared with cooperative agreements, licensing, and other forms of relationship. Joint ventures, however, require two partners. And where the former military sector is concerned (except in the case of dual-use technology) foreign investors are still reluctant to invest in Russian and East European manufacturing industries. They themselves explain that there are multiple investment risks, such as low return on investment and low survival rates. Indeed, it is reported that 80 per cent of Russian-American joint ventures failed to develop to achieve profitability, and the same was reported to a conference on East-West Joint Ventures organised by the Austrian Economic Chamber in Vienna in 1991.

How to explain this low survival rate? It appears that the majority of the new companies failed to reach their planned level of efficiency, or had not taken off for reasons other than technical, economic or hardware. These 'hardware' problems are, however, explained by Vassilopoulos (1994) as the results of more fundamental factors related to managerial issues, such as inadequate interpersonal communication, and other human resource problems. Critical among these have been issues arising from cultural difficulties.

Fig.1. Framework of cross-cultural inter-relations within a joint venture company

		Desire to maintain culture	
		High	*Low*
The culture of the partner	*Attractive*	Integration	Assimilation
	Not Attractive	Separation	De-culturation

Fig. 1 offers a schematic overview of four possibilities that arise when people of different cultural backgrounds and business cultures are brought together:

- Integration: both partners are keen not only to absorb and use the best of what is brought to their common business by their partner, but are also able to critically assess and modify those components of their background which do not fit the joint venture.
- Assimilation: the culture of one partner is so much stronger than that of the other that the latter completely accepts what is brought in - the latter becomes a weak replica of the former.
- Separation: each partner is too attached to their own traditions/experience to appreciate the achievements of the other. Communication channels are limited.
- De-culturation: each partner refuses to accept the other's culture, and is incapable of absorbing from the other. In this case, the company simply fails.

Examples from an analysis based on 33 Russian joint ventures show the optimal scenario to be that of 'integration': each partner enriches the other while being fully aware of possible cross-cultural differences (Lawrence and Vlachoutsicos, 1993). Failures in a joint venture's functioning are often caused by other possible scenarios among which the 'de-culturation' and 'separation' varieties are the worst. Without exact identification and alleviation of cross-cultural differences and the various possible clashes between them, the 'seeds of conflict' tend to grow faster than the company's capability to tackle negative consequences.

In Russia, several reasons commonly hinder the achievement of the desirable 'integration scenario' (Vassilopoulos, 1994). These stem not from inherent deficiency or intentional confrontation, but from ethnical, historical and religious features of the national background. For example:

- Eastern unpunctuality, which infuriates Western managers, can be understood in terms of different cultural conceptions of time;
- Western managers expect loyalty to the company, and equate the organisation's well-being with their own. An Eastern employee may regard the interests of the individual and of the organisation to be in opposition. Hence, staff in Eastern countries sometimes combine efforts against the company and, for instance, exchange confidential information such as salary levels;
- Another example, understandable in terms of history, is the Eastern practice of saying at meetings what is expected, irrespective of personal opinions. In consequence, it is common in Eastern Europe to say what the other expects to hear, but not, of course, actually to do it. Westerners, on the contrary, are more likely to mean what they say.

These examples are not meant to imply that Westerners are always right, but only that it is a mistake to expect Eastern firms to be carbon copies of their US/West European partners.

In this respect, it is interesting to compare the observations of two participants in the Budapest meeting who have practical experience of conversion from contrasting perspectives. One is the leader of the cooperation programme launched in Eastern Europe and Russia by the German firm Daimler Benz (Schmidt-Bischoffshausen (1994). The other is a professor from St. Petersburg, and Vice President of a small knowledge-based joint venture (Altshuler, 1994).

Conversion through commercialisation of military research: experience of a German partner

In 1992, Daimler Benz began a project on R&D cooperation and technology transfer with Eastern Europe and, particularly, Russia, focusing especially on organisations with identified themselves with the strategic secrets of the former USSR. It quickly became apparent that this was not a simple task, and that it could not succeed without complete commitment, ingenuity, sophistication and endurance. Indeed, it is vital to emphasise from the outset both partners' interest in long-term and stable cooperation, and mutual technology transfer.

There have been three aims for the joint R&D projects:

- Identifying and securing outstanding, already available, R&D results, with which Daimler Benz could accelerate its own product and process developments;
- Doing supplementary high level research with Russian and East European institutes and companies, using their specialised expertise and cheaper resources;
- Mutual learning and gaining new ideas and product concepts.

The process of cooperation starts with the identification of the most attractive projects. For a better understanding of this non-trivial question, one must understand the complex R&D situation in Russia.

Besides many university research institutes distributed all over Russia, the internationally known Russian Academy of Sciences employed about 160,000 people (as of December 1992) in about 420 research institutes and 270 establishments. Even the largest German research centres, in Karlsruhe and Juelich (with about 4000 employees) appear small compared to some of the Russian institutes. The military-industrial complex with its special high tech capabilities, but also its access barriers, comprised some 5 million employees in over 2000 companies, 20 per cent of which engaged in R&D.

Daimler Benz imagined initially that, in the centrally planned Soviet economy, there would have been computerised data banks and/or central planning departments that could be tapped to support its initial search process. Unfortunately, no such supporting sources were found. Therefore Daimler Benz tried several parallel approaches:

- using Russian consultants;
- using German consultants from the ex-GDR, with excellent connections to Russia;
- hints from the German Ministry of Research & Technology;
- hints from German industry associations which were cooperating already with Eastern Europe;
- direct contacts.

During initial contacts with selected partners, different approaches to technological innovation became evident. Daimler Benz increasingly learned to understand the R&D of its Russian partners and their ways of proceeding. It became obvious that, to a much greater extent than in Western countries, innovation has been dominated by technology push rather than market pull strategies. In Russia, too many technological innovations were looking for market applications, rather than market requirements seeking technological solutions. Reversing this pattern became a key goal for the future.

The lack of a 'time-urgent' competitive spirit among Russians has already been mentioned. It was hard to explain to them that technologies are often short-lived goods, which can quickly become obsolete, if they are not continuously developed further. Under present financial and planning uncertainties, many research institutes, and their technological competences, are endangered. Seen from a German perspective, it appears important that Russia reduces its huge basic research capacities and transforms them into new market oriented business areas with R&D intensive products and services.

For Daimler Benz, the most promising areas for R&D cooperation lie in areas similar to those independently identified by UNIDO in St. Petersburg, viz.: materials and engineering structures; surface technologies; energy technologies; information technologies (in particular software); laser technologies; physical and chemical technologies; scientific instruments and equipment development.

Since 1992, Daimler Benz has established many contacts and various cooperation projects of differing sizes. So far, results have been difficult to realise, and time consuming, relative to the efforts put in. Nevertheless, continuity and endurance provided mutual success. This indeed could be the guideline for future successful cooperation in technology transfer and commercialisation.

Some of the problems encountered include:

- The technologies and research results offered were not well-enough described for evaluation;
- Technology performance data and status of applicability were often unclear;
- Legal uncertainties;
- Unclear intellectual property rights on technologies;
- Vague cost estimates and price calculations;
- Inadequate telecommunication infrastructure;

On the other hand, the following quite encouraging observations were made while working with Russian partners:

- Increased readiness and flexibility to learn and to adapt to customer needs;
- Strong business engagement in privately organised activities (outplaced groups and entrepreneurs).

These positive observations created the basis for the further involvement by Daimler Benz in conversion programmes eastward from Germany.

Conversion through commercialisation of military research: experience of a Russian partner

This case study (Altshuler, 1994) describes concrete positive experience of cooperation between a Russian company and a West European private company in a high-tech field. The goal of collaboration was to acquire the leadership in the newly emerging market of laser dental drilling instruments, new instruments which could radically change attitudes to dentistry. The results of two years of joint work are very promising, but still reveal problems which are typical for the development of similar projects.

A principal factor in success so far has been the product itself, which has a certain appeal in the medical market. Lasers are already widely used in medicine, but not yet in dental surgeries. Yet dental research in Germany and Russia suggests that lasers could compete with mechanical drills: lasers work faster, less painfully, and have other potential advantages. As with any new medical technology, one can expect a powerful financial and intellectual wave to follow the scientific discoveries and launch the new instrument. With 5 million dental surgeries globally, and assuming a price per dental laser of $10,000, the initial volume of the world market is $50 billion. The rate of opening of this market depends basically on the investment volume. In 1994, global investments for development of laser drills and technologies related to dental tissue destruction totalled less than $30 million. A ten-fold increase could result in 20 per cent of European dentists being able to buy laser drills in only 3 years time.

Hence the government organisation, Laser Centre (LC) IFMO in St. Petersburg, and the private company, LMS in Vienna, decided to enter this market. LC has over 20 years of experience in the development and production of lasers for military and space applications, and 30 years in medical applications. LMS is a small private company established by Austrian and Russian shareholders in 1992 for the development, production and sales of medical lasers. Both companies had clear goals and interests in joint cooperation. For LMS they are the creation of high-tech production of laser drills in Austria, and the ownership of intellectual property for novel technologies. For LC, they are the profitable sale of intellectual property, participation in the production of laser drills, investment in new R&D projects, and maintenance of scientific and technical potential during the present hard times in Russia.

So the goal-setting step for this cooperative project was successfully accomplished. The market niche was identified and verified, the volume of production needed to fill it was assessed, the goals of the partners were non-contradictory and mutually complementary. Work began to develop a pilot product, a multiwave laser dental station, named ONYX. However, in order to design and manufacture ONYX, LMS and LC had to create a partnership network with several other companies worldwide - a factor often forgotten by Russian project sponsors. Hence, links were formed with an Austrian electronics firm, another Austrian firm that specialised in dental handsets, a Danish design firm, and an American optical components and fibres company. Altogether, nine companies in four countries have been approached, together with the West European EUREKA research programme.

In financial terms, the initial forecast expected investment costs to be recovered in two years. But until recently, the necessary venture capital would have been unavailable in Russia. In practice, funding has been assembled from three main sources: shareholders; soft credits from a combination of Austrian banks and regional funds; and government grants for LC.

LMS planned to begin selling ONYX in Europe and Russia in 1995. The first buyers were expected to be physicians who wish to create new methods and techniques of treatment. Training centres will be established in several countries. LC will produce and supply the laser heads and optics, drawing on eight Russian plants. This offers a real chance of conversion for these plants, enabling them to engage in competition with other producers of optics, especially in the United States. Only by engaging in such international competition will real progress with conversion be made in Russia. Already Russian plants have all the necessary technologies for production of complex optical and laser equipment but level of their products is lower than the best world models. Under the ONYX project, LC will order the same optical component from a Russian contractor and from one of the best foreign firms. By comparing the two components over quality, price and terms, the Russian suppliers will be able to evaluate their perfpormance against western standards.

Within the next two years the project partners expect to supply ONYX on the Russian market as well, by setting up production in Russia similar to that in Austria on the basis of the ISO-9000 standard. They hope that it will be one of the first optical companies in Russia working to Western standards.

Of course, the development of the project has encountered many difficulties. Some arise from the general legal and regulatory context, such as the lack of complete and consistent laws regulating such cooperation; the lack of lawyers specialising on Russian-Austrian relations; the absence of an appropriate insurance system; and the fact that the customs rules in Russia and elsewhere impede the free transfer of experimental models across state borders. Additional difficulty has come from the instability of attitude of potential funding organisations towards such projects, which changes with changing political conditions. Finally, difficulties have arisen from the different prior experiences, assumptions and outlooks of the partners, and from lack of clarity over approaches to resolve disagreements. These have not, however, prevented progress, and should become easier to deal with over time.

FOREIGN INVESTMENT AND CONVERSION

The two case studies presented just above illustrate the final feature of defence conversion, viewed from the East, that we wish to address here, namely, the importance of foreign direct investment (FDI). This feature emerged from numerous contributions to the Budapest meeting, some of which are reproduced in later chapters.

Numerous high-level meetings in Russia and elsewhere concerning FDI have emphasised, on the one hand, the potential attractiveness of Russia for foreign investment and, on the other, the lack of stability in the country, and problems related to legal protection, the mafia, bureaucracy, etc. Concrete business talks between potential partners at the enterprise level, which are critical to the creation of confidence, are still uncommon.

We can consider the attractiveness to FDI of a particular conversion project as the convergence of three factors (Boutoussov, 1994): the attractiveness of the industrial sector, the region, and the enterprise. We discuss the first two of these here, the third having already been much discussed in this chapter.

Attractiveness of the sector

The attitude of investors is based on their preliminary experience of the sector, the availability of credits, and the trade-off between investment and returns (both time- and money-wise). In Russia, under the influence of concern about instability, most investment flow is channelled into trade deals *(fast return)*, infrastructure and construction projects *(high profit and governmental support)* and exploration of natural resources *(high profit)*. The attractiveness of several sectors (like gas and oil) and the huge size of projects therein can strongly improve the outlook of an entire region.

The attractiveness of specific sub-sectors depends upon the balance between the investment needed and the potential market. Hence, investments in military conversion projects focus mainly on so-called dual-use technologies, where the returns are expected sooner and investments are not high.

The attitude of the Russian partners is another factor affecting the sectoral distribution of investment projects. In St. Petersburg, this distribution is 'capacity driven', i.e. Russian sponsors tend to promote those projects which they consider most important, with the results, as already described, of an overwhlming emphasis upon joint ventures.

Attractiveness of the region

Following the consultants Ernst & Young, we may assess the attractiveness of regions to investors in terms of the following factors:

- the role of the region in the national economy;
- the regional outlook (activity and reputation of industrial community, the policy of the local government etc.);
- the quality/availability of financial services;
- human resource/management development level;
- infrastructural development;
- international image (culture, hotels, sports, etc.).

On these counts, St. Petersburg emerges among the top ten investment prospects in the world, yet actual investment is far below this level. It is evidently not enough to have a big inflow of foreign visitors to become a top investment attraction. What is wrong with St. Petersburg, Nizhny Novgorod and Vladimir? Perhaps only that their time is yet to come? For the moment, Russia's well developed technological, R&D and human resource bases are not the most critical factors in the minds of foreign investors.

In this situation, the role of local governments is both clear and difficult: they must prevent the irreversible losses of their most vital resources, chief among which are intellectual resources and R&D potential. This point assumes considerable importance when viewed against the background of world trends in the location of industry (De Meirleir, 1994).

The economic revival of the countries of Western Europe after the war was largely based on investments by large American multinationals. Then, during the last decade, new markets opened in the Far East, and low labour costs became the main attraction for new indigenous and offshore investments. The multinationals moved production to these low labour cost countries.

However, it is unclear how long this eastward trend will continue. Indeed, as with Western Europe in the sixties, Asian labour costs have increased very fast. If productivity does not follow suit, these economies might face stagnation. Moreover, by introducing new production processes, re-engineering companies, and reducing the labour content by automation and robotisation, the cost of much western production has started to fall back towards Asian production costs. Thus, microprocessors were originally fabricated, manually, in the US in the sixties. In the seventies, chip production moved to Malaysia, Taiwan and Japan. In the eighties, manual production was already being replaced by a semi-automatic process and, finally, the chip came back to the West in fully automated plants in which 'the chip makes the chip'.

A similar trend is observed in the automotive industry, but this time in Eastern Europe. Ford, General Motors, Volkswagen, and other major companies have acquired existing Eastern Europe production facilities. Labour is available, trained, and hungry for money to spend on consumer goods. While the older generation might feel nostalgia towards the protected but low-standard life under the previous regime, the younger generation, exposed to the wealth of the West, has a different and more positive attitude.

Can, however, the economies of Eastern Europe continue this evolution without falling back into the cycle of recession, ten years from now, which the West has just gone through? In other words, what resources should be applied in order to avoid the consequences of the continuous growth of labour costs, not supplemented by productivity gains? Part of the answer is that the national intellectual potential, the R&D facilities of Eastern Europe, should be mobilised in order to provide the long-term stable growth of viable and productive industries. Hence, the future of the Eastern European economies and the CIS can only be assured if the decision-makers understand that the current lack of investment into indigenous R&D threatens economic development.

Further lessons can be drawn from recent West European experience, particularly their emphasis on regionalism, and on the role therein of SMEs (De Meirleir, 1994).

Regionalism: West European countries are encouraging their regions to increase their role in economic development. This has resulted in the reinforcement of the regional infrastructure for technological transfer. Hence we see the growth of science parks and R&D parks. For example, France had three technology parks in 1980, but more than 30 today. In Germany, some 40 Business Innovation Centres were set up in the 1980s. In the UK, two science parks in 1980 grew to 36 by 1990. In the same decade Japan set up 18 technology parks. The Southern European countries were somewhat slower in the development but are catching up fast. The European Commission has received 12 applications for new parks under the *Sprint* programme; Italy has had 30 projects under study since 1991.

The increased role of knowledge-based SMEs: Small and medium-sized enterprises play a greater role than large companies in innovation, job creation and exports. In Belgium, a country that could be compared in scale with a region of Russia, SMEs accounted for 52 per cent of production, 38 per cent of exports, and 54 per cent of investment in 1992. In the last fifteen years, national, regional and European authorities have increasingly emphasised the role of SMEs especially in the field of technological transfer. In addition, the new concept of Business Innovation Centres, which provide for the integration of research, development, production and marketing, has gained in importance as an instrument of regional policy.

Case study: regional policies in St. Petersburg and foreign investment.

Let us conclude once more with a specific case, and consider again the experience of St. Petersburg, this time focusing on policy instruments for attracting foreign investments, particularly for conversion projects (Naryshkin, 1994).

More than 110 laws have been adopted in Russia since 1987 to regulate foreign investments. Nevertheless, apart from the fact that Russian legislation allows foreign investors to participate in any form of privatisation, the formation of the Russian investment legislative package is not yet complete. In this situation, the Mayor's office in St. Petersburg has chosen to concentrate on those factors which can be controlled and optimised by the regional administration itself.

Hence, the regional authorities have sought to provide a higher degree of political and social stability as compared to Moscow. The costs of goods and services are also much lower than in Moscow. The geographical location of St. Petersburg offers certain advantages. It is the most important point in the mutual rapprochement of the East and West. The city has become virtually the only large transport, communication and commercial centre in western Russia. In addition, a certain city infrastructure providing for future economic growth is already developed. In particular, banking and communication systems already exist. A system of training centres which guarantee a high level of training, and the possibility of retraining for specialists, has also been set up.

With particular reference to attracting foreign investors, plans are underway to establish by the year 2000 ten customs-free zones and three export oriented production zones. The main objective of the St. Petersburg Free Economic Zone Programme is to increase economic activity by attracting investments, and by more efficient use of the local export potential. A number of economic and legal measures are to be taken during the establishment of the Free Economic Zones. These include establishment of a commercial taxation system; reduction or cancellation of Customs duties; introduction of accelerated depreciation rates, especially for hi-tech production; and reduction of fees for the use of land and other natural resources. All of this should increase the economic attractiveness of the region to investors. The land rent, for example,will be 70 per cent lower than usual for production zones, and 40 per cent lower for customs zones.

Finally, the St. Petersburg Mayor's Office, together with the city enterprises, have been active in promoting their region internationally. Examples of recent events which they have organised, or in which they have participated, include:

- International Conference 'Investments in Russia: New Regional Possibilities', St. Petersburg, November 1993;
- Leipzig Innovation Forum, Leipzig, March 1994;
- Third Annual Meeting of the Board of Directors of the European Bank for Reconstruction and Development, St. Petersburg, April 1994;
- Exhibition of Investment Projects from the Countries of the Eastern and Central Europe, London, May 1994;
- International Conference and Exhibition on Small Business in Russia, St. Petersburg, June 21-24, 1994.
- International Conference 'East-West: Investments, Conversion, Russian Hi-Tech' (under the auspices and support of UNIDO), September 1994.

CONCLUSION

The problems of defence conversion in Eastern Europe and the CIS remain formidable. In addition to the problems faced by western defence firms, who are already used to working within a market framework, their eastern counterparts have to grapple with the wider problem of economic and political reconstruction as well as the specific problems of defence conversion. Nevertheless, much experience has now accumulated of attempts at conversion. The picture that emerges is, naturally, mixed. But on the basis of the evidence presented in this chapter, there is good reason to believe that well-coordinated action at the levels of regions, industrial sectors and enterprises, together with support from the national level, can succeed. What is essential now is to learn from the experience accumulated to date and, in so doing, to build more

surefootedly and confidently for the future. As the possibilities for cooperation between east and west improve, defence enterprises, with their strong emphasis upon R&D and high technology, remain among the most attractive prospects for such new ventures.

REFERENCES

1. Altshuler, G. B.(1994) Joint East-West High-tech Company - A Practical Experience. Paper presented to the NATO Advanced Workshop 'Military R&D: Conversion and Technology Transfer'. 23-31 August, Budapest.
2. Boutoussov, M. (1994) Industrial Restructuring in Russia and Role of Foreign Investments. Presentation at the Conference 'Meet the Government of Russia', 22 October, Brussels.
3. Brzoska, M., and P. Lock (eds) (1992) *Restructuring of Arms Production in Western Europe*. SIPRI, Oxford University Press.
4. Czinkota, M.R. (1994), Changes in Eastern Europe- Is the West Ready?. Presentation at the meeting of the International Council of American Management Association, 8-12 October 1994, Budapest
5. De Meirleir, M. J. (1994) R&D: A Major Factor to Attract New Investments. Paper presented to the NATO Advanced Workshop 'Military R&D: Conversion and Technology Transfer', 23-31 August, Budapest.
6. European Parliament (1993) *European Armament Industry: Research, Technological Development and Conversion*. Final Report. Luxembourg:European Parliament, Directorate General for Research, November.
7. Kast, F.E., and J.E. Rosenzweig (1985) *Organisation and Management. A Systems and Contingency Approach*. McGraw Hill,.
8. Ivanov, V. (1994) Commercialisation of the Low-Orbit Satellite Communication System SIGNAL. Paper presented to the NATO Advanced Workshop 'Military R&D: Conversion and Technology Transfer', 23-31 August, Budapest.
9. Karczmarczyk, K. (1994) Three Years of Experience in Defence Conversion in St.Petersburg. Paper presented to the NATO Advanced Workshop 'Military R&D: Conversion and Technology Transfer', 23-31 August, Budapest.
10. Lawrence, P., and C. Vlachoutsicos (1993) Joint Ventures in Russia , *Harvard Business Review*, Jan.-Feb, pp.44-54.
11. Naryshkin, S. (1994) Problems of Conversion and Opportunities for Attracting Investments to enterprises under Conversion in St.Petersburg. Paper presented to the NATO Advanced Workshop 'Military R&D: Conversion and Technology Transfer', 23-31 August 1994, Budapest.
12. Schmidt-Bischoffshausen, H. (1994) R&D, Cooperation and Technology Transfer in Daimler-Benz with Russia. Paper presented to the NATO Advanced Workshop 'Military R&D: Conversion and Technology Transfer', 23-31 August, Budapest.
13. Skinner, C. (1994) Does Re-engineering Equal Success?, *Focus on Change Management*, No.1, January, pp.3-6.
14. Southwood, P. (1991) *Disarming Military Industries: Turning an outbreak of peace into an enduring legacy* London: Macmillan.
15. Vassilopoulos, K. (1994) Managing Across the Cultures: East-West. Paper presented to the NATO Advanced Workshop 'Military R&D: Conversion and Technology Transfer', 23-31 August, Budapest.

West European defence industrial policy after the Cold War

PHILIP GUMMETT*

Department of Government
University of Manchester
United Kingdom

INTRODUCTION

Until the late 1980s, the size and shape of western defence activities reflected the specific geopolitical circumstances of the Cold War. As these circumstances changed, the defence sector suffered not just a loss of demand, but a loss of coherence. The military strategies and force structures pertinent to defending against massed attacks from the East lost their relevance. It became less clear how to organise military forces in response to the more diffuse set of risks that have emerged. This is true in relation both to the possibilities of threats from weapons of mass destruction, and the use of national armed forces in multinational coalitions, such as the burgeoning United Nations interventions and NATO's intervention in Bosnia.

Defence planning has become extremely difficult. So, consequently, has the formulation of coherent policy towards the defence industries.

In sharp contrast to the countries of eastern Europe and the former USSR, which face corresponding problems, defence conversion has generally not been at the centre of western debates about the future of the defence sector. Of course, there has been analysis and political activity on this subject, as later chapters show. But within the market economies of the west, the defence industrial sector has to a considerable extent been treated as just another sector whose environment has changed (like steel, coal or automobiles), leaving it in need of restructuring and rationalisation according to well-established market principles. Moreover, in scale it has never dominated western economies as it has in the East. Accordingly, the consequences of reductions, while serious, have rarely been as catastrophic as in the East, at least at the national level, even if the same has not been true within certain regions. Instead, the western debate has turned largely on strategies for

P. Gummett et al. (eds.), Military R&D after the Cold War, 33–49.

restructuring the defence sector within the framework of new geopolitical and budgetary circumstances, and at a time of changing relations between technologies of military and civil origin. While not so central to national economic survival as the corresponding debates in the East, the western debate has, however, also not been easy to pursue.

Since the end of the Cold War, Western countries have found it difficult to identify military requirements in a coherent fashion, and then to find the necessary funds at a time of public pressure for cuts. When 'the threat' came clearly from the Soviet Union, it was possible to plan fairly straightforwardly. Moreover, because of the scale of forces assembled to deal with that threat, lesser defence problems could be managed with some configuration of forces drawn from the large total. But the single large threat has now been replaced by multiple smaller, but less clearcut, 'risks'. Not only is it difficult to know what to plan for, but the forces available will be much smaller than in the past, thus reducing the scope for withdrawing elements of the total to meet particular eventualities. If it could be confidently assumed by each country that it would meet all conceivable eventualities in the company of the same fixed set of allies, then a division of labour might be agreed. But even this seems implausible at present. Hence the profound uncertainty that grips defence planners and, by extension, those responsible for planning defence research and development (R&D) and for managing the defence industry.

Governments and international organisations are, therefore, facing profound challenges in the security field, including the need to:

- redefine national security and strategic priorities;
- reduce defence industrial activity while maintaining appropriate levels of capability, nationally and internationally;
- convert the capabilities that lie in the defence sector, so that they can flourish in the civil sector;
- control the international flow of militarily-related equipment and know-how without prejudicing legitimate trade and economic development.

Chapter one set the scene for the conversion debate with particular reference to Eastern Europe and the countries of the former Soviet Union. This chapter does the same for the countries of Western Europe and, to some extent, of North America. We shall not go in much detail into conversion strategies and practice, partly to avoid repetition of some of the more schematic material in chapter one, and partly to leave the empirical detail to the chapters in Part Two. We shall focus instead at a more general level on the ways in which western defence industries and governments have responded to the end of the Cold War, thus outlining the context within which discussion of conversion in the West can be understood. That is, we shall address certain themes relevant to the second and third of the problems listed just above.

IMPLICATIONS OF DEFENCE CHANGES FOR R&D

All the countries that were involved in the former Cold War have been making deep cuts in their defence forces and supporting structures. We shall not go into those here. The essential point to note, however, at least as regards western European countries, is *how little difference* these cuts are making to the shape of the inventory of new equipment requirements of the USA and the larger European states. There are some important exceptions, such as the new emphasis on command, control, communications and intelligence, on space surveillance and communications, and on defences against weapons of mass destruction, offset by some reductions in nuclear weapons. But most major programmes are being kept in place, albeit stretched out in time and often with a reduced number of units.

At the level of R&D, and especially 'R', governments responded initially to the post-Cold War conditions by asserting the importance of maintaining high levels of technological competence, if not necessarily pushing this through into finished products. For example, in a speech in September 1991, the then British Minister of State for Defence Procurement, referring to the importance of developing a 'reconstitution capability' as an element of defence strategy, suggested that 'we might also consider whether to give R&D greater priority within the defence budget.' (Clark, 1991). He added that he was not proposing a flood of new money, but rather was wondering

> whether we should not be researching new technologies and demonstrating them, while not automatically taking them into Full Development as before. We would therefore be thinking in terms of giving pure research, and technology demonstration, greater priority.

Such ministerial speculation gave pause for thought about assuming that defence R&D would necessarily be cut at the same rate as the rest of the defence budget. This position was also consistent with that in the USA where the ratio in 1985 of $1 spent on R&D for every $3 on procurement, was expected to change by 1995 to a ratio of less than one to two (Van Atta, 1994).

The overall turbulence of defence policy is making it difficult for clear lines of R&D policy to emerge. In addition, various indequacies of statistics, such as the very limited projections which most countries are prepared to publish, lack of information about industrial spending, and difficulties of accounting for dual-use projects, also complicate the task of analysis. Nevertheless, it does seem that western European governments are indeed protecting their defence research, at least relative to the rate of reduction of defence budgets in general (GRIP, 1993).

Let us review the position in selected countries, noting in passing, however, the important differences in relative scale of equipment and R&D spending that characterise these states, with the leading European spenders, France and the UK, being an order of magnitude below the world leader, the United States:

- In Britain, defence R&D is planned to fall between 1987 and the turn of the century by about one-third. However, within this total, defence research is expected to fall by only 15 per cent by 1998 (Cabinet Office, 1994, para.3.10). Spending on defence as a whole, in contrast, is expected to fall by 14% in real terms between 1992-93 and 1996-97 alone. Within these totals, there is to be a 'modest though noticeable shift away from areas of research on platforms (such as ships and aircraft) towards research on weapons and sensors.' (Ministry of Defence, 1994, para.437 and 505).

- In France, the defence minister aimed in 1992 to maintain defence research at at least 6 per cent of what, under the 1992 Loi de Programmation, was planned to be a slowly declining equipment budget (Info-DGA, 1992, p.5). Within this envelope, there was to be a marked switch from nuclear to space and intelligence related activities, and redundancies were announced at the main French nuclear weapons research establishment, though even here the cuts appeared to be concentrated in administration and production rather than research (Dawkins, 1991). There is no clear evidence of significant cuts otherwise in conventional defence R&D. Overall, French spending on defence R&D has remained for several years at about 33-34% of procurement expenditure. However, deeper cuts in the defence budget were proposed by the Juppé government in 1995, with as yet unclear consequences for defence R&D.
- In Germany, where the absolute level of military R&D spending has of course been much lower than in the UK and France, reductions are planned, but these are likely to be very much less than planned cuts in procurement. Thus, whereas procurement spending is expected to fall by about half between 1989 and 1994 (a much higher figure than for the UK), R&D spending is expected to fall by only about one sixth.

INDUSTRIAL DEVELOPMENTS

The future west European capability in defence technology depends not only on the policies of governments but also on the decisions of companies. This is not because of industry's role as a sponsor of defence technology, where it plays a minor part compared to governments, but rather because in every country it is in industry rather than government that most of the *physical* capability is to be found.

Industry responds to different pressures than those operating on governments. Accordingly, while the US and European governments have been gradually revising their defence policies over the past several years, defence industrial companies have been moving ahead more rapidly in order to try to maintain their own viability. In the European context, in particular, these developments are important at various levels:

- they influence the defence capability of Europe as a whole, as well as that of individual states;
- they affect the economic security of states, both in terms of direct effects (such as jobs) and by altering the general attractiveness of a country, or of regions of a country, for high technology investments, according to the 'cluster' theory of Porter (1990), and the arguments of Reich (1990) over the importance of maintaining a skilled workforce as a magnet for such investments;
- for both political and economic reasons, therefore, the protection of national defence industries is a natural concern of most governments, but this concern runs against those currents in European politics that are flowing towards greater integration;

- they influence the scope for shifting the balance of European technological capabilities more in the direction of dual-use technologies, as discussed further below.

We can summarise the strategies being followed by western firms as following three main (but not mutually exclusive) lines: sharply reduce the scale of defence operations through cuts in employment and plant closures; dig deeper into defence markets; and convert existing resources to new markets.

Cuts in employment/plant closures

Recent years have seen substantial 'downsizing' among western firms, even if, as de Vestel (1995) has pointed out, no significant company has gone bankrupt. A recent estimate for western Europe (Brzoska et al., 1995) calculates losses of 400,000 jobs between 1990 and 1995, a reduction of more than 30%. The largest absolute number of jobs was lost in Britain, while relative job losses were highest in Austria, Germany and Belgium. To illustrate with reference to just one company: in 1995 British Aerospace announced that 1350 jobs were to go over two years at its Dynamics division, which manufactures missiles. This will leave the division with only 2,500 staff, compared with 16,500 in 1990. (*Financial Times*, 16 March 1995). These numbers demonstrate that earlier estimates (Anthony et al. 1990), that were met with considerable scepticism at the time, were actually rather conservative.

These reductions are, in absolute terms, small compared with those in the United States: the fusion of Lockheed and Martin Marietta alone will cost 12,000 jobs and the closure of 12 manufacturing facilities between 1995 and 1997, although out of a workforce of 170,000 (*Financial Times*, 27 June 1995).

There has been some attempt to combine downsizing with diversification into non-military production. However, reliable and systematic data on this subject are not, to my knowledge, available. This is not surprising, given both the difficulty of collecting such data in practice and, more fundamentally, the difficulties in classifying products as military or civil once one gets some way down the production chain below the level of prime contractors and final assemblers. Anecdotal evidence suggests that smaller enterprises seem to have been more successful in diversification than larger ones, but hard evidence on this point is scarce, and indicates an obvious need for further research.

Data are available on the degree to which individual companies have reduced their defence dependence (percentage of turnover that depends on defence sales). The picture that emerges is variable, but shows most major defence firms choosing to concentrate more heavily on defence work (see below), and with data on subcontractors being less readily available. A company such as British Aerospace (Europe's leading defence contractor) has reduced its defence dependence over the past decade from above 50% to 37% in 1993 (SIPRI 1995, Appendix 13A). Its French counterpart, Aérospatiale, has similarly dropped from 68% defence in 1980 to 30% in 1993, and the aeroengine firme, SNECMA, has undergone a similar transformation (Hébert, 1995), though, interestingly, several of the other French firms cited by Hébert have maintained or even increased their defence dependence in recent years. In fact, in all these cases of apparent diversification it remains to be established what really has been going on: has there been genuine conversion of defence production into civil production, or merely a reduction in the proportion of defence production (achieved, as in some cases, through an increase in the percentage of civil production arising from the purchase of new, civil, businesses?

Strengthening their position in defence
Broadly speaking, most leading western defence firms have taken a strategic decision to aim to strengthen their position within today's smaller defence market. In addition to downsizing, and perhaps some diversification, they have also engaged in processes of industrial concentration, nationally and internationally, and have sought a larger share of the arms export market.

Concentration and Internationalisation: The past decade or so has seen considerable restructuring and concentration of firms at the national level. In the USA, this has reached the extreme of the merger between Lockheed and Martin Marietta, forming the world's largest defence company, with an annual turnover equal to about 15 months of French national procurement spending. On the European scene also there has been a steady process of national concentration, probably in fact running ahead of that in the USA, and reaching the point where, in Germany, for example, the overwhelming bulk of defence orders go to the Daimler-Benz group, while in Britain there was much speculation in 1995 about an impending 'end-game' between the two leading defence contractors, British Aerospace and GEC, following the latter's victory over the former in the battle for control of Vickers Shipbuilding and Engineering Limited, the submarine manufacturer.

The restructuring process has not, however, stopped at the national level. In a development that has been commonplace among civilian firms in an increasingly globalised economy, defence firms have latterly begun to form cross-border links. Their governments, moreover, have permitted this, having previously treated the defence sector as one of unusual strategic significance, and therefore as not appropriate for any form of foreign control. (Walker & Gummett, 1989 and 1993; Sandström and Wilén, 1993; Brzoska & Lock, 1992; Hébert, 1995). International restructuring has been particularly evident in the electronics and aerospace sectors. Restructuring of the warship and land equipment industries has tended so far to remain within national boundaries, although even this is changing.

Two main patterns of international activity can be observed. One pattern has been of major defence contractors taking over second tier firms in other countries. Examples include:

- in *aerospace*:Bombardier (Canada) and Short Bros (UK); Matra (France) and Fairchild Space (USA); SNECMA (France) and FN Moteurs (Belgium); Lucas Aerospace (UK) and Tracor Aviation (USA); DASA (Germany) and Fokker (Netherlands);
- in *electronics*: Thomson-CSF (France) and (among others) Hollandse Signaal (Netherlands), Ferranti International Sonar UK), and Pilkington Optronics

(UK); Siemens (Germany) and Plessey Radar and Defence Systems (UK); Dowty (UK) and Resdel Engineering (USA).

Further examples could be given in the small arms and ammunition sector, and yet more, although much fewer in number, in land and sea systems. For a more complete list, see Sköns (1993), who also shows the importance of transatlantic acquisitions.

Transatlantic links cease, however, to be so prominent when we move to the other, and arguably more significant, pattern of activity, namely, moves to establish international joint ventures between the major players on the European scene, particularly between British and French, and French and German, firms. Examples here include:

- in *aerospace*: Aérospatiale (France) and MBB (now Daimler-Benz Aerospace - Germany), to form Eurocopter; GEC-Marconi (UK) and Matra Defence (France), to form Matra Marconi Espace; BAe and Matra (to merge their missiles divisions);
- in *electronics*: GEC-Marconi and Thomson-CSF, to form GEC-Thomson Airborne Radar; a subsidiary of IRI (Italy) and Thomson-CSF, to form SGS-Thomson Microelectronic.

Again, these are the sectors that have been most prominent in this type of activity.

These developments, taken together, present the prospect of radical reshaping of the European defence industry, which might result in the formation of a few large multinational 'clusters' of fixed composition (Steinberg, 1992), but more probably perhaps will take the form of fluid coalitions of opportunity between divisions of the main defence firms (Walker and Gummett, 1989 and 1993). In either event, they will be smaller than their precursor firms, thus continuing the process of down-sizing. They will also be enthusiastic proponents of the other element of the 'deepen defence' strategy, namely, arms exports.

Arms exports: One crucial reason for the processes of internationalisation in the defence sector is the growing pressure of US firms in the international arms market. US firms, as already mentioned, achieve considerably greater scale at the upper end of the range than do European firms. This follows from the fact that the (unified) US domestic market is about twice the size of the (fragmented) west European arms market. Hence, although the US has long been the world's main arms exporter, the dependence of individual firms on exports has in the past been very much less than that of European firms, where exports have, on average, been as high as 30-40 per cent of production.

Now, however, as the global market (including the US market) shrinks (with growth at present only in SE Asia), US firms are competing much more actively for exports, both in Europe and in the markets where European firms have themselves traditionally exported. In response, the European firms are restructuring in an attempt to acquire the mass to withstand the American challenge (not to say the threat of US monopoly: see Kapstein, 1994), not least by seeking scales of production equivalent to those of their US competitors.

The problem is that an export-led escape from the problem of declining markets cannot succeed for all. Global decline, coupled with tougher competition all round, has raised the stakes enormously.

Conversion

What remains, then, is the strategy of direct conversion. This, however, is not a simple concept. We can distinguish its operation at at least three levels: those of the individual plant, the company as a whole, and the region within which the plant is located. (Southwood, 1991). That is, we can distinguish between:

- *Attempts to change what is produced in an individual plant.* Here we encounter all the problems that the literature on technology management, technological innovation, and organisational behaviour, would lead us to expect. That is to say, a firm is seen as a highly developed, organic entity embedded in its own history. If it is a successful firm, it will have optimised at all levels to its role. Change, therefore, is far from a trivial matter. The switch from military to civil production will involve all the familiar problems of identifying products, marketing them in an unfamiliar environment, and altering work practices at a variety of levels;
- *Attempts to alter the overall product range of a firm* comprising many individual factories. This, however, can come close to the diversification strategies discussed earlier. It may well not involve any direct conversion, in the sense of using the same personnel as previously, at the level of individual plants;
- *Attempts to generate new foci of economic growth in a region*, regardless of the fate of individual factories, in an attempt to absorb displaced labour into new jobs. This approach recognises the problems of plant level conversion and seeks instead to provide fresh starts for displaced workers. It offers perhaps more scope for intervention by national or regional authorities (as with the European Union's KONVER programme), through training programmes and support to new, especially SME, businesses, for example.

These more specific strategies are discussed in various chapters in this book, as are the very important differences that flow from the different economic systems within which conversion is being attempted. We make only two observations here. First, conversion, especially at plant level, appears to have been attempted more in the East than the West, for reasons perhaps to do with the different structures of industrial activity and, in some cases, the geographical remoteness of plants. Second, there is considerable confidence in the West that normal market processes, judiciously supported by government intervention, provide adequate means for industrial adjustment, as has happened in the past, notably in declining industries such as coal and steel, or even in the defence sector itself, as at the end of the 2nd World War. What emerges from previous cases, however, is the importance of the prevailing social and economic conditions. Thus, at the end of the 2nd World War, western Europe and the USA could reduce their defence labour force rapidly for at least three reasons: the large number of women who had been drawn into the war effort were willing to return home; many companies had switched from civil to defence production, and still retained the skills necessary for civil work; and there was pent-up consumer demand. Clearly, these factors do not apply today, so that even in the West the present defence downturn presents particularly difficult problems.

NEW CIVIL-MILITARY TECHNOLOGICAL RELATIONS

The management of technology for defence purposes therefore faces several challenges. It will be less well-funded than in the past. Production runs will be shorter, encouraging international collaboration and/or advanced manufacturing methods in order to keep prices within reach. The industry will be increasingly internationalised, making national control of technological assets more difficult. The international arms market will be more fiercely contested. And the traditional post-1945 assumption that military technology was somehow more advanced than civil is being reversed, in areas from electronics to structural materials, as the commercial sector, with its vastly greater size and its growing performance standards, is increasingly making the technological running (Gummett and Reppy, 1987; Gummett, 1991). This last point means, first, that defence suppliers have to learn how to draw more actively on the civil technology base (and may indeed be threatened by traditionally civil suppliers in the competition for defence contracts); and second that, again, the process of supply is becoming increasingly internationalised not only at the level of the prime contractors, but right down to the level of suppliers of components and materials.

How, in these circumstances, are governments and firms responding in terms of their policies for maintaining technological dynamism, and for securing defence equipment of adequate quality yet affordable price?

In considering this question, it is interesting to observe that Japan has become a major producer of high quality defence equipment (as well, of course, as a prime supplier of components to western defence equipment), without having developed a specialised defence industry. Hence, Drifte (1986) has described Japan as having defence production without a defence industry. That is, defence production is managed as a small part of the work of large, technologically dynamic companies, whose main competences and markets lie elsewhere. Friedman and Samuels (1992) and Samuels (1994) have extended this argument by showing how Japan's 'technology and security ideology' comprises the three elements of indigenising (that is, mastering locally), diffusing and nurturing technologies, thus creating independent capabilities that are available for application in both defence and civil contexts. Such an approach would also help to alleviate another potential problem that could arise from the present wave of industrial concentration, namely, how to maintain competition, if not within individual countries (which is increasingly implausible), then at least within Europe as a whole. By relying less on a specialised defence sector, and more on a generally strong technology and industrial base, the prospects for so doing would be improved.

Dual use technologies

This discussion is now organised in several countries around the concept of dual-use technologies. There has already been extensive analysis of this concept in the USA, as shown, for example, by the publication in 1992 of the results of a major study from the Harvard project on dual-use technologies (Alic et al., 1992). Since the election of President Clinton, the theme of dual-use technologies has moved from the level of analysis to the level of policy. It has become a central pillar of defence technology orthodoxy (Van Atta 1994; Gansler 1993), with the 1995 Department of Defense budget containing over $2 billion for work of this type. Similar emphases are apparent also in Russia, though their follow through into practice is rendered more difficult by the problems of limited demand for civil high technology (Cooper 1993).

What is the scope in western Europe for serious development of dual use technologies, as the basis for both defence and civil activities? To the extent that European governments and firms do address the concept of dual-use technologies, do they do so in the spirit of aiming towards the 'Japanese model', in a spirit of conversion, or of simply seeking new forms of financial support for a besieged defence sector? Are European firms capable organisationally of working in the 'Japanese' way, or is the habit (found more strongly in some countries than in others, it must be said) of organising defence production separately from civil too strongly entrenched? In practice, a variety of positions can be seen in Europe, deriving from different conceptions of the status of defence affairs, at one level, and of the relations between the defence and civil sectors, at another.

In certain respects, *Britain* seems to be becoming increasingly active on this subject. Industry can be seen to be pressing strongly for a greater national effort in the development of dual-use technologies, notably through the programme operating under this title, sponsored by the CBI on the initiative of British Aerospace (Coghlan, 1994). Industry has also called for a wider national role to be played by the Defence Research Agency (DRA) in the form of support for the overall science and technology base rather than a narrow concentration on defence purposes only. The same theme arises in a paper submitted to the Ministry of Defence (MOD) by the Defence Industries Council in late 1993 (Defence Industries Council, 1993) which calls for a study of future technological requirements that seems not unlike that conducted in France in 1993 for the Commissariat général du plan (1993 - and see below).

These moves run in parallel with measures being taken in UK government in general, and the DRA in particular, to develop new Dual Use Technology Centres, and related initiatives which will align the programmes of the DRA more closely with those of industry (House of Lords, 1994; Coghlan, 1994). However, just as it is not clear how far the outcome of the industrial initiatives will in practice be confined to bolstering existing defence firms, so the motives behind the governmental initiatives are also mixed. Specifically, they arise at least as much from the DRA's need to cut its fixed costs by rationalising its facilities onto fewer sites, while also attracting cooperative industrial support for these facilities, as from any clear policy lead by the MOD. They are, therefore, concerned with conversion only to the extent that, in cutting costs and reducing staff, the DRA is keen to maintain critical mass in key technologies by developing links with industry.

The then procurement minister did say in September 1991 that

> In the future I see the MOD making increased use of commercial off-the-shelf technology wherever we can. Our R&D will be increasingly targeted on producing military derivatives of basically civil technology, and on those areas where civil technology is not suitable or simply does not exist. In the constantly extending border area between military and civil technology there will be scope for MOD to become a more eclectic - though discriminating - patron and customer of work with potential for civil application. (Clark, 1991).

However, this was something of an exceptional remark. Even today, the UK MOD insists that, while it is content for there to be civil benefit from defence programmes, defence funds can only be spent on activities for which there is a clear and primary defence need, and this insistence appears to many observers to be inhibiting the scope for developing the dual-use approach. Much evidence on this score was given in 1994 to the enquiry into the DRA by the House of Lords Select Committee on Science and Technology, resulting in a recommendation by the Committee that the DRA be encouraged and enabled to play a more prominent role in national wealth creation (House of Lords 1994). It is worth adding that the Ministry of Defence and the DRA are also being increasingly drawn into wider discussions of the scope and direction of their research programmes by virtue of their involvement in the machinery of science and technology policy in the UK. Specifically, they now have to make statements of overall strategy for the annual *Forward Look of Government-funded Science, Engineering and Technology*, and are actively contributing to the Technology Foresight exercise, run by the Office of Science and Technology, which offers some possibility of harmonising MOD's requirements with other national scientific and technological efforts (Cabinet Office 1994)

A similar debate has also been underway for some time in *France*, but in a tone altogether more positive than in the UK. France has the largest military industry in western Europe, mainly still under state control and located within distinct national champions, but with an increasing proportion of it facing privatisation. This industrial strength is supported by a strategy of independence which, however, gets harder by the year to maintain, and has come under much greater pressure in 1995. France is already dependent on foreign suppliers for various materials and components, and partly in response to this position plays an extremely active role in European defence, and defence industrial, collaboration.

Expenditure on military R&D has remained fairly stable as a percentage of procurement expenditure since 1982, varying between 31% and 36%, but typically being around 33-35%. The Ministry of Defence also funds more research in companies than any other French ministry.

The Ministry concentrates its technical expertise on armaments questions within the Délégation Générale pour l'Armement (DGA), within which a division called the Direction des Recherches et Etudes Techniques (DRET) oversees the research programme, performance of which is distributed thus: 63% in industry; 7% in universities and research centres of other ministries; and 30% in research organisations under the supervision of the Ministry of Defence. (Source: Memorandum by Professor Alain Pompidou, in House of Lords 1994).

The figure for intramural research expenditure in France of only 30%, compares with one of more than double that in the UK. The consequent predominance of industry in the performance of defence research, together with the volume of contracts placed by DRET directly with firms is seen in France as creating a dense network of links between public and private laboratories. This, some say, is 'a guarantee of the best use of dual-use technologies' (Pompidou, in House of Lords 1994, memoranda).

More than this, however, is the explicit attention that has been given in France to the development of dual-use technologies. Thus, for several years there have existed large annual meetings to draw together defence and civil scientists (so-called *Entretiens science et défense*). Civil agencies, such as the national space agency (CNES) are much more closely involved with defence programmes than would be the case in, say, the UK.

The tone of the French outlook can be seen in the following quotation, taken from an editorial in the house journal of the French DGA, in introducing in 1991 a special issue on 'Les Technologies Duales':

> Le temps n'est plus où les contraintes de secret et de spécificité conduisaient la Défense à mener des recherches isolément, en espérant, peut-être, des 'retombées' civiles. Les conditions économiques et techniques d'aujourd'hui imposent de mener recherches et développements en pensant dualité: ce que je cherche n'existe-t-il pas ailleurs? ce que je trouverai ne sera-t-il pas utile ailleurs?
>
> [The time is past when the constraints of secrecy or of specificity could lead to defence research being conducted in isolation, hoping perhaps for some civil spin-off. Today's economic and technological conditions require R&D to be conducted in a spirit of duality, asking: Does what I seek exist elsewhere? Can what I discover be used elsewhere?] (*L'Armement*, 1991, p.3).

The willingness to place defence interests unashamedly in the forefront of wider national technological development is a theme that was continued, and much developed, in the November 1993 report of the Groupe de stratégie industrielle of the French Commissariat général du plan. (Commissariat général du plan, 1993).

This is a book-length report written by a group of over 60 (named) officials from the DGA and other ministries, industrialists, trade unionists, academics, and others. Among other things, it reasserts the importance of the defence sector to the French economy in general, and to French industry and technology more particularly, calls for a policy of active development of dual-use technologies, with new government-industry consultative procedures to drive it. It reviews in some detail the future importance of a range of technologies, and calls for them to be divided between the three categories of those that it is critical to retain in France;

those that could be maintained through European cooperation; and those that could be acquired from a broader range of suppliers.

Whether these recommendations are appropriate or not, the interesting point of comparison from a British perspective is between British concern to ensure that defence funds are sharply focused on defence purposes, and the French approach which, as in this case, not only ranges more widely but is also prepared to permit defence officials to associate themselves publicly with this position.

That this is characteristic of the French approach is confirmed in evidence given to the UK House of Lords Select Committee on Science and Technology by Professor Pompidou. scientific counsellor to the Prime Minister, who observes

> 'Our constant concern is to have regard ever more attentively to the osmosis between civil and military research. A continuous dialogue is maintained between the staff of the ministry of defence and those of civil ministries' (House of Lords, 1994, vol.2, p.290).

Not all commentators, however, regard these developments with equanimity. Thus, Chesnais (1993) questions the wisdom of the renewed emphasis upon maintaining an arms economy, and upon keeping defence interests at the heart of French technology policy at a time when technology of civil origin is increasingly setting the pace. Similarly, Serfati (1996), referring to the report by the Groupe de stratégie industrielle, observes that these (self-identified) members of the 'meso-system' (the French equivalent of a military-industrial complex) argue that they can count only on their own strength and so must tighten the links between themselves, while also increasing the links between themselves and civilian technology. Their call for more focused programmes of civilian technology, with the DGA playing a larger role in the formulation of relevant policy, can therefore be interpreted as having more to do with the reinforcement of the defence sector than with any desire to promote the concept of dual use technology as such, or to engage in conversion.

Germany, with the most powerful economy in Europe is also, in sharp contrast to France and Britain, one of the most heavily constrained politically in terms of defence equipment spending, relative to its size (Rohde and Schmidt, 1995). Germany has, moreover, had to cope not only with the massive problems of reunification but also, more parochially, with significant changes in the organisation of defence procurement. One aim of this reorganisation is to draw upon civilian technology more intensively in order to reduce costs and improve quality, although in fact it has already been policy since 1985 to draw on civilian-developed technology as far as possible (Lock and Voss, 1996).

Indeed, in contrast to the USA and UK, Germany has not maintained large state-owned defence research establishments. Instead, it makes heavy use of private companies or (to the tune of about one-third of the R&D outlays) other research institutions with primarily civil interests (such as the Deutsche Forschunganstalt für Luft- und Raumfahrt, and the Fraunhofer Gesellschaft). Industrial contracts for R&D are heavily concentrated in a few firms.

Expenditure on research and technology, as a percentage of the sharply declining procurement budget, has seen a fairly secular rise from about 18% in 1985 to 21% in 1989 and 30% in 1994, but with nevertheless a decline in real terms. Staff numbers are being correspondingly reduced at relevant research institutes. No clear trend exists in terms of new orientations for military research and technology, and the various research institutes meanwhile are seeking more work from non-MOD customers.

Since the Second World War, the practice in Germany has been for all military development and production to be done in private firms. These firms themselves have been engaged in extensive restructuring, both nationally (especially with the fusion of Deutsche Aerospace into the Daimler-Benz group) and internationally, and in downsizing. They are on the whole less militarily dependent than their British or French counterparts, and in that sense much more like Japanese defence producers. By the same token, they face less serious conversion problems, on average, than British or French defence manufacturers. The global orientation of German industry, and its proximity to the territories of the former Soviet Union and its allies, also offer intriguing prospects for cooperation and new departures to German firms, though in these respects the evolution of German and European arms export policy will be important, given the strong resistance to arms exports among large sections of the German electorate.

Among the smaller defence spenders of western Europe, where the volume of defence R&D is already quite limited, there has also tended to be implicit if not explicit attention to the cultivation of dual-use approaches, which now are being reinforced. Thus, in Sweden new dual-use networks are being created to link civil and military R&D organisations (Hagelin 1996).

Overall, therefore, there is evidence of significant debate on the possibilities for a greater emphasis on dual-use technologies in western Europe. It bears adding that, beyond the advantages already mentioned, a stronger emphasis on dual use technologies would also help with another problem which faces defence planners, namely, how to establish a '*reconstitution capacity*' for defence equipment. The issue here is partly the classical one of having a 'surge capacity', that is, a capacity to expand production of certain items rapidly in a time of emergency. But the concept of reconstitution goes deeper. It acknowledges the point that the ability to design, as well as to build, complex technological systems takes time. This time varies from one type of system to another. The skills needed for design and for project management, as is so often argued when a project is faced with cancellation, are difficult to re-assemble once dispersed. Defence ministries on both sides of the Atlantic are known to be considering this problem, trying to assess the time scale on which various design and production capacities could be re-established, and to estimate, on certain defence and foreign policy assumptions, what facilities they should aim keep in existence under their own control, what they could expect to be able to draw from allies, and what might be available from the general national or global technology and industrial base. It seems probable that a shift in the direction of dual-use technologies, by rooting defence activities within a more general technology base, could help with this issue also.

CONCLUSION

Defence conversion has not attracted the same level of attention in the west as in the east, for various reasons. In the first place, the dependence of western economies on the defence sector was less than in the east. In addition, existing market-oriented procedures for industrial adjustment have been expected to apply to the defence sector, as to other sectors. The processes of industrial downsizing, national and international concentration, and limited diversification and conversion have been industry-led, albeit needing at least tacit acceptance by governments in what remains a particularly politically sensitive industrial sector. The context of debate and action has also been influenced by an appreciation of the changing relations between technologies of defence and civil origin, and the consequent need, for defence purposes alone, to build closer links between the defence and civil sectors. Western defence conversion, therefore, is perhaps better characterised as one element among several in a general process of repositioning of the defence industrial sector in the light of the end of the Cold War and the globalisation of technology and of industry.

---

* This chapter arises in part from work done in a longstanding collaboration with William Walker, University of Sussex, UK, Judith Reppy, Cornell University, USA, and Josephine Anne Stein, of PREST, University of Manchester, UK; from work done with support from the UK Economic and Social Research Council; and from work contributed by other colleagues in the CREDIT (Capacity for Research on European Defence Industry and Technology) network.

REFERENCES

1. Alic, J. et al. (1992) *Beyond Spinoff: military and commercial technologies in a changing world.* Boston, Mass.: Harvard Business School Press.
2. Anthony, I., Allebeck, A., Wulf, H. (1990) *Western European Arms Production: Structural Changes in the New Political Environment.* Stockholm: SIPRI.
3. Brzoska, M., Lock, P. (eds) (1992) *Restructuring of Arms Production in Western Europe.* Oxford: Oxford University Press for SIPRI.
4. Brzoska, M., K. Kingma & H. Wulf (1995) Bonn International Center for Conversion, *Demilitarization and Conversion*, Report No. 6, Bonn.
5. Cabinet Office (1994) *Forward Look of Government-funded Science, Engineering and Technology 1994.* London: HMSO, April.
6. Chesnais, F. (1993) Commissariat général du Plan: un rapport critique ... critiqué, *Damoclès*, No. 49, pp.30-31.
7. Clark, A. (1991) Speech on 'Defence and the high technology industries'. London: World Economic Forum, 4 September; Ministry of Defence News Release 106/91.
8. Coghlan, A. (1994) Stony ground for Britain's ploughshares. *New Scientist*, 22 January, pp.12-13.
9. Commissariat général du plan (1993) *L'avenir des industries liées à la defense*, produced by the Groupe de stratégie industrielle. Paris: La Documentation Française.
10. Cooper, J. (1993) Transforming Russia's Defence Industrial Base. *Survival*, vol.35, no.4, Winter 1993-94, pp.146-62.

11. Dawkins, W. (1991) French N-research to shed 4,000 (sic) jobs. *Financial Times*, 9 November. (The 4,000 must be a misprint, and would make no sense given the scale of the military applications division of the CEA; the figure of 400 is given in the body of the article).
12. Defence Industries Council (1993) *Government and the Defence Industry: Working Together*. London: DIC.
13. De Vestel, P. (1995) *Les marchés de défense en Europe: L'heure des politiques?* Paris: Institute for Security Studies, Western European Union, forthcoming in Chaillot Paper series.
14. Drifte, R. (1986) *Arms Production in Japan: The Military Application of Civilian Technology*. Boulder, Colorado: Westview.
15. Friedman, D., Samuels, R. (1992) How to succeed without really flying: the Japanese aircraft industry and Japan's technology ideology. Paper presented at National Bureau of Economic Research conference on 'Japan and the US in Pacific Asia', San Diego, April. Massachusetts Institute of Technology, mimeo.
16. Gansler, J. (1993) Transforming the US Defence Industrial Base. *Survival*, vol.35, no. 4, pp.130-46.
17. GRIP (1993) *European Armaments Industry: Research, Technological Development and Conversion*, Final Report for European Parliament/STOA. Brussels: European Parliament, Directorate General for Research.
18. Gummett, P. (ed.) (1991) *Future Relations Between Defence and Civil Science and Technology*, A Report for the (UK) Parliamentary Office of Science and Technology. London: Science Policy Support Group, Review Paper No.2, ISBN 1 873230 02 8.
19. Gummett, P., Reppy, J. (eds) (1988) *The Relations Between Defence and Civil Technologies*. Dordrecht: Kluwer.
20. Gummett, P., Stein J. (eds) (in press) *Construction, conversion and control of defence technological capabilities in Europe*. (Chur: Harwood)
21. Hagelin, B. (1996) The Swedish case, in Gummett and Stein (forthcoming).
22. P Hébert, J-P. (1995) *Production d'armement: mutation du système français*. aris: La Documentation Française.
23. House of Lords (1994) Select Committee on Science and Technology, *Defence Research Agency*. London: HMSO, HL Paper 24, session 1993-94.
24. Info-DGA (1992) interview with Pierre Joxe, no. 46, June. Paris: ADDIM.
25. Kapstein, E., (1994) America's Arms Trade Monopoly, *Foreign Affairs*, vol. 73, no.3, pp.13-19.
26. *L'Armement: Revue de la Délégation Générale pour l'Armement* (1991) Paris, No.29, October.
27. Lock, P., Voss, W. (1996) The German case, in Gummett and Stein (forthcoming).
28. Ministry of Defence (1994) *Statement on the Defence Estimates 1994*. London: HMSO, April.
29. Porter, M. (1990) *The Competitive Advantage of Nations*. London: Macmillan.
30. Reich, R. (1990) Who is US? *Harvard Business Review*. January.
31. Rohde, J., Schmidt, P. (1995) German Armaments Policy: its Consequences for the Armaments Industry. *Defense Analysis*, vol.11, no.3, 269-77.
32. Samuels, R. (1994) *'Rich Nation Strong Army': National Security and the Technological Transformation of Japan*. Ithaca, NY: Cornell University Press.
33. Sandström, M., Wilén, C. (1993) *A changing European defence industry: the trend towards internationalisation in the defence industry of western Europe*. Stockholm: National Defence Research Establishment, FOA Report A 10054-1.3.
34. Serfati, C. (1996) The French Case, in Gummett and Stein (forthcoming).
35. Sköns, E. (1993) Western Europe: internationalization of the arms industry. In Wulf, 1993.
36. SIPRI (1995) *SIPRI Yearbook 1995*. Oxford: Oxford University Press, for Stockholm International Peace Research Institute.
37. Southwood, P. (1991) *Disarming Military Industries: Turning an Outbreak of Peace into an Enduring Legacy*. London: Macmillan.
38. Steinberg, J. (1992) *The Transformation of the European Defence Industry: Emerging Trends and Prospects for Future US-European Competition and Collaboration*, Santa Monica: RAND, Report No. R-4141-ACQ.
39. Van Atta, R. (1994) US Dual Use Technology Policy. Presentation by the Special Assistant for Dual Use Technology Policy, Office of the Assistant Secretary of Defense, USA, to the Foundation for Science and Technology, London, 16 February.

40. Walker, W., Gummett, P. (1989) Britain and the European Armaments Market. *International Affairs*, vol.65, pp.419-42.
41. Walker, W., Gummett, P. (1993) *Nationalism, Internationalism and the European Defence Market.* Paris: WEU Institute for Security Studies, Chaillot Papers, No. 9.
42. Wulf, H. (ed.) (1993) *Arms Industry Limited.* Oxford: Oxford University Press, for SIPRI.

Concepts Of Military Technology: Contesting the boundaries between the civilian and the military

TARJA CRONBERG

Unit of Technology Assessment
Technical University of Denmark
Denmark

The technologies of the Cold War have been destabilised. The political and social relations of the arms race countries have been disrupted and institutions dismantled. New concepts are being negotiated to better reflect the emerging networks around military R&D and military technology. This process of negotiations takes different shapes in the East and the West. Although the arms race produced parallel technological innovations in the former Soviet Union and the US the interface between what is considered military and what is civilian technology differ.

In this paper I shall discuss concepts of military technology in the West and East. The end of the Cold War makes the differences between the way military technology has been embedded in society in the US and the Soviet Union increasingly visible. Consequently, the conversion problem i.e. how (if at all) to transform the military technologies into civilian use, is posed in a completely different manner. The analysis shows that military technology does not follow a predetermined universal technological trajectory, but is rather situated in a local context and constructed in negotiation among actors (Bijker et al., 1992).

The results presented in this paper originate from the research programme on Military Conversion and the Technological Edge of the Unit of Technology Assessment, Technical University of Denmark, during the period 1991-1997. Empirical studies have been carried out in the Los Angeles region in California (Aeroe 1992, 1994) and in the Perm region in the Western Urals (Cronberg 1992, 1994a, 1994b). Innovation economics and social studies of technology form the theoretical platform of these studies.

THE INSTITUTIONAL BOUNDARY

In order to understand conversion or the transformation of military resources into civilian uses in a broader context it is necessary to define what is meant by military technology and military production. In the West, particularly in the US, this definition is

P. Gummett et al. (eds.), Military R&D after the Cold War, 51–62.

largely *institutional*. Military technology is technology which is produced in accordance with rules defined by the Ministries of Defence.[1] In the US the Department of Defense (DoD) defines not only technical specifications for military products, but also the cost accounting systems and the quality control procedures to be followed by military enterprises. Furthermore, as the Department of Defense also acquires the property rights, i.e. the right to transfer knowledge and know-how to competing firms, this fact has led to a situation where a number of civilian enterprises refrain from military work.[2]

This institutional definition of military technology also integrates a number of civilian technologies into what is considered 'military'. The DoD has also drafted specifications for cookies, toilet seats and the like. The definition between what is considered military and what is civilian is one of specifications and procedures rather than one of technological know-how or technologies. The boundaries of what is considered military and what is civilian are continuously negotiated.

As a consequence of this there exist, in the United States, two industrial and technology bases[3], one for the military and one for the civilian. The linking mechanism, spinoff, was based on the assumption that technologies developed for the military, automatically or at least without any state intervention, diffused to the civilian sphere. This notion has increasingly been contested, and integration of the two industrial and technology bases is on the agenda (Alic et al., 1992; OTA, 1991).

The very strong influence of the DoD (Department of Defense) upon the structure and function of the defence industry, makes it relevant to define this industry from its decisive relationship to this single customer relationship rather than by its products (Reppy 1983, p.25):

> The nature of this governmental customer is the single most important determinant of the characteristics of the industry, because the DOD's monopsony power permits it to set directly the specifications of the products sold in the market and the rules under which business in transacted. This is not to argue that the private defence firms have no market power, but only that they exercise their power in the context of the rules set by the government.

Given this institutional definition of military technology as technology produced in accordance with the specifications of defence departments, *procurement reform* is the natural focus of negotiating new boundaries between military and civilian technologies.

---

[1] Definitions of what is in the West considered as military or defence technology have been reviewed in *Future Relations between Defence and Civilian Science and Technology* (1991).

[2] In CSIS (1991) the differences between civilian and military production are further elaborated.

[3] 'A defense industry and technology base is the combination of people, institutions, technological know-how and facilities used to design, develop, manufacture and maintain the weapons and supporting defense equipment needed to meet the US national security objectives'. The civilian or commercial base is the one responsible for the same outside this domain (OTA 1991, p .39).

PROCUREMENT REFORM

Contrary to market transactions, jobs from the DoD are acquired on the basis of bidding for government contracts or allocated directly to firms within the military industrial complex. More than 65 percent of all defence contracts are routinely awarded without competitive bidding (Stowsky 1986).

The Pentagon's procurement of defence goods is regulated by the government's procurement regulations, which are both defined and implemented by the Pentagon. These behavioural rules are defined in the *Armed Services Procurement Regulations* and *The Defense Procurement Handbook*. The procurement regulations comprised 100-125 pages when they were introduced in 1947. In 1973, they were expanded into 3,000 pages and they continuously expand (Stowsky 1986).

The Pentagon's procurement regulations not only indicate product specifications but affect often in detail also the production organisation and the product development process. Often the Pentagon allocate their people to the production plant to closely monitor the development and production process. The firm's own room for influencing the production and hence the defence technological development consequently becomes rather limited. Further, the required accounting procedures are also very influential on the organisation of the US defence production. In consequence, firms involved in both defence and civilian production often have to divide their production between two separate units, each with their own accounting system. (Cronberg & Aeroe 1995).

Results and innovations arising from DoD contracts belong to the DoD, and the inventing firms are, as a point of departure, not allowed to exploit these in their commercial production. The strictly regulated environment for defence production involving intense testing combined with very restricted use of the findings for commercial purposes and a very bureaucratic book keeping system all contribute to an erosion of the contractors' commercial competitiveness, and consequently hamper their ability to penetrate the commercial markets as countermove to reduced defence spending.

Today procurement reform is on the agenda. In 1992 the Defense Conversion Commission, which presented its final report in December 1992 recommended that efforts to foster commercial-military integration be strengthened, expanded and accelerated considerably. The Commission suggested transfer of technology originally developed for defence from federal laboratories to commercial activities. It promoted the idea of dual use technologies and 'manufacturing extension centers', where manufacturers can obtain information and advice on improving their production processes.

According to *Adjusting to the Drawdown* (1992, p.24) the Defense Conversion Commission suggested that the Department of Defense should work closely with Congress and other Federal agencies, reduce or eliminate the statutes and regulations which prevent greater commercial-military integration. Furthermore, the commission proposed that 'the Secretary of Defense should require that DoD use commercial specifications, standards and buying practices for all procurement actions except those for which he or she has approved military-unique practices on the basis of a demonstrated, compelling need'.

This, however, means fundamental rethinking not only the procurement system, but the American political system as a whole, or as pointed out by Alic et al. (1992, p.163):

> Because the barriers between DoD (and its contractors) and the commercial sector are deeply rooted in the American political system, closer integration will require a fundamental rethinking of competing policy objectives. Greater integration would mean relaxed procurement requirements and greater discretionary authority for procurement officials - both of which are likely to be politically contentious. If such changes occur, they will reflect the recognition that DoD 's isolation now threatens its technological edge, as it did not when defence technology was superior to anything the commercial sector could provide.

RESOURCE ACCESS AS BOUNDARY

In the Soviet Union *all* technologies were defined by ministerial procedures and specifications. Technical documentation was drafted and approved by the state, not only for the military but also for the civilian production. Procurement rules may have been different, but the whole procurement system as such was similar. While civilian and military production units are separate in the US they were often combined in the Soviet Union. Only in the later stages of production did specialisation occur. Furthermore, the idea of defining technologies as arising from the civilian or military sectors could not be applied in the same way as in the USA because so much civilian productions was managed by the military industrial complex.[4]

The objective of this transfer of civilian production into military industry was not to create technological spinoffs, but to raise the quality of civilian production. The military 's image of high quality and high discipline production combined with special management methods were to rub off onto civilian production, so often plagued by low quality and mismanagement. This transfer led also to a de facto integration in the plants, with civilian and military productions were carried out in the same plants and controlled by the same groups of people. The secrecy attached to military production was not limited to military technologies alone, but to all production in the military industrial complex, including the production of washing machines, videos and the like. Thus whole industrial plants were closed off.

When asked about the basic difference between military and civilian technologies the enterprise managers we have interviewed in Russia without exception underlined the questions of *access* and *price*. Military technologies were of 'gold', civilian production could also be of 'steel' to cite an often quoted expression. Consequently, when trying to transcend the gap between military and civilian technologies, the Russian engineers and scientists, who have inherited the Soviet system, face a different set of problems from their American collegues.

The military sector as a whole had the highest priority in society. The Military-Industrial-Commission with representatives from the Politburo, Academy of Sciences and

---

[4] [4] Even during the Gorbachev period industries were transferred to the Military-Industrial Complex. The Ministry of Machine-Building for Light and Food Industry and Household Appliances was discontinued in 1988 and 220 of its individual plants were transferred to defense industry ministries (Alexander 1990, p.20).

the Defence Departments had the highest power and authority in the country to allocate resources. Nine military ministries channelled the resources further to around 2,000 enterprises, which completed the tasks of weapons development and production. These enterprises, including research institutes and design bureaus, were allocated the best raw materials. The best brains were reserved for weapon development and working in the military sector implied a number of privileges including higher salaries.

Quality control also differed between the civilian and the military sectors. In the latter, designs and prototypes were carefully finished and tested. The technical documentation was checked and the personal responsibility of the chief engineer in the design bureau enforced. Barriers to the transfer of know-how were bridged by giving institutions the power to coordinate efforts or by setting up special agencies for weapon development programmes (ballistic missiles, nuclear weapons) (Evangelista 1988).

American literature on conversion from the 1970s and 1980s[5] also refers to this gap, to the 'performance at any cost' approach of the military and the failures in utilising military technologies in civilian spheres due to lack of market thinking and cost optimisation. However, this problem is much more dramatic in Russia today. It also defines the conversion problem as one of transformation from a high tech, high cost and high status sector to a low tech, low quality and low cost one. This technological transformation is to take place in a context, where the economic system is being transformed to a market economy and where changing prices of raw materials, energy and other resources are creating a chaotic situation.

THE BARRIER OF PROFESSIONAL PRIDE

In this situation it is not astonishing that many of the scientists and engineers in Russia working on conversion focus on the quality/price gap. Using military technology for example in advanced composite materials or military testing equipment, should give an advantage for the civilian sector. The scientists and engineers are willing to lower the quality of the military technology, while at the same time expecting to increase the level of corresponding civilian technology.

In our interviews in Perm in March 1992 this was the main direction in which a number of military companies were searching for new products.[6] Design bureaus, which had previously worked on missile engines, artillery or steering systems, were contemplating producing glass-fibre pipes for the chemical or the food industry. A space technology composite materials research institute looked for consumer composite products, such as canoe paddles, crutches and the like, i.e., things which require more than normal strength. Typically, in these cases the chief engineer or the scientist in charge had worked out a specification describing the technical details of a possible product. In our March interviews in 1992 these descriptions were devoid of any market oriented information. The expectation was of automatic demand as better technical quality for example in piping would be

[5] See for example Melman 1983, 1986, 1988 and Lynch 1987. For a review of the literature see Cronberg & Haugbølle Hansen (1992).

[6] For a more detailed analysis of this search process, see Cronberg 1994.

available. By November 1992, however, there were already efforts to provide a rough market assessment.

This 'closing the gap' approach was well summarised by one of the managers of a new small company (emerging from a military enterprise) who was considering producing machinery for artificial surface materials. According to the director, they were offering a high quality product even though their civilian clients desired only lower quality ('customers say: "thank you, we only need this level"'). When confronted with the fact that his potential customers did not need the higher quality, the director answered: 'We *know* they need it, but they are not willing or able to pay'.

This type of 'social construction' of civilian technologies by military engineers and scientists had been dominant in the Russian military enterprises during the conversion process in 1992-1994. It was due not only to the lack of market orientation and contact with civilian customers as is clearly demonstrated by the above example where a producer-user contact did in fact exist. It was also, and maybe foremost, a question of professional pride by the engineers and their traditions in the culture of military production. Consumer-oriented products are often 'little things', which optimise the cost-benefit ratio and do not require large scale tasks to be achieved. Conversion, to produce commercially viable, simple but marketable products such as knives and forks or shampoo is not the kind of complex technical task the Russian military scientists and engineers are proud of solving.

The scientists and engineers employed in the military enterprises are professionals. They have successfully competed with the world's leading technology, that of the United States, in the arms race. Although targets have been set by technological advances in the United States (Evangelista, 1989), they did achieve technological parity. Or to quote one of the scientists, 'It was the nature of our bureaucratic system. Even if we created new things, and new ways of doing things, our bureaucratic system told us to do the same things the Americans did. But to do it better or cheaper'. Russian scientists were not only proud of their world class performance in weapons technology and innovation. They were also proud of being able to reach this level more cheaply than the Americans. The above cited scientist pointed out that 'what took 5 billion dollars for Americans to achieve, we did for 30 million. We simply did not have the resources'.

'Equivalent to the world class' was the quality mark of technology in the Soviet Union, both in the arms race and elsewhere. Russian scientists and engineers from military enterprises, when presenting their proposals for cooperation and joint ventures during our interviews, never forgot to emphasise that their product/technology meets world standards. Lack of more specific targets, lack of contact with civilian clients and the 'world level tradition' of military technology has made 'the world level' a goal even in conversion.

Early state programmes for conversion underline the point that not only should conversion efforts maintain the core of scientific and technological potential of the defence industries but that they should also 'work in the directions in which the world class results have been scored and where achievements from promising a big commercial success are expected'[7].

---

[7]The programme for broadening the economic reform, Russian Government, 1992 (The programme is presented in Conversion, RICA, 10 July 1992).

A DETOUR TO WEAPON EXPORTS

Given the barriers to conversion both in the East and the West weapon exports are an alternative to civilian production given defence budget cuts. In the United States this has been argued for as a strategy for some companies to adjust the reduced defence spending. Since the collapse of the Soviet Union, the American defence industry has undergone substantial restructuring with a number of mergers and aquisitions. Those remaining in military production have consolidated their position also in weapon exports. However, the Defense Conversion Commission notes that:

> In all likelihood, companies will find it increasingly difficult to export defence products in the 1990s, as global markets for defence products decline. The end of the Cold War, of the war between Iran and Iraq, and of Operation Desert Storm as well as global pressures to reduce defence spending, should reduce demand for exported defence goods. While the market is shrinking, it is becoming more competitive. Many NATO countries plan to increase reliance on defence exports to bolster their domestic defence industries, and Russia and other former Soviet republics seek to sell arms in order to obtain hard currency for economic development projects. (p. 35)

While the United States does warn about the difficulties of exporting defence products in the 1990s, weapon export is time and again proposed as an adjustment strategy in Russia. Both government representatives and industrial leaders have argued for conversion to be financed through the sale of weapons. Already in the spring of 1992 Yeltsin declared that weapon sales were essential to obtain foreign currency for conversion, while his adviser Mikhail Malei expressed the view (in Conversion, RICA, 19 May 1992) that:

> For a long time the military industrial complex has been absorbing large sums from the state budget. Now the task is to make the military industrial complex a source of budget revenue. If the military industrial complex is not ready to export non-military products, it should start earning hard currency for the state by exporting weaponry.

Military production is not argued for here on security grounds, but on economic grounds. The task is to integrate Russia into the world economy.

On the other hand, the incomes to be generated by export sales have been questioned as prices have been held artificially low due to the privileged position of the defence sector for raw materials and supplies. Stopping arms production and selling raw materials might be a more economic way of earning the funds necessary for conversion. Export incomes in the past have often come from totalitarian regimes, and been more in the form of credits than actual payments. Finally, the question is whether arms sales would have a negative impact on world opinion, and divert potential support to the conversion process in Russia.

Arms exports from the former Soviet Union continued to decline in 1992 although less steeply than in 1989-1991. According to Gennadi Yanpolsky, General Director of the Defence Industry Department of the Ministry of Industry (September 1992), exports accounted for 30% of sales by the Russian defence industry in 1991 and 7.2% of sales in the first half of 1992. Estimates indicate that Russia exported arms worth $23 billion in 1989 and $7.8 billion in 1991. Sales for 1992 were around $3 billion, and since then have been nowhere near the levels of the 1980s (SIPRI *Yearbook 1993*, pp.447-9).

Military exports could, after the Cold War, have been a common trajectory for the survival of the military industries in the East and the West. Shrinking world markets and the way military exports have been built into the social and political context in the US and in Russia do not promote any universal solutions. Even here trajectories diverge.

TRANSFORMATIONS

New patterns of social relations will emerge, as the separation between the civilian and military sphere is no longer maintained as a specific sphere supported by its own language, institutional structure and practices. In the future we may no longer be able to talk about military and civilian technologies, as weapon systems will incorporate commercial products produced by commercial enterprises available on commercial markets. This does not, of course, exclude the continuation of residual military technologies and products produced in government-owned and/or maintained arsenals. The claim here is only that the bulk of weapons production will be outside the realms of these arsenals. Military production will in the future be less isolated and secret, but also more difficult to control.

The dual use/critical technologies strategy devised in the United States as a way to integrate the military and the commercial technology bases and to promote economic growth, is thus also a strategy to manage a boundary between the military and civilian sectors. A basic assumption in this strategy is that there is no difference between these two types of technologies and production or at least that the technologies with minor modifications may be rendered dual use. Rather than focusing on the differences, which was the case during the Cold War, the similarities are underlined. Critical technologies ' lists drafted by the Department of Commerce and the Department of Defense show in fact, that at least on a general level they the overlap: military and commercial R&D may be combined, is the official US conclusion in its technology policy after the Cold War (OTA, 1991; *Adjusting to the Drawdown*, 1992).

The second underlying assumption is that the interests of the military and commercial spheres are compatible. Not only do critical technologies overlap, but at the development stage also military and civilian requirements coincide. Advanced composite materials, advanced optics, sensors and measuring techniques will not have diverging properties for military and civilian uses, at least not at the outset. The critical question here then becomes: at what stage of the development process do commercial and military requirements diverge? And what about those commercial or military technologies which at the outset do not have military applications.[8]

The policy of weapon exports in Russia is also a strategy to manage the boundary between the military and the civilian, given that the enterprises have not, in the short time since the collapse of the Soviet Union, been able to go over to civilian production. The

---

[8] Critisism has been raised against the 'dual use high tech track' in Branscomb (1994), Marcussen & Yudken (1992) and Yudken & Black (1991).

unstable business environment, lack of monetary support, inexperience in working in a market environment, foreign competition and other reasons have made the goal of transforming the economy to civilian production an unachievable one on this timescale. Weapon exports are supported for economic rather than military or security reasons. They should earn the country hard currency, and in the end help the enterprises in their conversion efforts. Continued weapon exports would also maintain the high tech base of the country, not necessarily for the development of future military technologies, but above all to avoid the total disintegration of the technology base.

As the United States has filled the void left by earlier Soviet weapon exports, it is difficult to criticise this strategy on moral grounds. Its weak points as a conversion strategy are rather to be found in the lack of efforts to actually secure the funds for conversion, the potential inability of the Russian military enterprises to reproduce themselves and their know-how base under the current conditions without state aid, and the difficulty for any country to increase its share of the world weapons market in current conditions.

Both the dual-use strategy and the military exports strategy will, potentially, increase the share of civilian production and reduce the permanent military production of the two countries. The dual-use strategy also implies increased openness of the boundary between the military and the civilian and a more fluid divide between the two, a divide which, moreover, is being continuously renegotiated. The consequences of the Russian weapon export strategy, which is more clearly within the military sector, are more difficult to assess. Most likely this will mean a sharper divide between the two sectors. Negotiations of the borderline will be fewer and mainly directed to the use of economic resources gained from exports. While there exists in Russia today a discussion on dual use, the quality gap between the two sectors up to now, makes an immediate implementation of this strategy a difficult, if not impossible task.

CONCLUSION: A STRUCTURATION

In summary, I would like to present a matrix for the transformation processes currently going on in the East (Russia) and West (the United States). In a four field table of *military and civilian producers and users* we find a hard core of military production in the square of military production for military users. Products made by civilian enterprises and used in military applications, and products made by military enterprises and used in civilian applications, form two borderline cases, where either the producer or the user is civilian. Both types of production exist, particularly in areas where information is not classified and military secrets are not endangered.

Russian military enterprises today produce more civilian than military goods. In the same way American military enterprises have civilian divisions, even though they are separate from military production, due to, e.g., different cost accounting systems. Civilian enterprises have produced, albeit only to a very limited extent, products for the military. Such cases have, however, been mostly for civilian-like applications within the military, such as food, transport vehicles, furniture and the like, i.e., products not used directly in weapons and weapon systems.

		PRODUCER (P)	
		Military	Civilian
U S	Military	$U_{U.S.}$ ← P ↓	← $P_{U.S.}$ The US conversion policy
E R (U)	Civilian	↓ U_{Russia} The Russian conversion policy	(The Peace Economy - a No Man 's Land?)

The implications of this structuration become clear when comparing conversion in Russia and the United States. In the United States the focus of future conversion strategies is for the commercial producers to become more involved in producing for the military. The thrust is, rather than to have the military produce for military use, to encourage civilian enterprises to engage themselves in the military. This is the core of the new dual-use/critical technologies approach, the intention behind ARPA's efforts to draw in the US manufacturing sector, and the ultimate goal of the technology reinvestment programme.[9]

In Russia, on the contrary, efforts are focused on increasing the civilian production of the military producers. Although some of the military enterprises have been privatised and transformed into civilian producers, the expectation is that military enterprises will continue military as well as civilian production. This is the essence of the military export drive where integration into the world market is primarily expected to go through military exports, both as a vehicle of earning hard currency and subsequently as an instrument of conversion. The second strategy has been to expand the existing civilian production which has consisted of household appliances and home electronics. And the third strategy, although not very successful, is the 'closing the gap' approach.

The strategy selected for managing the boundary between military and civilian technologies will also determine the location of *the technological edge* in the future. The current conversion efforts, both in the United States and Russia, fully demonstrate the double bind of the previous technological race. Material resources and human capacity have been

[9] The Conditions for this programme are spelled out in ARPA, 1993.

invested in military R&D and production. The results of these efforts are difficult, if not impossible, to apply within the civilian sector. The particular field where these difficulties abound is that of conversion of military high tech to civilian high tech. As the direction of conversion in the US lies in the use of commercial technology for military purposes, this in itself is evidence of the military's inability to sustain technological advances in the modern world. Similarly, Russian efforts to convert directly from military to he civilian production via production of very low tech consumer goods is also an indication of the same problem.

The question to be raised here, referring once again to the diagram, is why the category of 'military producing for the military' is not being transferred to the fourth field, namely, civilian producers for civilian users? One answer is that the current conversion process is not necessarily aimed towards a 'peace ' economy, but rather represents an adjustment to the post Cold War security situation. That is to say, military production and procurement are to be secured, but not necessarily at the level of the Cold War. The possibility of conversion back to larger scale military production has to be secured by maintaining the capabilities for military R&D and production. 'Technological surprise' does seem to have lost importance, as new kinds of enemies such as terrorist attacks emerge. On the other hand, 'technological surprise' is gaining increasing importance in another race, that of economic competitiveness. Increased focus on the 'economic war' is built into both US and Russian conversion strategies, although in historically contingent ways.

What concepts of military technology will dominate in the future is impossible to forecast. What may be concluded from the analysis in this paper, however, is that a dual use strategy will have very different meanings in the US and Russian contexts, and hence may well have yet further meanings in such other contexts as Japan and Europe. The search for universal dual use technologies in critical technologies lists, or by other means, is at best a difficult endeavour, as the boundary between the military and the civilian is continuously renegotiated.

REFERENCES

1. Aeroe, A. (1992) Coping with Reduced Defense Spending. Conversion within the US Military Industrial Complex in the 1990s, *Technology Assessment Texts. No. 7.* Lyngby: Unit of Technology Assessment. Technical University of Denmark.
2. Aeroe, A. (1993) Technology Management View of Conversion from Defense to Civil Production: Experiences from Southern California, *Technology Analysis & Strategic Management*, Vol. 5, No. 3.
3. *Adjusting to a New Security Environment. The Defense Technology and Industrial Base Challenge.* (1991). Background Paper. Washington D.C.: Congress of the United States. OTA.
4. *Adjusting to the Drawdown* (1992) Report of the Defense Conversion Commission. December, 31, Department of Defense Conversion Commission. Washington DC.
5. Alexander, A.J. (1990) *Perestroika and change in Soviet weapons acquisition.* USA: Rand Corporation, June.
6. Alic, J., Branscomb, L.M. et al., (1992) *Beyond Spinoff. Military and Commercial Technologies in a Changing World.* Boston: Harvard Business School Press.
7. ARPA (1993) *Programme Information Package for Defense Technology Conversion, Reinvestment and Transition Assistance.* Washington D.C.
8. Bijker, W. and J. Law. (eds.) (1992) *Shaping Technology/Building Society. Studies in Sociotechnical Change*, Cambridge, MA: MIT Press.
9. Branscomb, L. (1994) Targeting Critical Technologies, *Science Technology Industry Review*, no. 14. Paris: OECD.
10. Conversion RICA (1992), May 19.
11. Cronberg, T., Aeroe, A. (1995) *Jobs without Guns: Innovation and Industrial Restructuring in Post Cold War US and Russia.* (Forthcoming).

12. Cronberg, T. (1994a) The Entrenchment of Military Technologies. Patriotism, professionel pride and Everyday Life in Russian Military Conversion 1992-1994. Paper to the BICC/CISAC Workshop 'Conversion of the Defense Industry in Russia and Eastern Europe', Bonn, 10-13 August.
13. Cronberg, T. (1994b) Civil Reconstructions of Military Technology: The United States and Russia, *Journal of Peace Research*, Vol. 31. No. 2. May.
14. Cronberg, T. (1993) *Enterprise Strategies to Cope with Reduced Defense Spending: The Experience of the Perm Region*, Paper to the Stanford University Workshop on Russian Economics, 22-23 November.
15. Cronberg, T. (1992) The Price of Peace. Military Conversion on the Enterprise Level in Russia, *Technology Assessment Text No. 10*. Lyngby: Unit of Technology Assessment, Technical University of Denmark.
16. Cronberg, T. & Haugbølle Hansen, K. (1992) From Military to Civil Production. A review of recent literature on military conversion, *Technology Assessment Text No. 5*. Lyngby: Unit of Technology Assessment, Technical University of Denmark.
17. CSIS (1991) *Integrating Commercial and Military Technologies for National Strength. an Agenda for Change*, Washington, D.C.: The Center for Strategic and International Studies.
18. Evangelista, M. (1988) *Innovation and the Arms Race. How the United States and the Soviet Union Develop New Military Technologies*, Ithaca N.Y. Cornell University Press.
19. Future Relations between Defence and Civil Science and Technology (1991) A report for the Parliamentary Office of Science and Technology. Prepared by the ESRC/SPSG Defence Science & Technology Policy team, London: SPSG Review Paper no. 2.
20. Gansler, J. (1988) Integrating Civilian and Military Industry: the Segregation of the Defense and Commercial Economies is Hurting Both, and Only Government Can Break Down the Barriers to Cooperation, *Issues in Science and Technology*, Vol. 5, Fall 1988, pp. 68-73.
21. Gansler, J. (1993) Industrial Contraction: Facing the Paradoxes of the Post-Cold War, *SAIS Review, A Journal of International Affairs*, Winter-Spring 1993/Vol. 13, no.1.
22. Gleditsch, N.P. and Njølstad, O. (1990) *Arms Races. Technological and Political Dynamics*, Oslo: PRIO and Sage Publications.
23. Kaldor, M. (1982) *The Baroque Arsenal*, London: Sphere Books.
24. Lynch, J.E. (ed.) (1987) *Economic adjustment and conversion of defense industries*, Boulder, Colorado & London: Westview Press.
25. Mackenzie, D. (1990) *Inventing Accuracy. A Historical Sociology of Nuclear Missile Guidance*. Cambridge, Mass.: The MIT Press
26. Markussen, A., and J. Yudken (1992) *Dismantling the Cold War Economy*, New York: Basic Books.
27. Melman, S. (1988) *The Demilitarised Society: Disarmament and Conversion*, Montreal: Harvest House.
28. Melman, S. (1986) Swords into Ploughshares: Converting from Military to Civilian Production, *Technology Review*, Vol. 89, pp. 62-71.
29. Melman, S. (1983) *Profits Without Production*, New York: Alfred A. Knopf.
30. Office of Technology Assessment (OTA), US Congress (1991) *Redesigning Defense: Planning the Transition to the Future US Defense Industrial Base*. OTA-ISC-500. Washington, D.C.: US Government Printing Office.
31. Parrott, B. (1983) *Politics and Technology in the Soviet Union*, Cambridge, Mass.: MIT Press.
32. Popper, S.W. (1990) *The Prospects for Modernising Soviet Industry*, Santa Monica: Rand.
33. Reppy, J. (1983) The United States, in Ball, Nicole and Milton Leitenberg, *The Structure of the Defense Industry. An International Survey*, London: Croom Helm.
34. SIPRI (1993) *Yearbook 1993*, Oxford: Oxford University Press.
35. Stowsky, J. (1986) *Beating Our Plowshares into Double-Edged Swords: The Impact of Pentagon Policies on the Commercialisation of Advanced Technologies*, The Berkeley Roundtable on the International Economy. Working Paper 17. Berkeley: University of California.
36. Yudken, J. and M. Black (1991) Towards a New National Needs Agenda for Science and Technology Policy: The Prospects of Democratic Science and Technology Policymaking, in G.A. Bischak, ed., *Towards a Peace Economy in the United States. Essays on Military Industry, Disarmament and Economic Conversion*, London: Macmillan, pp. 160-201.
37. Zaichenko, A. (1988) Risk and Independence of Innovative Activity, *Voprosy Ekonomiki*, No. 1, January, pp. 41-51; in *Soviet Union Economic Affairs*. May 12, 1988, pp. 27-33.

New Challenges after the Cold War

JÁNOS FARKAS

Department of Sociology
Technical University of Budapest
Hungary

Some three years ago the editor of the daily newspaper *Népszabadság* invited me to write an article about the new post Cold War motive factor in technical development. I declined, explaining that I had no clear perception of the problem. Undoubtedly the Cold War was an enhancing factor in R&D and technological progress. In advanced industrial countries military accomplishments have been relatively quickly adopted by the civil sector, which led to a major increase in the development of transport, telecommunications, computer-technology, etc. In the Soviet Union and the former socialist countries of Eastern Europe - because of the political and economic climate - there has not been a similarly open relationship between the military and civil sectors. But even in this region, with slight time lags and many complex transfers, military and space research have made their mark on technical progress.

Since 1986 the geopolitical situation has changed dramatically. The Warsaw Pact and the CMEA (Council for Mutual Economic Assistance) have collapsed; the former socialist countries have gained independence from the Soviet Union; the Soviet Army has been withdrawn from most of these countries; the Soviet Union's federal system has also collapsed; the united Soviet Army no longer exists; its previous nuclear potential has been split up among four countries - Russia, Ukraine, White Russia (Belorus) and Kazakhstan. The NATO forces of Western capitalist countries won the Cold War without a single shot. With the collapse of the Warsaw Treaty the world became in practice a unipolar place.

But at the same time new challenges arose, and it soon became clear that this apparently unipolar world is in fact a multilateral place. The Soviet Union disintegrated. Ethnic and religious dissent broke out, in and among its newly independent countries. Civil wars, riots, massacres and wars between nations began. The number of disorganised actions dramatically increased and it is not uncommon that the Russian Army - often encouraged by the West - is asked to intervene, to make and keep peace. Greater Yugoslavia has also disintegrated. The ethnic and military conflicts are still raging, and it is difficult to anticipate the outcome of the situation in Bosnia. Ethnic tension has increased among the former socialist countries of Eastern Europe. Hostility among the dominant nation and its minorities is on the rise, which then makes a mark on official foreign policy, and relations between the neighbouring

P. Gummett et al. (eds.), Military R&D after the Cold War, 63–72.

countries. In parallel to these political problems, the number of environmental challenges has also increased. Professionals, examining our rapidly disintegrating planet, have pointed out the main global problems: the thinning ozone layer, global warming, depletion of natural resources, the green-house effect, perishing rain-forests. Examining air, water and earth pollution the Brundtland report introduced the term 'sustainable development', in 1987, which was accepted - in theory - at the 1992 UN world-conference in Rio de Janeiro. Unfortunately political practice has not yet matched theory and rhetoric in this respect.

During the last few years, experts have attached considerable expectations to the transfer of military R&D potential to the civilian sector. Conversion has become a central research issue, and many proposals have been made suggesting ways of using the energies invested in military activities for peaceful, civilian purposes. The issue of technology transfer can now be seen from a different aspect, focused upon the idea of conversion.

These are among the problems that are discussed in this book. In this chapter, I will outline a general frame-work within which to locate this debate.

SCRIPTS FOR THE FUTURE

In this section I introduce one of Ervin László's recently published papers, which gives us a pessimistic picture of what may happen to the world in the event of nothing but market mechanisms surviving the collapse of the old ideological boundaries of politics. His forecast applies to the following periods:

1995: China, India and the role of other over-populated developing countries. The technology they use to produce goods has a high level of energy and raw material consumption which heavily contaminates the environment.

2000: Commercial politics leads to an economic war. The largest companies cooperate and increase their output. Many companies go bust while others achieve monopoly positions. Owners and directors increase their profits. Unemployment increases around the world, causing major social conflicts. As governments intervene more, to influence market trends, businesses become more cautious and uncertain. The market dwindles as natural resources diminish and, therefore, social problems increase. The already intense competition is further aggravated by these factors.

2005: Even the wealthier countries have problems with satisfying their citizens' needs. Poverty is on the rise, the number of homeless increases. Governments resort to violence and the size of the police force increases while more prisons are built.

2010: Governments are incapable of solving the social and economic crisis. Democratic parties are replaced in power by extremist ones. The natural environment reaches a critical state.

2015: Food-production is surpassed by the increasing birth-rate. The land is destroyed by wasteful management. Refugees from South-Asia, Central and South-America, Africa and China emigrate to developed countries, which causes extreme social tension. The world is split in half. Some developed countries still obtain a high standard of living, while the rest become impoverished. The affluent protect their existing privileges, while the poor revolt against the intolerable inequalities.

2020: The leaders of wealthy nations perceive the danger they face. They decide to take control, and oversee all walks of life. They clamp down on free trade and replace the free market with a tightly controlled economic system. The industrial countries form an alliance, as individually they become powerless. The alliance is formed by the European Union, the North American Free Trade Agreement and the Asia Pacific Economic Cooperation. They establish a common monetary organisation and currency. Food-production is encouraged. Non-desirable activities are taxed or penalied. International trade is strictly controlled. Price restrictions are enforced and import-export quotas are set up. Taxes are imposed on those using energy sources, and fines for dumping. The international monopolies oppose these measures. 80 per cent of the world's population remains outside this economic block, and perceives itself as the victim of the situation.
2025: Developed countries use force to stop emigration. World stability falters as the affluent minority rules over the impoverished majority.

Such an outcome is self-evidently unacceptable, based as it is on short-term interests and the logic of political power. But is there any other option? The Earth has enough food and minerals to supply mankind. This, however, requires the preliminary conditions of a decrease in the world's birth-rate and the consideration of the Earth's capacity in proportion to the goods we manufacture and the natural resources we use. Market mechanisms alone cannot solve this problem. The birth-rate has already slowed down, but not yet stabilised. In the next 30 years mortality will still remain below the number of births. The world, however, can withstand a slow increase in the birth-rate. We have to make sure that the world's inhabitants use the resources and possibilities nature offers, in a more effective way. We need to find a way whereby 75 per cent of the world's population can by-pass the era of polluting, energy and raw material demanding technologies, while the developed industrial countries should move on to post-industrial production and consumption. Rather than continually increasing the material base of living standards, the quality of life should be improved instead.

We should be looking for a new scale of values, and new goals to replace the faith put into the market. The market is insensitive to the capacity of reserves and the increase of wastage. In the neo-classical economy there is no mention of limits to exchangeable values, nor of boundaries to economic growth. Nature, in economic terms is a 'finite sector' which, as a subsection of the whole system, can be replaced by others. This, however, does not fit reality. Through the mechanism of distribution, market forces regulate the balance between supply and demand. But they do not achieve an equitable distribution of material goods. Moreover, the system will only be sustainable if we distinguish between permissible and excessive production. The economy's energy and raw material consumption, waste discharges and pollution, must not be allowed to reach the limit of nature's regenerating capacity.

The neo-classical economic approach has to be replaced with something else. It is the economy that should be subordinate to nature, and not the other way round. The goal of economic activity should not be to maximise value exchange but to increase value within a self-supporting system. Effective and well balanced distribution has to be achieved. To get the right proportions an additional value dimension is needed, that of sustainability, which is superior to the classical value exchange in not mistaking short-term advantages for long-term disadvantages. Such an approach could also take into account the sustainability of the market itself, for economic rationality and the market cannot be eliminated. Rather, both of these factors have to be placed in their proper context. If we disregard these connections, the law of the market will exhaust the reserves. The value of sustainability has to determine the demands of the market in all respects.

Let us now examine some specific problems faced by the countries of the old East-West divide.

QUESTIONS CONCERNING THE EUROPEAN UNION

The creation of common European market has suffered a set back through the economic recession sweeping across the continent. The member states have had to rethink their development strategy. *Growth, competitiveness, employment - challenges and the roads leading to the 21st century* is the title of the so-called *White Book* that summarises the problems and the proposals for solutions.

Unemployment has increased to 11 per cent (17 million). Then President Delors initiated a re-examination of the current model and the Community's economic policy. Initially a flexible social model was drafted, which entailed a liberal economic approach. Later this had to be modified - in the Keynesian tradition - by more state intervention. This created a mixed economic philosophy. The White Book gives the following answer to the problem of unemployment: by improving macro-economic conditions, GDP growth can be set back to 3 per cent. A healthy world economy and free trade is necessary to achieve this. In addition, investment levels must be sustained. The European Community's investment ratio in the 1960s and 1970s was 24 per cent, falling to 21% in the 1980s and to 19% today. The target set by the *White Book* is 23-24% once again. To achieve this, government savings have to be increased (by funding national budgets), the profitability of investments has to be improved, and business confidence strengthened. Private, but also state, investments need to be intensified. But the Community's budget of 20 billion ECUs is just half a percent of the European Union's total output. The change to a Keynesian approach is, therefore, both symbolic and negligible. Also many liberal-monetary factors have remained in the Community's economic policy (upholding stabilising monetary policies, reducing budget deficits etc.)

It is difficult to co-ordinate successfully the variables of *employment*, *growth* and *productivity*, as a quick review of the arithmetic will show. Because it is such a critical matter, competitiveness will not be compromised. This requires the maintenance of an annual 1.8-2% increase in labour productivity, which means that a 2% increase in GDP will still not reduce unemployment. The 2% level is forecast for 1995, but until then unemployment is expected still to rise. As the supply of labour increases half a percent annually, the growth ratio would have to exceed 2%. But even if annual growth were to reach 3-3.5%, only 10 million new jobs would be created by the year 2000, instead of the targeted 15 million. Restructuring labour-power has been suggested, particularly the development of the trained labour-intensive service sector. The higher level, life-long training is seen as an intellectually based investment. Flexible working hours, part-time jobs, and the winding up of the rigid, conventional working patterns are the ways in which a balance can be achieved on the labour market. Nevertheless, the unemployment ratio is unlikely to fall below 5-6%.

The European Union's example therefore offers a lesson to Central and East-European countries: economic growth cannot be based entirely on either supply or demand factors. Both sides have to be treated equally. Basing growth on investment - infrastructural investments in particular - is also a model idea. Another lesson to learn is that competitiveness cannot be sacrificed on the social altar of job creation. In the countries of Central and Eastern Europe, the service sector and infrastructure can still be significantly increased and thus jobs created.

The *White Book* proposes a new development model in the spirit of contemporary environmental economics. It proposes the widespread use of 'clean technologies' Economic growth would, therefore, occur with the moderating use of specific sources of energy and raw materials. It reduces pollution and increases economic competitiveness. This approach, however, is not yet reflected in the proposed plan for an economic policy.

Beyond the questions of economic management, Eastern European countries currently face the double problem of when and how to join the European Union and NATO alliance. It is known that both these acts have a number of obstacles. East European countries have to tackle under-development and defence problems that restrict them from becoming members of the European Union. The EU associate membership and the NATO *Partnership For Peace* programme are merely the first steps down this road.

Some member states prefer 'deepening' integration within the Union (France, Germany, Benelux countries, Italy), while others (Great Britain, Denmark) would rather 'widen' it, by hastening the admission of East European countries. Understandably, from our region, we perceive the latter choice as ultimately requiring less sacrifices from the Union. We believe that, by being permanently kept out, the East European countries - lacking a strong economy and an advanced democracy - are doomed, and will fall victim to chaos. It is understandable that the Union members most opposed to the admission of East European countries are those that also have development problems. The 1996 EU intergovernmental conference on reform of the Union will no doubt discuss the potential costs and benefits of 'deepening' and 'widening'.

DEFENCE PROBLEMS IN EAST-EUROPEAN COUNTRIES

According to the Hungarian foreign policy expert Dávid Meiszter (1993), the perception of a post-Cold War security vacuum is misleading. It was commonly believed that the Warsaw Treaty was a safety guarantee. Since it has collapsed we seek refuge in another organisation, namely NATO. Many have not yet awoken to the fact that the bipolar world no longer exists, and that the organisations of the remaining side are being transformed. The concept of a security vacuum is based on an incorrect situational judgement. The fundamental feature of the Eastern European region is not a vacuum, but change. This change is inseparable from uncertainty and instability. The main source of danger is instability. The one way out of this situation is by eliminating it. This can be achieved by hastening the change towards democracy in all states of the region.

The meaning of the term *security* has changed in the last few years. Its military aspect has been displaced by political, economic and human rights issues. In guaranteeing security, the non-military factors have taken the dominant role. With the collapse of the divided world, security that had been based on confrontation is replaced by the recognition of mutual values (pluralist democracy, the respect of human rights, constitutional state, free market economy) and cooperative security arrangements. The most important form of representation is the theory of indivisible security, which says that the security of each (European) state is internally linked to the security of all states. *Security* is an objective situation in which a country is not threatened by internal pressures, while external conditions do not hamper democratic progress and threaten its sovereignty. The *feeling of security*, however, is subjective, and can be manipulated by the media and government programmes.

During the Cold War the *sources of danger* were based on the mutual fear of nuclear strikes. Major crises arose over the following issues: Berlin crisis in 1953, Hungarian revolution in 1956, Cuban missile crisis, the shooting down of Powers' reconnaissance plane, invasion of Czechoslovakia in 1968, war in Afghanistan, deployment of intermediate-range nuclear missiles.) The sources of danger have now changed and the question of security has become a lot more complex. Meiszter believes that the following points are the *new sources of danger*:

- the imperceptible nature of general instability (the unpredictability of situations);
- unstable state formations, disintegrating powers, aggressive forms of nationalisms emerging from the ruins of federations;
- massacres on ethnic and religious grounds;
- growing militant Islamic fundamentalism;
- regional conflicts;
- mass starvation and an economically divided world;
- unmanageable mass migration;
- waves of political refugees, escaping the violation of human and minority rights;
- humanity's deteriorating health problems (AIDS, drugs);
- irreversible damage to the natural environment (global warming, nuclear disasters);
- international terrorism;
- proliferation of military technologies;
- nuclear weapons in undesirable places (illegal acquisition, purchases, production based on gathered information)

In Eastern Europe we face additional new *sources of danger*. The lack of law and order is typical of this region. The necessary tools and mechanisms are limited. The common will required to deploy them is divided between conflicting ideas. Early warning systems are ineffective. East European countries are unstable and their security is fragile.

To this list must be added the concomitant symptoms of collapsing state formations. Balance has to be regained among the more than 50 differently motivated new states that have replaced Europe's former three groups of countries. Political change is not always peaceful. Western Europe is integrating while Eastern Europe is disintegrating. For ethnic reasons the possibility of a 'spill over' cannot be excluded. The weakness of the post-Soviet Union and its disintegration is also becoming a security problem. Local conflicts break out in which - understandably - the West is reluctant to intervene. Yet by encouraging the Russians to restore order, they legitimise their presence in Russia's 'near abroad'. The Ukraine is also toying with the idea of becoming a nuclear power. (Ukraine has 176 intercontinental ballistic missiles to launch 1240 nuclear warheads, and 41 strategic bombers with 328 nuclear warheads; although, it has signed documents with Russia on disarmament). A new 'Berlin wall', the wall of poverty, is being built, which can be exploited by extremists on both right and left. Because the region is generally underdeveloped the degree of environmental damage is tragic (natural waters are polluted, forests are desolated, large areas are radioactive). Many poorly constructed power stations can be found in this region, which can be put down to the lack of industrial discipline (Meiszter, 1993)

The contemporary concept of security policy takes into account the fact that the dangers faced are not primarily military, although they can become military when mishandled. Security can only be guaranteed when all factors have been taken in account and deployed. The correct order of these factors should be: a) economic; b) political; c) human rights; d) environmental; and then e) military. If conflicts sprang up among East European countries, it is hardly likely that the West would intervene. T.G. Ash wrote in one of his articles that the West's heart did not beat in tune to a mutual European interest, freedom, suffering, and historic injustice (*Nepszabadsag*, 24 July 1993). The USA's reaction to the Yugoslavian civil war was similar. Max Jacobs writes the following: '...Western societies today have no stomach for military action outside their borders unless vital national interests are at stake, as in the Gulf, or an intervention can be carried out without significant casualties, as in Somalia. This is a fact of life Europe will have to live with' (*International Herald Tribune*, 1 March, 1993).

CONVERSION OF THE ARMS INDUSTRY

The 'catch 22' of world security is the conversion of the arms industry. The arms race led to a military sector that grew beyond economically tolerable measures. As the confrontation disappeared, many contemplated the conversion of the arms industry and the release of a large and instant peace dividend. Expectations were particularly high in countries with weak economies. However, instead of the expected economic boom, conversion deepened the recession, for the following reasons:

- it is a technically complex, and economically costly, exercise;
- the initial phases require major financing, with only long-term returns;
- to begin with, it may cause or increase unemployment.

In February 1993, 23 nations each possessed over 1000 modern armed vehicles; 15 had 1000 kilometre range ballistic missiles; 25 states had chemical weapons installed. A possible conversion would cause social and economic problems. The size of the supporting industry that manufactures services, upgrades and designs the parts, is also relevant. A paradoxical situation has arisen in which it is difficult to decide whether continuing arms manufacturing, with the necessary monitoring and restrictions (which upholds the danger of the weapons being used), or promoting conversion (thereby causing social tension) would cause the larger crisis.

Conversion has also met strong opposition from the *arms industry*. The industry is non-competitive and has no interest in the reduction of production costs; lobbying, and corruption among ministerial organisations and arms manufacturing companies is common; modern marketing is unknown. It lacks good information on the civil market. Rather, it has one customer, who also determines and oversees the work: the ministry of defence. Engineers working in the arms industry are in a highly bureaucratic environment; production is hesitant compared to the civil market's; there is a continuous demand for the latest technology; productivity and efficiency of arms manufacturing companies fall behind civil companies; the means of production cannot be used for civil purposes without alteration (Szabó, 1993)

Withdrawing the Soviet Army from foreign territories and the international monitoring of significant arms reduction poses a similar problem. President Clinton's plans to close US military bases may also meet strong opposition. Statesmen will have a tough ride putting across the motto: 'momentary losses for future returns!' Steps like this can increase instability in under-developed countries, and lead to a propensity to re-arm. This is how, paradoxically, the safer world can become more dangerous.

The possibility of nuclear proliferation is also a major concern. In the past, controls such as the Nuclear Non-Proliferation Treaty could to some extent be imposed on countries. Now, the number of nuclear weapons states has increased from five to eight (with Israel, Pakistan and India). Seven others have the potential to become nuclear powers (Argentina, Brazil, Iraq, Iran, North and South Korea and Taiwan), and three others (Algeria, Libya and Syria) are thought by some to be able to obtain nuclear weapons with producing them themselves. The Soviet Union's disintegration causes further serious problems: in 1992 more than 100,000 people worked in its nuclear industry, among them 10-15,000 researchers, engineers and designers, who possess information on arms manufacturing, and 2-3,000 who have knowledge of the manufacturing technologies. If these people disperse in all directions, the monopolistic nature of the knowledge surrounding nuclear arms productions will dissolve.

From the point of view of conversion, the technological transformation of the Los Angeles conurbation is an illuminating example. Previously it had been the USA 's principal base for arms manufacturing. Currently 3500 companies work here in the production fields of computer hardware and software, pharmaceuticals and civil R&D. Surprisingly the traditional textile industry has also recovered in this region. In addition, entertainment industry companies concerned with environmental R&D, as well as production, are prospering. Former arms manufacturing companies equip cars with radars which improve the highway information system. The combination of high-tech and conventional industries may well be one solution to the problem posed by conversion.

CONCLUSIONS

1. The utmost must be done to prevent the occurrence of the sinister situation described in my introduction. With international cooperation, by harmonising market and government forces, planned changes must be induced.
2. Western countries have to overcome the recession. Tackling unemployment has become an increasingly important task, which first and foremost requires new investment policies.
3. The East European security problem must be solved, with the help of the West. The organisational prerequisite is EU and NATO membership.
4. Close economic integration is necessary to achieve conversion. Non-military security factors can prevent dangerous situations from occurring.
5. Armed forces will have to be maintained in the future, but history has taught us that deploying military force has rarely led to lasting solutions. Among the 180 wars that followed World War Two, many were 'recurrent ' ones. Furthermore, the defeat of one belligerent party does not necessarily solve the problem. It can lead to new conflicts.
6. Information and technological transfer is a precondition, and the most effective form of economic cooperation, in which the more developed countries must offer disinterested help to the less developed ones. As a matter of fact it is in their strongest interest to do so, since conserving or deepening underdevelopment can regenerate vulnerability and conflicts. The most important area of knowledge and technological transfer is finding solutions to the ecological problems, with international collaboration.

REFERENCES

1. Berend, T. (1994) 'Hightech' és hagyományos ipar együtt: a dél-kaliforniai kiút, *Napi Gazdaság*, 2 April.
2. Burgess, A. The Use of External Pressure to Safeguard Minority Rights. (Unknown source).
3. Brown, G.E. (1992) *Report of the Task Force on the Health of Research*. (Chairman 's report to the Committee on Science, Space, and Technology U.S. House of Representatives. Washington, D.C.: U.S. Government Printing Office, July.
4. Gazda P. A védelem és a gazdaság konverziójának dialektikája, *Kézirat* (No date).
5. Gazda P. (1992) A hadigazdaság konverziójának problémái. *Kérirat*, 18 May.
6. Héthy, L., Szabó, J., Ungvár, Gyula (1992) Defence conversion and economic transformation in Hungary. NATO - C and EE Defence Conversion Seminar, Brussels, 20-22 May.
7. László E. (1994) A stabilitás és a piac, *Népszabadság*, 28 May.
8. Meiszter D. (1993) Biztonságpolitikai filozófia egy alternatív gyakorlathoz *Politikai Tanulmányok Intézete Alapítvány*, Budapest, November.
9. Merényi M (1994) A növekedés európai dilemmái: Beszélgetés Báger Gusztávval a PM fôosztályvezetôjével az EU Fehér Könyvérôl, *Népszabadság*.

10. Mogee, M.E. (1991) Technology Policy and Critical Technologies. A Summary of recent reports, *Discussion paper number 3*, The Manufacturing Forum, December.
11. Murphy, P. (1994) Unemployment fall-out, *Living Marxism*, June; and, Real Unemployment 10%, 20% or 60?, *Living Marxism*, August.
12. Opstal, D. van. (1993) Integrating Civilian and Military technologies: An Industry Survey, The Center for Strategic and International Studies, Washington, D.C., April.
13. Rabkin, Y.M. (1994) Science and technology in Russia. Position papers submitted to the OECD country review, Montreal, January.
14. Renner, M. (1993) Preparing for peace, L.R. Brown (ed.), *The State of the World*, Washington, D.C., Worldwatch Institute.
15. Szabó, J. (1992) Human conversion problems of the Hungarian defence force. Paper presented at international conference, Brussels, 3-4 December.
16. Szabó, J. (1993) The Hungarian defence sector in a time of change. Case study, Budapest.

Shock Therapy – Is There Really No Alternative?[1]

PAUL REDFERN

London School of Economics
United Kingdom

INTRODUCTION

The title of this paper is deliberately somewhat tendentious. The experiences of the former communist countries since 1989 have been so diverse that the historical record alone should have demonstrated, contrary to much conventional economic wisdom, that alternatives to so-called 'Big Bang' shock therapy for conversion of economies from communist to capitalist modes of production do exist, and are being followed (Estrin 1994a). Thus, while this paper is concerned with the problems of conversion in Eastern Europe and the former Soviet Union, its point of entry is via the rhetorical strategies employed by economists concerned with such issues. Hence the title.

To talk of the rhetoric of economic advice may appear to be a frivolous distraction given the urgency of the problems which need to be addressed in conversion issues. However, as the distinguished economic historian Donald McCloskey has pointed out, rhetoric is indispensable to any argument, economic or otherwise (McCloskey 1990). Invoking Aristotle's tetrad, he argues that rhetoric consists of four components - metaphor, narrative, fact and logic - none of which can stand independently of one another. In the economic context, he argues, models of economic behaviour act as metaphors

[1] This paper has its roots in a longstanding research interest in questions of economic theory. I am grateful to Prof. Michel Boutoussov of UNIDO and to the organisers of the NATO Advanced Studies Workshop for giving me the opportunity (and the incentive!) to push this interest in a more practical direction.

P. Gummett et al. (eds.), Military R&D after the Cold War, 73–92.

for human behaviour. Moreover, the accuracy of any metaphor may only be judged in the context of some narrative of human behaviour. Thus a model of consumer's preferences, say utility theory, is a metaphorical representation of actual behaviour, which depends on there being a co-existent narrative, which in the case of utility theory would consist of a story of how human beings always prefer more to less, but how they all face opportunity costs in the use of their time and resources, so that they are always forced to choose between alternative ends. Narratives not only support metaphors (and vice versa), however; they also criticise them. Similarly with facts and logic: 'if my grandmother had wheels, she'd be a tram' might be a logically impeccable statement, but one which could never be verified factually.

Viewing economic writings, and the policy prescriptions that flow from them, as rhetorical devices may seem unpalatable, but McCloskey demonstrates, from a brave analysis of his own earlier writings (and those of others) how such a dismissive stance towards questions of rhetoric cannot be avoided. The problem is, however, that such a dismissive stance is extremely widespread and deeply held amongst the economics profession. The title of this paper therefore refers not so much to the historical evidence concerning the diversity of conversion strategies as to the refusal of governments' economic advisers to to see this diversity as anything other than an unfortunate deviation from the true path.

Professor Paul Ormerod describes the mindset of such economists in the following words:

> Teams of economists descend on the former Soviet Union, proclaiming not just the virtues but the absolute necessity of moving to a free-market system as rapidly as possible. Such prescriptions involve the establishment of market economies of greater purity than those contemplated by Ronald Reagan and Margaret Thatcher. But despite governments in the former Soviet bloc doing everything they are told, their economic situation worsens....
>
> Academic and consultant economists from the West – of which Jeffery Sachs of Harvard, who acts as an adviser to the Russian government, is perhaps the most prominent example – descend on Eastern Europe proclaiming the urgent need to move to free market economies as soon as possible....
>
> In an article in the British newspaper *The Independent* in October 1993, Sachs argued that the failure of 'shock therapy' – his phrase – in countries such as Russia and the Ukraine was not due to the idea itself being wrong, but due to the fact that it had not been implemented with sufficient rigour. (Ormerod 1994, pp.1 and 63).

The 'insufficient rigour' argument is, as Ormerod also points out elsewhere, the refuge of cultists everywhere:

> Sociologists and psychologists have documented many case studies showing the reactions of groups when views which they hold about the world are shown to be false. In such situations, far from

> recognising the problem, a common reaction of individuals is to intensify the fervour of their belief. (Ormerod 1994, p.5)

Indeed the reaction of Sachs and his colleagues to the failure of conversion policies to hold to the one true path would be comical were it not for two factors. First, the degree of power which this particular cult holds, in particular as exercised through international financial institutions such as the IMF, the World Bank and the OECD. Second, the degree to which, given the collapse of all the institutional and ideological certainties in the societies of the former Soviet bloc, this proselytising of this particular cult has found such fertile ground in those societies. Both these factors are illustrated in Batt's observations on the politics of privatisation:

> Post-communist governments embarking on privatisation ... have only one consistent, effective and organised source of pressure in support of the policy: the international financial institutions backed by Western governments, which insist on the inclusion of privatisation as a condition for financial support and technical and economic assistance. On the domestic front, they are weak and embattled. The choice of approach ... is conditioned ... as governments search for allies and struggle to maintain their credibility and authority. (Batt 1994, p.89)

Conversion of economies from communist to capitalist modes of production is conventionally seen as incorporating a number of linked issues: macroeconomic stabilisation following price liberalisation; opening of economies to foreign trade and competition; institutional reform including that of the legal system and the state; and privatisation of previously state-owned assets (Estrin 1994b, p.3). Crucially, however, in the case of the countries of the former Soviet bloc, they also include changing the focus of industrial output from military to civilian consumption (Bush & Yeltsin 1992, Bakhar & Fillipov 1993; see also Brun, Baehr & Karpe (eds) 1992). This it would seem, almost inevitably requires what Shafiqul Islam calls a sectoral approach. Indeed he argues that

> the conventional [sector-blind] strategy intended to accelerate the transition [from communism to capitalism in the former communist countries] ... appears to be accomplishing the opposite by ... jeopardising the sustainability of the reform process' (Islam 1994, p.339).

In this paper I present arguments on international trade and investment strategies for development which endorse Islam's call for a sectoralist approach, and what US Labor Secretary Robert Reich calls 'managed' or 'fair' trade, not free trade. However, in the very volume in which appears Islam's eighteen-page argument in favour of sectoralism as opposed to 'Big Bang', there also appears a contribution by a very senior OECD official, in which it is baldly stated that:

> it is necessary that CEECs [Central and Eastern European countries] ... clarify the model of integration [into the OECD] they want to

> pursue.... [S]ome general criteria should be met. First, integration should be based in the market place and on market opportunities.... The second criteria [*sic*] is that ... by pursuing a high degree of external openness, they would spur the economic system to find its proper place or specialisation in the international division of labor.... Third, the new pattern of specialisation should not be decided by the government or directly promoted.... Authorities have limited knowledge of the market while enterprises are better placed to assess their comparative advantages in trade. Government intervention must be limited to creating the general conditions under which enterprises can arrive at undistorted decisions on their specialisation pattern and can have access to the capital, labour and technology inputs required to carry out their production plans. (Zecchini 1994 pp368-369)

An immediate retort to such a policy presription would be to invoke countries such as Japan, Korea, Singapore and Taiwan, where governments have directly, and successfully, promoted patterns of specialisation.

For the purposes of the present argument, however, let it be observed that not even neoclassical economic theory would make such bold claims for the superiority of enterprises' knowledge of the market over that of the 'Authorities'. As Estrin concedes: 'Traditional neo-classical economic theory can offer few convincing arguments for privatisation, or indeed for preferring any one ownership form over another' (1994b p.14). What matters for the neoclassicals is not ownership but competition. The Austrian school of von Hayek *et al.* do insist that private ownership is the *conditio sine qua non* of a dynamic economy, but the logic of their argument, in support of entrepreneurship, would suggest a focus on new enterprises rather than privatisation of existing state-owned ones.

A second observation is that both Islam and Zecchini were presenting papers at a UNDP–sponsored conference (the second Round Table of the UNDP Development Study Programme, Bucharest 1992), yet they appears to have held a dialogue of the deaf (see also Ormerod 1994, pp.7-8). It appears that no matter how cogenct the arguments presented in criticism of 'shock therapy' approaches, the major international institutions have but one response, more of the same, with countries which fail to meet the requirements of 'the model' being berated for 'inadequate action' (Zecchini 1994 p366).

As already noted, however, the pressure for shock therapy appears to come not only from without but also from within, from domestic acolytes of the cult. The evidence I have for this is only anecdotal and personal, but time and again, in conversation with economists from the former communist countries, when I have tried to suggest that such and such a theorem in neoclassical economics is of dubious theoretical or practical validity, (and I shall discuss some of these in later sections) I have been met with accusations that the implications of such criticisms would be to return them to the bad old days of state planning. For these economists, the West means market economics, and neoclassical economics is the economics of the free market.

As I shall argue below, neoclassical economics is nothing of the sort, but the issue is not one really for economic debate but for political scientists, sociologists and anthropologists. On the one hand, as Edward Gibbon noted, also writing about the collapse of a regime, 'officers of the police and revenue easily adapt themselves to any form of government' (Gibbon 1903, p.75, quoted by Scott 1994, p.310). In this instance, read 'economists' for 'officers of the revenue'. On the other hand, and more generally and less cynically, the desire to believe in the policy prescriptions which are peddled by the Western economists who have descended on the countries of the former Soviet Union is reminiscent of the cargo cults of the South Pacific, where totems in the form of radios are constructed and worshipped in the belief that if enough devotion is rendered to them, the cargo will surely come. The purpose of the remainder of this paper is to let daylight in upon the magic of free market economics, and so help make room for a more considered response to the problems of transition from communist to capitalist modes of production.

CONVERSION AS PRIVATISATION

I have already briefly noted Estrin's comments that there are no compelling reasons in economic theory, of whatever hue, that require the privatisation of state-run enterprises in order to establish an efficient and dynamic economy. Estrin does claim to present some arguments from economic theory to support privatisation as the means of ensuring the establishment of an efficient and dynamic economy, but as he himself admits (1994b, p14.) 'the reasoning is subtle'. It relates to the issue of motivating managers to carry out restructuring. On the one hand, in 'the Anglo-Saxon countries', stock market valuation imposes a discipline on firms' managers, with bankruptcy 'the ultimate sanction for managerial deficiencies' (ibid.) – this presumably is the same financial discipline responsible for the chronic 'short-termism' which has so hampered investment in R&D in these countries (Cowling & Sugden 1994, pp.70-71). Such a discipline is lacking in the transition economies because the state-as-owner is both too involved in the running of the enterprise *and* not involved enough. Because it has wider interests, such as the provision of social security and the need to maintain social order, state involvement is likely to slow down restructuring. On the other hand, ministers in transition economies may 'be disinclined to use their authority to direct or influence managers at all' (Estrin 1994b, p.15). Estrin concludes:

> The debilitated and dispirited state apparatuses in these countries cannot fulfil the function of owner, and weak managerial motivation means that the micro-economy may not respond as necessary to reform programmes. (Estrin 1994b p16).

'Weak managerial motivation' in this instance means managers working

> in the interests of ... the labour force as a whole (including management itself); the local community, to which the firm may be a major supplier of public goods, services and housing as well as jobs; and perhaps even to suppliers of intermediate inputs. (Estrin 1994b, p.15).

One could easily imagine most Westerners (apart from their economists) wishing that *their* managers had such motivational problems!

It is not hard to think of situations in which there would be no *prima facie* reason to expect a state-run enterprise to do any worse than a privately owned one. If, for instance, government revenues came solely from profits from enterprise, there would be no reason to assume that the 'Authorities' would have any less limited knowledge of the market than anyone else. They would then be *ipso facto* in a position, by Zecchini's own arguments, 'to assess their comparative advantages in trade' (1994, p.369). Similarly, there is nothing *a priori* wrong with the fact that, as Zecchini complains 'In the CEECs the government ... is at once the owner of the majority of enterprises and the regulator of the economy' (1994, p.370). This is a situation to which every capitalist firm aspires. This is why, on the one hand, governments in capitalist economies have anti-monopoly legislation and, on the other, why business leaders are always praising or castigating governments for their pro- or anti-business approaches, which usually means the structure of corporate taxation. In other words businesses seek to influence government to regulate the economy on their behalf. This is of course a perfectly normal and legitimate activity but it does beg the question as to why, when business leaders successfully influence the regulation of the economy, that should conflict with their ownership of industry. Indeed, most observers attribute Japanese economic success to the particularly close links that exist between business and industry in Japan (Cowling & Sugden 1994). It is not then immediately obvious that ownership and control should automatically be a good thing when concentrated in the hand of a private owner, yet constitute 'two conflicting functions' (Zecchini 1994, p.370) when they are concentrated in the hand of a government.

Turning away from economic arguments, Estrin argues that the 'fundamental political reason in support of privatisation relates to securing the irreversibility of the reform process' (1994b, p.18). Given the difficulties in establishing a purely economic case for privatisation it is not hard to conclude that securing the irreversibility of the reform process is not only the fundamental *political* reason for privatisation, but the fundamental reason for privatisation *tout court*. Indeed, even in his so-called economic arguments, Estrin concludes by citing the 'need *rapidly* to introduce some weight in decision-making to the consequences for the level of profits' (1994b, p.16; emphasis added). However, it is clear that this argument relates more to political than purely economic questions.

Once it is accepted that there are no compelling reasons in any economic theory in favour of one form of ownership of productive assets than another, then it is possible to put the question of ownership in its proper context. The former communist countries are undergoing a twofold transition, from communist to capitalist modes of production and from military-dominated economic outputs to consumption-good dominated outputs. Communism failed because it was unable to deliver on its promise, made so famously by Khrushchev, to bury capitalism under the weight of the consumer goods that it would produce. Communist regimes were unable to buy off discontent with consumer goods, and in many instances further weakened their positions by turning to foreign loans to cover the deficit (Estrin 1994b pp8-9). The mounting problems of popular discontent, foreign debt and economic stagnation all led, once the former regimes had finally collapsed, to the decision to adopt capitalist modes of production, in order that the promise of higher personal consumption and gains in material wealth for the majority of the population might finally be met. Privatisation is an unavoidable concomitant of that decision.

In the West, capitalism is inextricably bound up with a capitalist class, with wide income differentials both between capitalists and workers and within the classes also. In seeking to introduce capitalism into formerly communist economies 'reformers are in a position ironically reminiscent of Lenin and the Russian Bolsheviks in 1917; ruling on behalf of a class which as yet hardly exists ... the entrepreneurial class, upon whose appearance the economic as well as the political success of the reform will depend'as Estrin (1994b, p.19) aptly puts it. Policy in the transition economies has consequently therefore often been primarily concerned with establishing a capitalist system while at the same time attempting not unfairly to favour one section of society over another – an attempt at producing capitalism without capitalists. The debate on vouchers offers a good instance of this. On the one hand, since the assets to be privatised nominally belong to the people, then it is only fair that they be offered shares in the title of these assets. On the other hand if every single citizen or worker is a shareholder, and exercises their rights as shareholders vigorously, then the environment in which the management of enterprise is conducted will hardly have changed. Almost inevitably, social considerations will be given at least as much weight as capitalist, or profit-oriented ones. One way out of this dilemma, in the Czech and Slovak lands and in Poland at least, has been the establishment of investor funds (Perotti 1994) - an attempt at a short-cut to the way capitalism has been developing in the West, whereby the major investors are less and less old-style capitalist-entrepreneurs and more and more institutional investors such as insurance companies, and in particular, pension funds.

However, there is more to capitalism than simply private ownership, individually or corporately, of productive assets. The problems of establishing clear title to assets is also bound up with the rights of creditors and the obligations of debtors, as (Perotti 1994) makes clear. Once we move into questions of title, rights, credit and debit, we are moving inevitably away from economics, away that is from questions of prices, incomes and growth, into law and accountancy: it is accountants, not economists, who draw up the balance sheets and otherwise provide the information on how the well the enterprise is performing and, as Harcourt (1965/1982) points out, there are significant and non-standardisable differences in accountants' and economists' definitions of rates of return[2].

Secondly, the purpose of capitalist production is to make profits, not to satisfy consumers' needs. Historically, profits have best been achieved, in the West, by the manufacture and sale of consumption goods. In other parts of the capitalist world they have been achieved by exploitation of natural resources for export to the West and with little spin-off benefit to the domestic population of these countries in the forms of gains in material wealth or higher rates of personal consumption. In opting for capitalist development, the countries of the former communist countries have taken a gamble that their development path will follow that of the West and not that of the Third World. However gambling is of the very nature of capitalist development. New product lines take time and money to set up and it is not until those products arrive in the shops and start to be sold that the question of whether the gamble has paid off can begin to be assessed.

As it is for the enterprise, so also is it for the governments of the former communist countries: the move to capitalism itself *is* a gamble, no matter how short the odds may appear to be on it being a successful one and note that nothing in what has been said so far is intended to disparage the validity of taking this gamble. The purpose of this section has been to demonstrate that there is nothing, however, in any economic theory which entails the necessity of capitalism for the purposes of establishing an economic system which is efficient and dynamic, still less one which will inevitably produce rising consumption and material wealth.

SUPPLY, DEMAND AND RATIONAL ECONOMIC MAN

In order to win any credibility for their policy proposals, all economic theories have to offer plausible accounts of the three basic concerns of economic life: a theory of relative prices, a theory of income distribution, and an account of economic growth. Moreover, they have to do all this within the overall context of social science explanations which, on the one hand, have to demonstrate the existence of a system, a theoretical framework or perspective within which social phenomena can be interpreted and classified while, on the other, permitting room for the operation of individual agency – allowing both that individual choices can make a difference in the way in which the system

---

[2] owing to the fact that economists in their models have knowledge of all prices, especially values of stocks and assets, while accountants have to devise conventions for estimating these, and these conventions differ between countries (cf. Chadwick 1993)

behaves *and* allowing individuals to behave in a way which is contrary to the overall pattern without destroying either themselves or the perspective which the system offers. This is a very demanding set of environmental conditions, and one which economists often explicitly or implicitly ignore. A good example of an explicit ignoring of the problems of agency is von Neumann's famous 'Model of General Economic Equilibrium' (1945-46), in which consumption is fixed and labour simply allocated amongst the various branches of production in order that a model of endogenous economic growth might be constructed.

In the von Neumann case, the purpose of the exercise was to show how a model of economic growth might be constructed. In many ways it is a direct descendant of the models of expanded reproduction in Marx's *Kapital* Vol.II. It has generated many useful developments (cf. Goodwin & Punzo 1987, Pasinetti 1991). However, it was never intended to represent the workings of any real economy. By contrast, neoclassical economics, with its elaboration of the laws of supply and demand and of utility theory, and its celebration of the consumer, does claim to embrace agency. However, the essence of agency lies in Giddens' useful expression, the ability 'to do otherwise' (Giddens 1987, p.220). In the economic context, one means of expressing this 'could have done otherwise-ness' character of agency, is through Nuti's (1970a) remark that there can be no forward markets in labour under capitalism. People are free to choose where, when and if they work. The same freedom of choice that exists in consumption exists also in production. This freedom of choice drives a coach and horses through neoclassical economic theories.

To see why this freedom of choice poses such a problem, it is necessary to turn to the way in which neoclassical economics deals with the three fundamental issues of relative prices, income distribution and growth. Relative prices are established by the interaction of supply and demand, income distribution by the marginal theory of production and growth is left indeterminate[3]. Supply and demand schedules are also calculated through marginalist principles: supply is determined by marginal cost and demand by marginal utility. The intersections of the marginal cost and utility curves of suppliers and consumers of all goods and services establishes a set of relative prices in which, in equilibrium, all markets clear. All goods and services are sold, no more are forthcoming at those prices and no more would be consumed if they were to be produced. This includes the market for labour, therefore the marginal productivity theory of distribution is an extension of

---

3

It is possible to call upon Keynesian macro-economics to determine a level of output, but even then growth can only be inferred, by use of the method of comparative statics, or comparison of two equilibrium positions, one with a higher level of output than another, but this is an addition to the theory, and one which has never sat very comfortably with the basic scheme.

the marginal cost principle underlying all other economic transactions. The marginal cost of capital equals the profit rate, the marginal disutility of labour equals the wage rate[4].

The set of relative prices thus established not only clears the market for produced goods but, during the course of the bargaining process between suppliers and consumers leading to its establishment, the prices perform a *signalling* role, co-ordinating supply and demand decisions.

So far, so good, but the problem arises in attempting to fit new goods into the scheme. Supply and demand schedules only arise as a *response* by buyers and sellers to *currently* available goods and services. New goods mean new markets, but *until* prices (and thus revenues) are established in these new markets, the new resource allocations which need to be set in order that these new goods be supplied *cannot* be signalled by the price system, a Catch-22 situation. In the absence of any prices established in the consumer good market, resources cannot be allocated to the production of the good, not if the price system is to be regarded as the co-ordinating mechanism for supply and demand situations, yet, without the good, there can be no price. This is the point at which Rational Economic Man has to be invoked in order to bridge the horns of this particular dilemma. In order to maintain the fiction that the price system acts as a resource allocating and co-ordinating mechanism, it has to be assumed that *all* goods and therefore *all* markets are known about at time zero. It is often claimed that Rational Economic Man is merely a convenient simplification, an abstraction which enables the salient features of the economy to be understood without unnecessary distraction; relaxing the assumptions made about him would merely complicate the exposition without necessarily adding anything to the basic model. In fact it is *only* with the aid of this abstraction that the price system can perform its dual role of the co-ordination of supply and demand and the allocation of resources.

The degree to which the Rational Economic Man exerts his hold on neoclassical economics can be seen in the notions of rational expectations and efficient markets. Rational expectations holds that economic agents discount the future in such a way as to anticipate future changes in price, consequently 'the economy systematically exhibits equilibrium' (Phelps 1992, p.130) while the efficient market hypothesis states that 'all new information is immediately and fully reflected in market price' (Peters 1989, p.32). Both of these notions have been described by their proponents as revolutions, but it may be seen that they are no more than sophisticated elaborations on the principle of Rational Economic Man.

---

4 To be precise the nominal, or money wage rate. The real wage rate is the nominal wage rate divided by the price level. The overall level of prices is determined by labour productivity, ie, the marginal productivity of labour. The interaction of the two determines the level of employment, i.e, whether the labour market clears or not.

The perfect foresight of *guarantees* that supply will equal demand. Hence every piece of neoclassical analysis begins with a list of supply factors $S = S(x_1 ... x_i)$, a list of demand factors $D=D(x_j ... x_n)$ and the instruction 'let S=D'[5]. If we concede the rationality of Rational Economic Man, and give him perfect foresight, then we cannot avoid having supply automatically equal demand, but in so doing we have completely undermined any possibility for claiming that economics is concerned with choice. There are no possible choices available, nor can there ever be if it is to be argued that the price system is the mechanism by which scarce goods are allocated to alternative ends. Once we let the genie of choice out of the bottle, then neoclassical economics has nothing to tell us.

Similar difficulties arise in the theory of demand. If consumers' preferences are to be aggregatable, then consumers can never change their consumption patterns with growth in incomes. They follow what are termed straight-line income-consumption paths, or Engel curves (Brown & Deaton 1972). They simply consume more of the same. To put it more starkly, when they are poor they drive small Rolls-Royces, and when they are rich they drive large ones. This is not a considered a failing in the theory, however; in fact it is considered to be one of its strongest results, as Silberberg (1978) makes clear in his discussion of the corollary 'substitution postulate'. Neoclassical demand theory does make a distinction between goods which are complements, such as bread and butter, and goods which are substitutes, such as guns and butter. In the final analysis however, all goods are considered to be substitutes for one another. An agent with bread will trade with an agent for butter. Silberberg discusses the 'substitution postulate in the following terms:

The substitution postulate is an explicit denial of the 'priority of needs ' fallacy. Politicians and pressure groups are forever urging that we re-order our priorities i.e., devote more resources to the goods they value more highly than others. While it is useful for such groups to talk of needs and priorities, it is fallacious for economists to do so. The notion of a 'trade-off' is inconsistent with one good being 'prior' to another in consumption. (Silberberg 1978, p.220).

In the real world, of course, there are clearly priorities of needs, or hierarchies of demand. While, clearly, with increase in income, more is consumed of previous consumption items, the real focus of interest is on what new items of consumption will be chosen. Thus, one does not enjoy the use of a video until one has the use of a TV. Nor does one enjoy the use of a TV

5

followed by a lot of algebra in which variables come to be expressed in terms of parameters and a functional expression for some variable or unknown aspect of the economic model under consideration is expressed in terms of parameters and variables for which information is available.

until one has achieved a domestic environment in which to watch it. This of course works both ways. Not only are consumer goods expenditures ordered in a sequence according to growth in income, but new lines of production are only introduced and marketed in response to increases in the overall increase in consumers' income. The development of new lines of production, as opposed to the improvement of old, is therefore the development of complements to the existing set of use values.

The paucity of the neoclassical analysis of demand is revealed by any standard textbook on demand theory, such as that of Lipsey (1981), which reveals that

1) Quantity demanded is influenced by the price of the commodity
2) Quantity demanded is influenced by the prices of other commodities
3) Quantity demanded is influenced by the size of the household's income and wealth
4) Quantity demanded is influenced by various 'sociological' factors
5) Quantity demanded is influenced by the household's tastes
6) (Lipsey 1981, p.75).

The next four pages are spent discussing these five aspects of demand, although only two lines are devoted to aspect (4) and one paragraph to aspect (5).

Neoclassical demand theory thus bundles up and throws away, as 'sociological factors' and 'tastes', exactly those aspects relating to questions of economic development which are crucial to the problems of economic conversion. Yet in doing so, neoclassical economics (in the shape of Lipsey's textbook) undermines its own rationale for pursuing its particular concerns, the exchange of already produced goods and the establishment of prices on these goods:

When there is a change in tastes in favour of a commodity, more of that commodity will be demanded, even though its price, the prices of all other commodities and household incomes have not changed. When there is a change in tastes away from a commodity, less of it. (Lipsey 1981, p.79).

To concede this however is to concede everything. If these supposedly 'non-economic' factors can so disrupt the ability of the price system to regulate the interaction of supply and demand, then their exclusion from what Lipsey *et al.* are pleased to call economic analysis renders that analysis irrelevant to all except the most restrictive of cases. That is to say, cases in which time periods are very short, and changes in tastes are not at issue in the analysis. A good example is the theory of consumer's surplus as expounded by Marshall, who uses variations in small quantities of tea to illustrate the principle. This care in the choice of the example does not prevent neoclassical economics, in this as in so many other instances, from extending the scope of the original theory so widely, and wildly, that the original purpose of the analysis is quite forgotten (both by its proponents and by its critics – Linder 1977, Ch.15).

Again it may be seen that, once again Rational Economic Man is lurking behind the scenes. Given perfect foresight, all consumption paths will be known. But again there is no possibility of the exercise of choice. Because neoclassical economics asserts that choice is being studied, the implication is that choice exists in the system under study, but in fact in all crucial cases, the exercise of choice is ruled out, because the implications of the existence of choice would be too damaging to the fundamental notion that the price system co-ordinates supply and demand.

LEARNING AND THE PROBLEM OF CHOICE IN ECONOMIC THEORY

It should be clear from the foregoing discussion that opposition to sectoral strategies for conversion by the major international financial institutions arises from the same straitjacket in which neoclassical economics operates. If it is assumed that the price system automatically and simultaneously co-ordinates resource allocation and clears the commodity markets, then there is no reason why governments should interfere to promote one sector over another. For exactly the same reasons that neoclassical economics opposes the promotion of hierarchies in consumption, so it also opposes hierarchies in production.

However, it should by now be clear that these arguments have little validity. Neoclassical economics fails in the basic claim to knowledge for an economic theory, namely a plausible account of the derivation of relative prices and income distribution. In this section, I outline some general points concerning the nature of capitalist production from a Keynesian perspective. In the section following, I then turn to consider the question of conversion, where the case for a sectoral strategy would seem to be overwhelming.

The conversion to capitalism is intended to lead to greater efficiency in production Efficiency in production means either producing more output from a given quantity of input, or producing the same output from less inputs. Efficiencies in production can therefore arise only if the existing techniques of production change. Even if the quantity and composition of the final demand product were to remain unchanged, there would inevitably be changes in the production of primary, intermediate and joint products. In any society which is accumulating material wealth through increasing its productivity and efficiency, there is a constant reorganisation of its means and methods of production.

The purpose of increasing efficiency in production is not simply to produce existing goods more cheaply however, but thereby to free resources of labour and capital for the production of new lines of output. Complementary to learning in production is learning in demand. The changing structure of production provides continually changing contexts for the consumption of products. The constant reorganisation of production involved in accumulation is accompanied by continual restructuring of demand. The fact that the creation of new products depends on the context of previous material production means that their consumption similarly depends on the context of previous material production. Consequently developments in consumer demand cannot be decided solely by reference to individuals. The context of the state of social development as a whole must be taken into account.

If economic growth is thought of as an ongoing learning process, as it is in Pasinetti (1981, 1993), learning which is represented by the very existence of such hierarchies of production, then it must also be recognised that it is the stocks of knowledge possessed by its labour force which ultimately forms the bases of a country's wealth. However, learning is precisely what is ruled out by the invocation of Rational Economic Man. He already knows he all he will ever need to know. That is why he has no need of money. His investments will always be productive.

However, not only does neoclassical economics have no real theory of demand, neither does it have a theory of production. It is a theory of a barter rather than of an industrial economy. Stocks are given, not produced, and money is not required to finance credit between the time of investment and the time of sale of the finished good, or as a hedge against failure of expectations, brought on by changes in production, rendering a technique obsolete. Neoclassical models describe in great detail the type of economies that Keynes set out to show in *The General Theory of Employment Interest and Money* (1936) were irrelevant to the analysis of a modern capitalist economy.

The problem that choice poses for neoclassical economics was recognised by a leading practitioner, Roy Radner in 1968. Radner (1968) showed that if any new markets (by implication, any new products) are introduced at any later date, agents will never have enough information to evaluate the full set of alternative strategics that they might pursue. Economic agents in general need to ensure that the goods and services that they offer for sale may be sold at some positive price. In an economy with futures trading, agents need not only to be able to compute *all* possible outcomes of the pattern of sales and purchases for *any* set of prices which will maximise their profits (given the price sets of all *other* goods and services), but furthermore the prices to be considered include not only all those possible *now*, but also all those possible in the future. Even under the assumption that knowledge of all future markets exists in the present, the burden of information required by the general equilibrium approach is severe. Once the possibility is introduced that spot markets might come into being at some future date, the burden of information is so severe, that the general equilibrium approach 'breaks down completely' (p.35) in the face of it. Agents will *never* have sufficient information to evaluate the full set of alternative strategies. A demand for liquidity as a hedge against non-realisation of plans will arise. Furthermore, this demand for liquidity will itself be indeterminate!

The introduction of liquidity into the discussion leads naturally to the discussion of Keynesian theories of the economy. In a justly famous passage, Keynes explains what is meant by 'a demand for liquidity against non-realisation of plans':

> Money, it is well known, serves two principal purposes. By acting as a unit of account it facilitates exchanges without it being necessary that it should ever itself come into the picture as a substantive object. In this respect it is a convenience which is devoid of significance or real influence. In the second place, it is a store of wealth. So we are told, without a smile on the face. But in the world of the [neo-]classical economy, what an insane use to which to put it! For it is a characteristic of money as a store of wealth that it is barren; whereas practically every other form of storing wealth yields some interest or profit. Why should anyone outside a lunatic asylum wish to use money as a store of wealth?
>
> Because, partly on reasonable and partly on instinctive grounds, our desire to hold Money as a store of wealth is a barometer of the degree of mistrust of our own calculations and conventions concerning the future. Even though this feeling about Money is itself conventional or instinctive, it operates, so to speak, at a deeper level of our motivation. It takes charge at the moments when the higher, more precarious conventions have weakened. The possession of actual money lulls our disquietude; and the premium which we require to make us part with money is the measure of the degree of our disquietude. (Keynes 1937, p215-216).

Radner's admission is consequently of great significance for Keynesian and post-Keynesian theories of the economy, theories which take as their starting point the conflict between the need to commit resources to the future in order to produce goods, and the fear that the future will not live up to expectations; a conflict whose state is measured in the degree of liquidity preference at any time.

Nor do Keynesian theories require that the price system act as a co-ordinating mechanism in economic decision making. Much of the Keynesian theory of involuntary unemployment and lack of effective demand demonstrates quite clearly the failure of the price system to co-ordinate activity at the level at which all resources could be most fully and profitably employed. Rather the price system operates, as it does in the real world, as an *accounting* mechanism whereby the success or failure of the gamble on investing, or continuing to invest in a particular product line may be assessed. To restrict the role of prices in this way may seem an unacceptable retreat in economic theorising, but it must be asked which is worse, a theory in which the price system plays this limited role, or one in which money plays no role at all?

In this regard, it is also worth noting that as well as having no theory of production or demand, neoclassical theory has little or no theory of the firm. Since economic activity in capitalist, or any, industrial society is organised through firms, this would seem to be a startling oversight. There are formal Keynesian models of the firm dating back to Marris (1972) Eichner (1973) and Moss (1976), in which managers have to run their firms with one eye to their shareholders and the other to their workers. Firms, however, tend to be black boxes as far as neoclassical economics is concerned. They do not operate internal markets, by and large, and therefore they are only of interest to neoclassical economists as economic agents, players in the resource and commodity markets.

The fact that firms operated a planned economy was first noted by Coase in 1937. If, as neoclassical analysis has it, production is co-ordinated via markets, he asked why do alternative forms of co-ordination, namely firms, arise? Cowling & Sugden (1994) argue that this is the wrong way to proceed – 'it analyses from markets to firms and it focuses on market versus non-market activity' (p38). They even go so far as to suggest that Coase himself would agree with that criticism, since they quote him as saying that:

> there has been an undue emphasis on the role of the firm as a purchaser of the services of the factors of production, and on the choice of the contractual arrangements which it makes with them. As a consequence of this¼ economists have tended to neglect the main activity of a firm, running a business.
> (Coase 1991, cited in Cowling & Sugden 1994, p.38).

Right-wing commentators have gone so far as to argue that, in their internal procedures, firms themselves operate a planned economy, and that they should introduce market relations within the firm itself (Parker & Stacey 1994). Such thinking underlies the National Health Service and British Broadcasting Service reforms, as well as the British Rail Privatisation. However, the recommendation that they do operate internal markets is one which has a touch of self-interest to it. If firms did operate internal markets, then they would become of greater interest to neoclassical economists.

CONVERSION AND DE-MILITARISATION

Were the economic problems of the former communist countries simply those of moving from one mode of production to another then, as suggested above, the question could safely be left to lawyers and accountants. Where economic theory does have a role to play is in the problem of how to ensure that the economies of the former communist countries or, as we might now title them, the new capitalising countries, will follow the path of Western rather than Third World economic development. The principal economic problem facing these countries is how to switch their output from its present military-dominated composition to a consumer-good orientation, and to ensure that those goods are sold.

Unfortunately the economic theories presently being peddled around Eastern Europe are highly unlikely to help in this venture. The fundamental reason for this is that they resolutely refuse to take into consideration the central fact of capitalist development, namely that profit-making is a gamble. There are no cast-iron assurances that supply will meet demand. Even more emphatically there are no assurances that even if supply did meet demand, we would have 'result happiness', as Mr Micawber would say. In the world of neoclassical economics, supply always meets demand unless and except that universal villain of the piece, government, interferes. However, everyone, including neoclassical economists, expects governments to regulate the economy. There is a cognitive dissonance here which needs to be overcome.

In the previous two sections I have argued that neoclassical economics is in fact incapable of providing any policy advice for the problems of conversion both from communism to capitalism and from military to consumer products, and have argued for the adoption of a Keynesian perspective, in which prices do not have a co-ordinating role, but money represents an important resource. It is now time to see how this perspective can be brought to bear on the question of restructuring.

There are two key problems to be faced. The first, and most intractable, is what to produce next. To repeat, this is always going to be a gamble, and I am in no position to offer detailed policy recommendations, except in the negative sense of suggesting policies to avoid. The second problem is that of financing conversion. This problem obviously depends on the scale of the conversion required. In the case of the former communist countries, this scale is bound to be substantial and require the aid of external finance, yet this aid is likely to come with conditions, which, as Islam noted, could actually be detrimental to the ultimate goal of the conversion strategy.

International financial institutions are, as has been seen, generally antipathetic toward the notion of sectorally based strategies for conversion. However, the fact that the scale of the financing is likely to be so large, makes it possible that they will be forced to concede on this point. With Professor Lord Desai, I have recently developed a model of a trade cycle as a neo-Austrian model of a frustrated traverse, from one line of production to another (Desai and Redfern 1995). In this model, the banks withdraw their financing before the new production processes can be completed, forcing the economy to return to its previous methods of production at great loss to all concerned. This cheery tale could easily be applied to the problem of conversion. Faced with the consequences of failure, and a return to military production, because of the lack of financial assistance, it is possible that a more limited, and therefore sectorally based set of targets for conversion might be chosen.

In the absence of sufficient external finance, governments and industries will have to finance these conversions by entering the export market. Here, however, it is vital that the industries which participate in the export trade fulfil the correct conditions. Free trade is not an unqualified good (Pasinetti 1981, p.253ff., Ormerod 1994, p.8). Paradoxical as it may seem, international trade only benefits a country when those industrial sectors engaged in trade are of low productivity growth, compared to productivity growth in the rest of the economy. Note that it is not the absolute level of productivity which is at issue, but the rate of its growth.

The reason is that a sector whose productivity is growing faster than the others in its domestic context will see the price of its goods fall with respect to the prices in the other sectors. In the domestic context this is all to the good.

Should, however, the output of this sector be primarily for export, then the benefits of that fall in price go not to the domestic but to the importing economy (Pasinetti 1981, 1990). Consequently, the terms of trade worsen for the exporting country, simply because of this fact. It is always a great temptation for a country to seek to obtain foreign exchange through process of export-led growth, and to use its most advanced sectors to achieve this goal. But if its advanced sectors have higher productivity gains than the remainder of its economy, unless this sector is regarded as a loss leader, then the net result will be a loss of foreign revenues as terms of trade move against it, the more productivity increases in this sector compared to the rest of the economy.

Having issued this warning, however, it is important to stress again that it is the *rates of change*, not the *absolute levels* of productivity which are the key variables here. In the case of the former communist countries, it may well be that the productivity of the military sectors is considerably higher than the productivity of the remainder of the economy. However, if the productivity of the military sector is already as high as it can go, and the rest of the economy is catching up, then it would make sense to support the military industry and use it in an export drive in order to obtain foreign exchange in order to finance the conversion of other sectors to capitalist forms of production, and the conversion of other enterprises in its own sector. Of course, there are many reasons why military exports ought to be discouraged, but former communist countries have already been turning back to military exports in order to secure foreign exchange. Only detailed analysis can say whether or not, economically speaking, this is a wise move.

In the long run, financial gains from international trade are far less significant than productivity gains from learning. Unless international trade continues to expand, the gains from trade become simply a one-off benefit. This, however, will only happen if overall productivity in the countries engaging in trade continue to grow. If, as Pasinetti puts it, international trade is going to 'hamper the process of learning, or deplete the stock of accumulated technical knowledge' then the gains may prove illusory (1981, p.257). For any economy whose wealth depends ultimately on learning, that is, any industrial economy, a large part of the success or failure of its businesses lies in its R&D. In very many cases, it is a question of 'no design team, no more business'. While, clearly there is little point in maintaining research centres which continue to be oriented toward Cold War military objectives simply for their own sake, equally there are great risks in failing to support centres of R&D which are attempting to re-direct their attention to civilian opportunities. Unless such centres are protected from the effects of international trade during this transitional period, the course of capitalist development in the former communist countries will lead them towards the Third World rather than the First. This of course is to advocate not merely sectoral strategies in favour of development, but also protection for 'infant industries'. What this paper has attempted to demonstrate is that there are superior theoretical arguments for such strategies than those currently employed to oppose them.

REFERENCES

1. Artis, R., & Nobay, A., (eds) (1976) *Contemporary Economic Analysis* Manchester: Manchester UP.
2. Bakhar, V., & Fillipov V., (1993) The managers' perspective: Star Wars to high-tech consumer goods, pp.71-76 in Claudon and Wittneben (eds).
3. Batt, J., (1994) Political dimensions of privatisation in Eastern Europe, pp.83-91 in Estrin (1994a).
4. Brown, A., and Deaton, A., (1972) Models of Consumer Behaviour, *Economic Jnl* 82 1145 -1236.
5. Brun, Baehr & Karpe (eds) (1992) *Conversion – Opportunities for Development and Environment* Berlin: Springer-Verlag.
6. Bush, G., & Yeltsin, B., (1992) *Joint Russian–US Declaration on Defense Conversion* Washington, D.C.:US Government Printing Office.
7. Claudon, M., & Wittneben, K., (1993) *After the Cold War: Russian-American Defense Conversion for Economic Renewal* New York: New York University Press.
8. Coase, R.H., (1937) The nature of the firm, *Economica* IV, 386-405.
9. Coase, R.H., (1991) The nature of the firm: influence, in Williamson & Winter (eds).
10. Cowling, K., & Sugden, R., (1994) *Beyond Capitalism: Towards a new world economic order* London: Pinter.
11. Desai, M. & Redfern, P., (1995) Trade Cycle as a Frustrated Traverse: An analytical reconstruction of Hayek's model. To be included in *Money & Business Cycles* London: Edward Elgar.
12. Eichner, A., (1973) Theory of the determination of the mark-up under oligopoly, *Economic Journal*, vol. 83, pp.1184-1200.
13. Estrin S.,(ed.) (1994a) *Privatisation in Central and Eastern Europe*, London: Longman.
14. Estrin S., (1994b) Economic transition and privatisation: conceptual issues, pp.3-29 in Estrin (1994a).
15. Giddens, A., (1987) *Social Theory and Modern Sociology* Cambridge: Polity in association with Blackwell.
16. Goodwin, R., & Punzo, L., (1987) *The Dynamics Of A Capitalist Economy* Cambridge: Polity in association with Blackwell.
17. Harcourt, G., (1965/1982) *The Social Science Imperialists and other essays* Cambridge: Cambridge U.P.
18. Harcourt, G., (1972) *Some Cambridge Controversies in the Theory of Capital* London: Cambridge University Press.
19. Harcourt, G., (1976) The Cambridge Controversies: Old ways and new horizons – or dead end?, *Oxford Economic Papers*, vol. 28, pp.25-65.
20. Islam, Shafiqul (1994) Dialectics of Transition from Communism to Capitalism, pp.324-342 in Kirdar & Silk (eds).
21. Keynes, J. M., (1936) *The General Theory of Employment Interest and Money* London: Macmillan.
22. Keynes, J. M., (1937) The General Theory of Employment, *Quarterly Journal of Economics*, vol. 51, pp.209-223.
23. Kirdar, U., & Silk, L., *A World Fit For People* New York: NYU Press.
24. Linder, M., (1977) *Anti-Samuelson* New York: Urizen Books.
25. Lipsey R., (1981) *Introduction to Economics*: London:Weidenfeld
26. Marris, R., (1972) Why economics needs a theory of the firm, *Economic Journal*, vol. 82, pp.321-352.
27. McCloskey, Donald N. (1990) *If you're so smart...? the narrative of economic expertise* London: The University of Chicago Press.

28. Moss, S., (1976) The Firm, Finance & Equilibrium in Economic Theory, pp.261-276 in Artis & Nobay (eds).
29. Nuti, D., (1970a) 'Vulgar economy' in the theory of income distribution, *De Economist*, vol.118, pp.363-369.
30. Nuti, D., (1970b) Capitalism, Socialism and Steady Growth, *Economic Journal*, vol. 80, pp.32-57.
31. Ormerod, P., (1994) *The Death of Economics* London:Faber & Faber.
32. Parker, D., & Stacey R., (1994) Chaos, Management and Economics: The implications of non-linear thinking, *Hobart Paper 125* London: Institute of Economics Affairs.
33. Pasinetti, L.L., (1981) *Structural Change and Economic Growth: A Theoretical Essay on the Wealth of Nations* Cambridge: C.U.P.
34. Pasinetti, L.L., (1991) *Structural Economic Dynamics: A Theory of the Economic Consequences of Human Learning* Cambridge: C.U.P.
35. Perotti, E., (1994) Corporate Governance in Mass Privatisation Programmes, pp.54-68 in Estrin (1994a).
36. Peters, E., (1989) Fractal Structure in the Capital Markets, *Financial Analysts Journal*, July-August.
37. Phelps, E., (1992) Expectations in Macroeconomics and the Rational Expectations Debate, pp.129-38 in Vercelli & Dimitri (eds).
38. Radner, R., (1968) Competitive Equilibrium under Uncertainty, *Econometrica*, vol. 36, pp.31-58.
39. Samuelson, P., (1962) Parable and Realism in Capital Theory: the surrogate production function, *Review of Economic Studies*, vol. 29, pp.193-206.
40. Silberberg, E., (1978) *The Structure of Economics: A mathematical analysis* New York: McGraw-Hill.
41. Scott, N., (1994) Economies in Transition, pp.301-315 in Kirdar & Silk (eds).
42. Vercelli, A., & Dimitri, N., (1992) *Macroeconomics - a survey of research strategies* Oxford: Oxford UP.
43. von Neumann, J., (1946) A Model of General Economic Equilibrium, *Review of Economic Studies*.
44. Williamson, O., & Winter, S. (1991) *The nature of the firm: origins, evolution and development* Oxford: Oxford University Press.
45. Zecchini, S., (1994) Integrating East & West, pp.364-373 in Kirdar & Silk (eds).

Innovation and technology policy in the East European transformation - the Hungarian case

PAL TAMAS
Institute for Social Conflict Research
Hungarian Academy of Sciences
Budapest

INTRODUCTION

In order to analyse the scope for conversion of the military industries, and of military technology, in Central and Eastern Europe, it is essential to appreciate the broader industrial innovation and technology policy context which forms the foundation for current debates. This chapter aims to provide that context, with particular reference to the case of Hungary.

From the 1960s, Central and Eastern Europe - including Hungary - entered a new phase of modernisation. The system arrived at a peculiar crossroads of development. The dominant socio-political system - even its liberalised version - was a major structural barrier to further development. However, neither the geopolitical surroundings nor its own past made it possible for the elite of the regime to consider a radical transformation of the system. It is also evident that during the past two decades a new industrial structure has come into being in Hungary - just as in the other countries of Eastern Europe - but owing to its structure, its conditions of operation and its efficiency (it had to confront the realities of the world economy) it has been to a significant extent devalued in the eyes of the local elite and, of course, also by international commerce. Consequently, the system had to resort to non-traditional, though not defiantly disruptive, measures in preparing for the future.

The Hungarian attempt of 1968 to introduce a new system of economic management represented, in fact, only one of such attempts. The state socialist regime of this period developed a programme aimed at reforming the system while preserving its essential features. One of its significant elements was that it tried to return Hungary to the world market and connect it with the major international trends of technical and scientific development. As part of a specific socio-political experiment to conclude something of a pact, the formation of a new - and loyal - middle class began. The crucial role was to be assigned to the new technical-managerial elite, in keeping with

P. Gummett et al. (eds.), Military R&D after the Cold War, 93–106.

the 'an sich' technological orientation of the state socialist regimes, and the technological optimism of the sixties, which could be observed in other countries also.

The efforts to promote reintegration with the world economy - despite their partial results - were doomed to failure in that period, owing to the systemic peculiarities of state socialism, the weakness of the large new industrial enterprises and the divergent, even opposing, interests of the large multinational companies. Nevertheless, small 'islands of modernisation' succeeded in 'holding their own' in the international system, and in so doing diversified their technical-managerial elite. These experiences of modernisation are now available for utilisation by the new models of technological policy in the nineties, though political complications, including often hysterical reactions from newly arisen groups aspiring to power, impede this process.

The new emphases in thinking about technology policy seem to be connected organically with the transformation of the overall system. Technology policy has become in various dimensions a crucial part of the reform process.

First, technology (and the underlying science) had direct political functions in the overthrown state socialist regime. The Hungarian establishment was less repressive than those of the other socialist countries, but even here one could often hear (though less often than in East Germany or Czechoslovakia) of the 'scientific-technological revolution', the 'advantages of socialism in the international technological competition' or the 'potential of scientifically building a socialist society'. And since these highly ideologised technological programmes failed, the prestige of domestic science and technology has fallen to an extent that endangers even the basic conditions for this kind of activity.

Secondly, science and technology constitute par excellence the field of activity of the intelligentsia that has become the most active participant in the transformation process. Although the primary role has been fulfilled hitherto by the intelligentsia of the humanities, the importance of the business elite has also increased. This fact, together with the efforts to expand the autonomy of the intellectuals in the scientific organisations, and the increasing rationality of the various decisions, greatly strengthened the position of the technocratic intelligentsia. In this context, the politics of technology became a special reserved field of these groups. Since the majority of those groups that enter the realm of politics are made up of amateurs, the field with which they became acquainted in their pre-political life is bound to become a kind of 'life jacket', a reserved field.

In the near future, those specialists who have failed as politicians but who remain on the political scene will probably become active in those fields where they can regard themselves as specialists. Those who have suffered serious political defeats may well seek compensation through professional success. Consequently, the upgrading of certain specific areas of politics will represent a natural phase in the process of transformation. It remains to be seen how effectively the members of the new elite who are forced out of politics will work here, but one thing seems to be certain: they will try to do something in this field and this is bound to contribute to the strengthening of the position of the technological issues.

Thirdly, in the foreseeable future, two specific fields are expected to come into the limelight: the formation of strategy concerning external economic relations; and environmental policy. In both, their implicit technology content is decisive. Thus the latent politics of technology will be even more important and will dispose of larger financial assets than the traditional sphere of research and development (R&D) did.

THEORETICAL BOUNDARIES - RESTRICTIVE SURROUNDINGS

In the debates on the state socialist regimes of Eastern Europe, various concepts and interpretations have been formulated concerning the issues of technology and the role of specialist intellectuals and economic elites. The concepts which have been used largely reflect the mini-cycles of this age: the period of the formation of the late-Stalinist system after World War II, the subsequent attempts at reform and then, after their (partial) failure, the continuously diminishing role of the technocrats in the 1970s and 1980s and the simultaneously increasing criticism and rejection.

Late Stalinism has been viewed similarly both by internal ideologues and external critics in terms of the Manichean struggle between Good and Evil. The system copied the industrial revolutions of the last century in many respects, for example in its strategy of accumulation, its emphases on the crucial elements of development, or in its *étatism*. However, it differs significantly from the classical model - partly because of the autarchy imposed by the Cold War, and partly because of the Soviet-type logic of implementing political power - in respect of choosing, training and controlling the intellectual elite. Those technocratic views which expect the birth of a new social entity from the alliance of the political elite with the new technologies are also characteristic of the system.

But the planners of the new industrialisation programmes were well aware that of those factors believed necessary for the 'take-off', i.e., capital, technology and a skilled labour force, they lacked the first two and so they shifted an excessively heavy burden onto the third. The new emphases are seen in the rapid expansion of higher education, expecially technical education. Simultaneously, the accelerating social changes create increasing demand for higher education; the transformation of the political elites necessitates also - at least in part - the utilisation of formal channels of education; consequently, the number of technical intellectuals has swollen, and become too high for the present capacity of the Hungarian economy. Since neither industry nor the independent R&D sector can absorb this group, many of these intellectuals find jobs in public administration. The East-Central European intelligentsia - at least a significant part of it - has always been employed by the state, even before state socialism experiment. Now this dependence, strengthened by the almost complete 'étatisation' of the economic sphere, tends to place the technical intelligentsia at the mercy of the state apparatus.

The sixties brought some remarkable changes in this respect. First, the sphere of politics became fragmented. The violently integrated policies of the previous period began to assert their independence as separate branches. At the same time there appeared important novelties both in theory and in the national policies of the East Central European countries. The framework of the totalitarian system began to be eroded, and a limited degreee of liberalisation occurred. In many spheres of decision-making, professional criteria gained ascendancy.

External analysts reacted to these changes in two ways. On the one hand, the assumption began to be challenged that these systems had an absolutely different quality - a view that had been formed in the totalitarian period. There appeared the first comparative analyses which regarded the state socialist scenarios as specific programmes of modernisation, and they tried to compare them with other programmes aiming at catching up with the developed countries.

On the other hand, in this very period, the all-powerful ideology of the totalitarian system was replaced by structuralist-functionalist interpretations of the political system and political culture. The influential representatives of political science in the period of liberalised state socialism called into question even the earlier constructed dichotomy of totalitarianism versus democracy.

The technology policy of this period began to think in terms of evolution, rather than earlier revolutionary metaphors. At the same time, its general logical models and ideological emphases were markedly future-oriented. This approach was reflected in the short-term social and economic reform plans (and occasionally in implemented reforms). It also manifested itself in long-term models which, in the orthodox forms, characterised the Soviet and East German conceptions of the 'scientific-technological revolution', while it had 'democratic socialist' versions as well, such as the humanistic approach to technology of Randovan Richta.

This period represents a turning point in the history of the state socialist systems. It was in this period that the economic and technical elites, which were loyal to the regime, realised for the first time that the state socialist system was unable to learn from its earlier mistakes and that its weaknesses characterised not merely certain isolated segments of the system but its entirety.

However, from the end of the sixties a conservative turn in policy began to appear. Socio-economic innovation, which tested both the capacity of the political elites to learn and the internal logic of the whole system, ran out of steam while still in the early phase of formulation. For a while the political reaction was to try to consolidate the original structures, but then the capacity of state socialism to cope with the new technological and economic challenges of the global world system began to diminish rapidly. The regime could not survive this 'deviant development' and, from the early seventies, its condition could be characterised as 'latent apoplexy'. The ensuing crisis lasted for two decades. Two stabilisation programmes emerged: a neo-conservative-isolationist version (Soviet-Romanian-East German-Czechoslovakian version) and a technocratic one (Hungarian-Yugoslav-'Giereckian' Polish version). The differences between the two kinds of programmes - in respect of the applied social engineering, their social bases and international connections and also regarding their ideological emphases - were so significant as to constitute - in our opinion - two different visions of the late state socialist system. At the turn of the eighties and nineties both approaches failed as systems, although some elements of the technocratic approach now seem capable of being utilised by the new economic strategies which seem to be guided by etatist principles. The isolationist approach, however, seems destined to disappear for ever.

THE TYPES OF INDUSTRIALISATION OF THE SEMI-PERIPHERY

The course of East European development was influenced from the 1960s in each country by two sets of conditions, which were independent of each other, and which generated unpredictable and unexpected consequences.

In the political realm, Soviet regional hegemony remained essentially complete, but in the economic sphere, during the period of detente, steps were taken to promote integration into the world economy. This new orientation - even if mediated through the logic of the prevailing system - helped to cope with the new challenges presented by the world economy. At the same time, the Soviet political hegemony to some extent shielded and distorted the impulses coming from the world economy. It made the new roles, functions and divergent structural constraints less conspicuous in a region that had not been fully integrated into the global system. There was no real debate about determining the place that could be occupied in this system by Central Europe. Thus public opinion in those Central European countries had a fairly homogenised view of the international system. Hence, although the Hungarians, the Poles, the Czechs experienced in some of their concrete dealings (such as business agreements, technological contracts, the beginning of emigration of intellectuals) the externally generated structural constraints which were to limit severely their capacity for action, they nevertheless attributed these constraints largely to the fact that they were partially excluded from the international system, rather than tracing them back to the structure of that system.

In what follows, the terms 'centre' and 'periphery' are used as in the writings of Galtung, McKenzie, and Wellhofer. According to such authors, the differences between the centre and the periphery manifest themselves in the quality of the units of the system, in the character of the currents between them, and in the different patterns of their interactions. The first dimension characterises the different levels of development, the second characterises the conditions of the ensuing unequal exchange, while the third dimension refers to the network of relations among the peripheries themselves, including the disrupted, centrally blocked relations within the peripheries, relations which are operative only through the mediation of the centres. It is worth emphasising the three main elements in the dynamics of the relations between the centre and the periphery; the labour regime, the spatial structure of production and pumping the profits out of the region. The areas between the centre and the periphery are usually called 'semi-periphery'. Belonging to the semiperiphery represents simultaneously a structural element within the international division of labour and a 'dependent way of development', leading from the periphery to the semi-periphery. The transition from the periphery to the semi-periphery can be relatively precisely connected with the structural changes in the movements of capital, characteristic of the import - substituting phase of industrialisation.

In the following section we offer a structuralist (neostructuralist) global theoretical framework for the technocratic version of East/Central European state socialism, or at least for those sub-systems which managed to integrate into the world economy to such an extent that the above-mentioned effect should not be left out of consideration in the final analysis.

By the beginning of the 1960s, the first phase of industrialisation, started immediately after the war, had been finished. During this phase a significant industrial capacity was created, though its technological level was for the most part backward.

In this period, remarkably few industrial products were manufactured that could be sold outside the region; the industrial system depended to a large extent on political protection; and its products served almost exclusively the needs of the domestic or regional consumers. Nowadays it is a commonplace to speak of the political determination of East European industrialisation, carried out after the war. However, it is remarkable that even after the late-Stalinist model of industrialisation had proved a failure, the more open phase of modernisation, starting in the sixties, could not implement basic changes in the accepted model of industrialisation either, though undoubtedly there were efforts to this end. Nevertheless, the dominant model did not change: it concentrated on the region, remained protectionist, and aimed at import substitution.

In the present work we consider Hungary in the 1960s and 1970s, a *semi*-peripheral country on the grounds that its exports outside the region consist mainly of foodstuffs and industrial semi-finished products. Indeed, within the Soviet bloc there developed no examples of wholly peripheral status, characterised by specialised exports and massive imports.

During the period in question, indigenous industry could not match the imported industrial input, necessary for development. Consequently, the development of industry depended on food and raw material exports. And since these branches of the economy were increasingly affected by the worsening exchange rate, their potential was limited and they could not provide the basis for industrialisation, based on the utilisation of imported technology. Another basic feature of the semi-periphery everywhere, and certainly also in Hungary, is that islands of modern technology are mixed with the remnants of a pre-industrial level technology. But it is clear even in this environment that the poles of development - regarding the origins of the various technologies, the organisational patterns, the utilised types of knowledge and also their markets - were everywhere integrated or at least they were better integrated in the international economy. We find no such success-story in the Hungarian economy, and very few in the other East European countries, that produced a significant breakthrough isolated from this economic environment. However, since technological breakthroughs characterise not the extractive industries of the semi-periphery but the manufacturing industries of the centre, this further widens the gap between the centres and the peripheries.

THE SYSTEM OF RESEARCH AND THE PROCESS OF INDUSTRIALISATION

By adopting new industrialisation strategies, the East European technocracies wished to solve two basic problems in the 1960s. On the one hand, it had become clear by that time that the development of an autarchic heavy industry had not resulted in an economic capacity which enabled integration into the international division of labour. Once, then, détente opened up the world economy to the small economies of East and

Central Europe, it became necessary to effect a change of paradigm in respect of industrial policy.

On the other hand, the events of 1956 in Hungary and Poland - together with other manifestations of protest in the region - had made it evident to the political elite that they lacked legitimacy. By the beginning of the 1960s it was already clear that they could not build their social base from the workers. Though initially these elites were rooted in precisely indentifiable groups of the intelligentsia, they clashed with the intelligentsia of the humanities and especially its elite. These conflicts became more and more bitter. True, there were attempts on the part of the elite to utilise this stratum as an ally and source of legitimation, with the help of which a much wider social base could be built. However, because in the societies of Eastern Europe this stratum traditionally created and distributed ideas, yet the political elite wanted to retain the monopoly of creating ideologies, there emerged a structural conflict that from the outset frustrated the efforts of the elite. At the same time it also became evident that the polarised dichotomy of 'politics' and 'society', of 'they' and 'we' greatly destabilised the whole system. The solution that was to be applied (how deliberately remains unclear) became evident only gradually: to create a new middle class. Such a middle class would be the primary supporter and, to a certain extent, the beneficiary of the new phase of industrialisation. The expected economic growth, and some specialised sections of the intelligentsia who were promoting this growth, and so were highly rewarded by the elite, together with part of the skilled labour force, were between them to constitute this new middle class and to become the means to stabilise the system.

The realisation of this notion was, however, severely hampered by such factors as the geopolitical situation, the international economy and the technological possibilities, not to mention the opposition of influential sections of the party apparatus. On the other hand, since this policy was rarely explicit (especially in its early phase) and since it did not challenge the foundations of the Soviet-type system, it did not to any great extent provoke a stifling response from the Soviet Union. The scope for action was, however, much more circumscribed by the international economic order and the level of technology which was at the disposal of the elite. In the Hungarian case the limits were set by the following factors:

- In the 1960s, in the centres of the international system, the introduction of the most modern technology resulted in the third wave of the formation of new industrial cultures. The industrial and innovation systems of Eastern Europe were unable to accommodate high technology systems in that period. Nor had the region any markets capable of absorbing them, apart, that is, from the military sector.
- It was recognised that the apparatus for pursuing R&D was unable to develop independently, without dramatic difficulties, large-scale technological systems, though it was suitable for the solution of a number of partial problems. Consequently, a policy of massive technology-imports had to be followed. Although the international market for technologies at that time was not so sensitive politically as it became in the 1980s, the number of potential sellers, technologies and partners was nevertheless limited.
- In those fields of technology where the Hungarian industrialisation had any chance of success, only large-scale mass production was profitable. Owing to the severely

limited internal market, the majority of the products had to be exported, primarily to the 'socialist markets', with most of the exports gsoing to the Soviet Union, because there was very little demand for them in the West. And the socialist markets, owing to the given strategies of development in each socialist country, could not be expanded optionally despite the chronic shortages.

- Hungary had only a limited number of regions where the level of infrastructure, the level of skills in the labour force, and the technological know-how made it possible at all to start such projects. These were the Budapest conurbation, and western and central Transdanubia.

All this delineated the scope and direction of the potential actions. Essentially the preconditions of the second wave of industrialisation - in respect of organisation, economic theory and technology - were clearly determined: food-processing, manufacturing industry and electronics at not too high a level, utilising 'second-hand' West European technology dating from the sixties and seventies in hierarchically organised large-scale state enterprises. The formation of the thus conceived chains of innovation had to be undertaken by the direct intervention of the state. The most important projects were to start in the Gyôr-Budapest-Székesfehérvár triangle, i.e., in an area where an island of modernisation, enjoying a relatively high level of infrastructure, could be created without too many difficulties.

In the contemporary West European programmes of 'catching up' (primarily, though not exclusively, in the French programme) special emphasis was placed on the so-called 'national champions'. According to this approach, national economies which wish to catch up with the leaders first have to build a large enterprise in a given technological field. After this enterprise has consolidated its position, with help from its government, it is bound to give impetus to its entire economic sector.

In the documents of the Hungarian technological policy of the period one often finds references to the French example - mentioned not as a direct source of inspiration but rather as a point of reference. The Hungarian efforts at concentration, which were much more marked than those in the West European models, had also - quite apart from the influence of the political culture of the state socialist system - functional roots. On the one hand, the scarcity of resources and, hence, the imperative upon the state to redistribute the national income, was much stronger than in Western Europe and thus without 'special treatment' there seemed little chance of success. On the other hand, there was no network of cooperation around the newly rising large-scale enterprises. Consequently, either the state tried to create this network by direct intervention or - and this was more often the case - attempts were made to 'internalise' it, that is, to make the enterprise as independent as possible of its potential partners. Though, in the success stories of the sixties and seventies, the decisions of the central state or party apparatus played a major role, these very stories displayed their limits as well. It is clear now that:

- The apparatuses were not homogeneous at all, but were structured in various ways. Within them, the hierarchical levels, political styles, modernising and reactionary trends, and personal networks of relations, left the industrial and territorial interest groups with a fairly wide scope of action.

- The apparatuses and their networks were encompassed, in connection with their structure, by a complicated system of patrons. Decisions concerning development were taken in this sphere, so that the success or failure of projects depended on the opinion of these networks, independently of original intentions.
- At the same time, despite their state socialist monopolies, the apparatuses themselves were weak in generating and maintaining processes of innovation. If we try to evaluate their acts along a theoretical continuum of actions and reactions then, in specific cases, it can be shown that the apparatuses were rather reactive, and that their acts could be classified as responses. Few only of their decisions (though these are well documented) could be considered to be truly the decisions of the administrative or party apparatus.

It was in this sphere that a new type of manager emerged at the end of the sixties. In evaluating models of the behaviour of this new manager, two approaches are used by the relevant literature. The dominant managerial roles of this period were deduced by economic and sociological studies, following the classic works of Kornai, from the structure of the economic system and the budget constraints which manifested themselves in this very system. Authors who felt an inclination towards the elite-theories of the political science, (e.g., Breslauer) interpreted the upper-and middle-level posts of leaders in the economy as essentially political roles, representing a special mixture of political and economic considerations.

The present paper takes the view that the types of the managers in this period resembled much more the first generation of 'industry-founders' in the developing countries. On this interpretation, there are - apart from the elements of the market economy - fragments of various models, for example those of local leaders, village teachers, community politicians and even of dictators. The role of the 'founding' industrial leader is a highly complex one. Economic success is, of course, an integral part of it, but according to its self-definition it is nearer to that of the social reformer. And this wave of industrialisation at last created in fact - at least partially - the much sought-after middle class. The behaviour and the value-system of this conglomeration, consisting of specialised intellectuals, enterprise managers and highly rewarded groups of skilled workers (a worker-aristocracy?), were determined by the conditions of its birth and initial socialisation. It was not conservative, but it was afraid of radical changes. It did not show much mobility in organisational, professional or political aspects. In its patterns of career it primarily wanted to achieve security. Its techniques in the power struggles were quite sophisticated, especially in the constant struggles within the organisations. Its value-system, however, undoubtedly contained a certain myth of rationality as well.

THE INNOVATORY MODEL OF THE RESEARCH INSTITUTE

In fact it was only in the sixties that the 'vocabulary' and 'mini-paradigms' of the organisation of science were created in the state socialist Eastern Europe. Here the analysis of the relations between industry and science constituted from the beginning a crucial aspect of scientific policy. However, when we speak here of the links between industry and science, the intentions, the objectives and even the concepts they use differ in two basic respects from what we observe in other regions of the world.

Firstly, in Central and Eastern Europe, the 'institutional-organisational' concept of science includes also the research laboratories, which on the 'American' model are considered to belong to the sphere of industry. When Americans speak of the relations between industry and science, they think primarily of contacts between research institutes and the production and research units of fims. In the Eastern case, enterprises which lack certain expertise turn to industrial research institutes, or to university or Academy centres, even for the solution of simple problems which - under different conditions - they could have handled themselves, if they had not lacked the capacity to tackle even routine tasks of modernising the production process.

Since those essential services which, despite having little to do with real science were nevertheless delivered by the system of organisations called 'Science', were after all provided for the sake of the enterprises, this connection became the basis of the relations between industry and science. In addition, in the majority of cases the initiators were not those who were directly affected but central authorities, offices responsible for the formation of technological policy, and the centres of economic power. The enterprises themselves did not understand clearly why their superior authorities, and the political control-offices, supported these types of relations so heavily, but they also endeavoured to maintain this network of relations - sometimes because of their needs for funds of modernisation, sometimes only out of conformism. Of course, the enterprises - except for those in the fields of drug production, electronics and manufacturing precision instruments - did not effectively need any real science. Fortunately, not too much of this was offered on the markets. Consequently, still in this period, in the 'zero' phase of relations, and with the exception of the above-mentioned fields, the chances of a more constructive relationship between the industry and science were stifled. And it is an open question whether the introduction of high technology has essentially changed the situation in the affected sectors of Central and Eastern Europe.

Secondly, it was in the period of the sixties that the political leadership tried to face up for the first time - simultaneously with the beginning of de-Stalinisation - to the extreme inflexibility of the economic system. And perhaps it was at this time that it first realised how difficult it was to transform these structures at one stroke. Thus, it began to search for support and this, in turn, led to the upgrading of the status of science. At the same time, a lot of illusions were born about the capacity of science to deliver economic benefits, and about its wider social role.

Meanwhile, the basic principles regarding the utilisation of scientific research were being formed in the centres of the world economy. In the core of this 'world system', the various centres (economic, political, commercial, scientific) are always better integrated and better connected with one another than in the peripheries of the system. Thus, in circumstances where interdependence is lacking, the points of contact will necessarily be different. The situation is determined - according to my hypothesis - by the following factors:

- While in the international centres of science and the modern economy these two spheres are closely connected, on the semi-peripheries of the 'world system' the situation is entirely different. Here the local units of both science and the economy are essentially divergent. According to their basic functions both are 'carriers' for their own global systems. And their interests, which seem to be quite coherent in the centres, are separated in the peripheries. This is not a matter of some kind of under-development. The functional cores of the 'world system', cores that are more or less connected with one another in the centres, have varying configurations, and varying domains of action. It is much more difficult to build horizontal links between these domains than to strengthen the links between the cores.

- Moreover, the roles of science and the economy are heavily ideologically informed, both in the centres and the peripheries. This circumstance makes it more difficult to interpret these roles correctly. A more thorough analysis may reveal that what appear at first glance to be the antagonistic value-systems of Science and Industry are guided by evident economic changes in the labour market. For example the pragmatic values cherished by the American universities have always included the tradition of training students for careers in the economy. Since research activity played a subordinate role to that of education, this training model necessarily influenced the whole character of university education. Moreover, this system of values was somehow reconcilable with the traditional view of 'academic freedom', even if it clashed with these values in some repects. However, after World War II, large-scale research work was introduced at the American universities, but now this work was required by the state and not by the economy. When - independently of this - the rapidly expanding university system began to require more and more teachers, the ideology of 'academic freedom' also changed; in a peculiar way it became upgraded, completed and absolute. Utilising the favourable environmental conditions, science became, to some extent, separated from the economy as it gained independence and developed an adequate ideology. There was some attempt at separation even in the Soviet-type state socialist system. The primary reasons were, however, different in this case. The underdeveloped industry and its poorly trained new managers did not need science in the early years of Soviet industrialisation, i.e. the late twenties and early thirties. Hence, the leadership of the state which had to consider long-term objectives as well, could hardly expect this managerial elite to become a good master of the newly established research apparatus. Of course, information is power, and those 'brains trusts' which were transferred from the sphere of the enterprises to the authority of national administrative offices contributed to strengthening the direct influence of the centre. On the other hand the intelligentsia (in the traditional East European sense of the term) needed places of shelter and 'hibernation' in the overpoliticised public life. These shelters had to be insulated locally as well as was possible. In this respect the ideology of Science could be utilised effectively. In fact, whatever practical considerations led to the creation of the network of academic research institutes, its significant self-organising capacity could be traced back to these social origins.
- If we analyse the expansion of the Hungarian research network in the fifties and sixties, the effects of both the highly industrialised societies and those of the Soviet model can be seen in the formation of the dominant ideologies - in a specifically

Hungarian combination. The academic and university networks were never as insulated in Hungary as in the Soviet Union of the thirties. And however much these networks were expanding in that period, they could not hope to have a labour market that could absorb large quantities of autonomous professional results, whereby the research intelligentsia became the beneficiary of the wave of innovation after World War II.

- 'The economy did not really need science'. There are various reasons for this, although probably no single one can offer a full explanation. Economic theorists use the Kornai-model to depict the value-system of the command economy. Other approaches emphasise the importance of the reward mechanisms favouring the anti-innovative roles and thereby influencing the behaviour of the managers in the formation of political culture. There are interpretations which explain the situation by referring to the technological content of the exports. Some studies allege that the low technical culture of the majority of the Hungarian enterprises constituted the main reason for their fear of innovation.

CURRENT ISSUES

Against that background, how are we to understand the problems of the eighties and nineties? Many analyses treat these problems almost exclusively as financial issues - or perhaps as dilemmas of organisation and personnel. I would like instead to emphasise that, though I do not consider these problems to be unimportant, their solution should be attempted by a comprehensive scientific policy which is capable of facing other theoretical dilemmas as well. In this respect three questions should be posed.

The first concerns the capacity of what hitherto has been a growth-oriented system of management of science to react to the new circumstances. Much has already been written to the effect that not only science, but also the whole economy and society of the socialist countries, lived under the illusion of constantly expanding resources and improving prospects of investment - in a word, under the illusion of ceaseless progress. These countries still cherish this illusion, despite all the difficulties. In specific policy areas, until the 1970s, preferences were realised by assigning much of the economic surplus to some of the affected groups, while others were given less - but what had been given to them previously was not withdrawn. This strategy was even more marked in the case of the management of science where, from the mid-sixties to the end of the seventies, the inputs to research expanded in all European socialist countries more rapidly than the national income.

Today, it is important to introduce, and justify to policy makers, managers and researchers, a policy of giving to some while also taking from others. This is a problem of value choice. But more than this, it also raises questions of the need for a mechanism for making such priority choices, which under the old system was unnecessary. This, in turn, becomes a question of the structure of power within science.In my opinion the remedy would lie, at least in part, in a new form of self-regulation and self-management in science, promoted by the new bargaining strength of the researchers.

The second issue is that of the current reduction in the number of jobs, where the question is, what can be given up without causing lasting and irreparable damage? The answers to this question vary not only from country to country, but also from one field of science to another and even from one institute to another.

Science policy will inevitably look for ways of retrenchment which are 'reversible'. But it is far from evident where the limits to 'reversible' damage lie, and how to recognise the point beyond which damage is already 'irreverisble'. Nobody disputes that it is a bad thing if no new instruments can be bought and the young talented researchers cannot be employed. Are we really able to assess what is worse: not to buy new instruments or not to employ new researchers? How long is the damage reversible, and how many years can pass until it becomes irreversible?

The answer cannot be definite even in concrete cases. No post-socialist country has significant experience in this respect. Nor, in Western Europe, where the situation practically resembles ours, are those who are responsible for the management of science examining this issue at the theoretical level. Rather, they are directing their energy to salvaging the system of research. Therefore it is only a tentative hypothesis on my part that, if I were forced to choose between creating jobs for researchers and modernising the instruments of research, *I would vote for increasing the number of researchers.* I know that there are views which are diametrically opposed to mine. According to them, only as many researchers should be kept as can be provided with the necessary means of research. But in those cases when the tasks do not require the use of certain strictly prescribed instruments, it is generally possible - sooner or later - to find instruments for the researchers - either in the country or abroad. Excluding whole generations from scientific research, or displacing them, may cause in all probability much more damage. However, we are faced with this phenomenon, though to varying degrees, not only in Hungary but also in the other half of Europe.

Consequently I think that the most advantageous tactics would be those which would lead, under the conditions of restriction, to reversible changes, and which would be based on external resources.

Thirdly, I call attention to the necessity of rethinking the relationship between elitism and egalitarianism within research. In the previous period a relatively favourable balance could be struck between these two principles in the dynamically expanding and relatively well-provisioned system of research. Each member of the community of researchers was given something. At the same time the professional elite, with reference to its achievement, was given more than the 'simple members'. The proportions of redistribution were far from being harmonious, but in the majority of cases there was no essential divergence from the picture, corresponding to the value-system of the affected people. However, the reduction of the available resources upset this seemingly peaceful balance. It seems that in this environment elitism has better chances of success. It is very difficult to dispute the principle of 'Let us give to those who have already demonstrated their talent', especially under the conditions of constantly dwindling resources. The other slogan says: 'We have to preserve the most valuable part of the researcher community until better times come!' Who would doubt the wisdom of this? Nevertheless I have to point out that *this principle favours the time-tested solutions and their representatives.* Consequently, it renounces those potentially new ideas and experiments which could be produced by new experts.

CONCLUSIONS

The social and economic transformation of Eastern Europe created very difficult conditions for science, technology and industry in this phase of industrialisation. Their high sensitivity to the social context has become evident, together with the fragility of their positions and rewards. The changes in the former Soviet Union resulted in the abolition of their traditional markets. Their leaders were forced to give up their close relations with the political elite - a connection which was formed under the conditions of late state socialism. Owing to the autocratic methods of internal management, utilised previously by the strong leaders of the relevant organisations, there was no 'second tier' to succeed these leaders. The birth of the elements of the market economy split the previously compact organisations of technology and led to the creation of independent units. In the meantime there have appeared the first elements of the third wave of industrialisation, characterised by high-tech industries, though the number of these elements cannot yet be considered sufficient for the desired qualitative breakthrough.

During the first two years of the transformation, the organisations analysed by us had to face crises threatening their very existence.

In the political and economic environment of the rapidly changing Eastern Europe, the 'neostructuralist' interpretation of national technological policy strategies will see its importance significantly increased. It will be used to re-evaluate what potential courses of action can be chosen by the Central and East European semi-periphery when the scope of manoeuvring is determined both by external factors, deriving from the global system, and by internal social changes. However, either there will be a new wave of industrialisation,or the traditional industrial potential will be reconstructed: the technological experiences, organisational cultures and bodies of experts which were formed during the previous wave of industrialisation surely cannot be simply eradicated. However, for the time being, we see no signs of a new process of industrialisation. The presently prevailing economic policies of this region of Europe resemble more the de-industrialising policy of the Argentinian or Uruguayan military juntas. The reinterpretation of the results of the previous phase of modernisation, even if these results are only semi-finished or only partially successful, and their utilisation in the new economic strategies, will perhaps indicate our coming of age in respect of political culture.

Critical Technologies, Policy and Security in a Middle Power Country: A Case of Avionics and Systems Integration in Canada

JOHN DE LA MOTHE AND GILLES PAQUET*
Faculty of Administration
University of Ottawa
Canada

INTRODUCTION

The nature of the international security environment is undergoing the most profound transformations it has faced since the 1940s. The certainties that governed strategy and diplomacy for decades have begun to rapidly dissolve. National agendas relating to East-West relations and arms reduction are being diffused. In the process, new concerns are arising, relating for example to regional dispute management, the rise of nationalism and the nature of 'peace-making', and the future roles of such international organisations as NATO and the UN. These new debates are not, however, being contained within the walls of national defense establishments but are indeed being carried out within the broader open context of government policy.

Throughout Europe and North America, military spending (including military R&D spending) is being reassessed and re-directed as are all other aspects of government activity (See National Science Board, 1993; European Commission, 1994). In part, this is due to the tight fiscal realities in which many governments are now finding themselves. This is also due to the growing consensus that the technology-economy nexus will increasingly drive the re-definition of security away from strictly military concerns and towards economic interests (See Roberts, 1992 & 1993; Tolchin, 1992; Lynn-Jones, 1993; Branscomb, 1993; Charlton, 1993; de la Mothe, 1996).

In recognition of this, many of the 25 OECD member countries - including the United States, Australia, Britain, and Canada - have recently undertaken a series of science and technology reports, reviews or re-organisations. The general context for these reviews is common: what would be called 'better government' or 're-inventing government' in North America or a push towards 'value for money' in the UK and Australia. Spinning-out government activities to industry, leveraging private sector funds, linking university research with industry needs, and so on are all, in part, a management reaction against the abuse of public procurement programs (such as 'the $8000 wrench') and a recognition of the new security agenda. These reviews have revealed a growing consensus (de la Mothe & Paquet,

P. Gummett et al. (eds.), Military R&D after the Cold War, 107–117.

1994; de la Mothe & Dufour, 1995). This consensus has gravitated, in technology policy terms, around (a) the agreement that technology has an important role of play in competitiveness; (b) that this has been bolstered by a growing economic and policy understanding of the process of industrial innovation; (c) there is a shift in the nature of defense-related and security issues;(d) there was a growing role for individual countries to define their technology policies in terms of critical, generic and dual-use technologies (Alic, 1992); (e) that there is a relative decline in the leadership and hegemony of the United States (thus creating new challenges and opportunities for middle power countries such as Canada) (Ostry & Nelson, 1995).

MIDDLE POWER COUNTRIES AND SECURITY

It has been said that the only thing that small and middle power countries have in common is that they are different. One thing that makes Canada different is that while it is a 'middle power' country technologically, it considers itself to be a 'big country' both economically (being a member of the G-7) and geo-politically. Clearly Canada falls within the ranks of the advanced industrialised countries, falling fourth in terms of per-capita Gross Domestic Product (GDP), fourth in terms of overall GDP and ninth in terms of actual expenditures on R&D. But there are several other factors besides overall economic performance that make science an important limiting factor in the technological competitiveness and security of countries such as Canada. To begin with, such countries tend to have limited domestic markets. This means that firms must export to foreign markets in order to gain economies of scale. Increasingly, they also need to justify heavy expenditures on R&D, for as technology increases the sophistication of products and processes, so the scientific, technological and economic resources and skills that are needed for development become more costly and complex. Furthermore, small and middle power countries tend to have less money, proportionately, to spend on R&D. They tend to have fewer research personnel per capita, and there is a considerable tendency for researchers from such countries to emigrate. In addition, small countries tend to have problems in concentrating R&D resources. They need to fund across the full spectrum of scientific research for educational purposes, but in so doing they typically fail to define their own technological niche areas - buying into, or falling behind, the research agendas of larger countries. (To some degree, this has happened in Canada, with its informal adoption of US critical technologies or priority areas.) As a result, and although it may be a specious exercise to generalise about small and middle power countries, technologically 'successful' countries seem to adopt an R&D specialisation strategy. They tend to seek market niches and they tend to pursue industries in which they already have strong multi-technology corporations. (As we will see below, this is the case with Canada's selected focus on avionics.)

Canada clearly fits the criteria of being a middle power country. It is a member of most international 'clubs' such as NATO. Its domestic market is confined to 27 million consumers, as opposed to 265 million in the US, 500 million in Europe and 123 million in Japan. Sixty-five percent of industrial R&D is performed by 100 firms in six industries. Canada's gross expenditure on R&D is 1.35% of GDP as opposed to 2.7% in the US.

Technological dependency is suggested by its 7 billion dollar high-tech trade deficit, its contribution to world science is roughly 4%, its technology share of world exports is roughly 3%, and its indigenous patents-to-labour-force ratio is one of the lowest of the industrialised nations. The anomalies created by Canada's economically advanced status but technologically immature development are highlighted by Canada's somewhat unique security situation in which its proximity to the United States, coupled with an extensive marine coastline (bordering on three seas) make a strategy of critical technology selection in which government partners with universities and industry a key future feature.

Critical Technologies

It is interesting that so many 'critical technology lists' have emerged from within the bureaucracies of the G-7 governments. In the US alone, estimates suggest that as many as 25 'lists' have been penned since 1989, each of which features as many as 36 'critical technologies'. These 'lists' can be used in the allocation of public and private investments into new technology development and to show where a government sees its priorities. These lists have the potential of providing a focal point for national technology plans that can guide government, industry and academic actions or responses. In Canada, the government has long relied on general areas as providing direction (informatics, biotechnologies, and new materials) and has 'borrowed' or taken note of the critical technology designations of its major trading partners (particularly those of the US and Japan). But, of course, the problem is not listing critical technologies - it is more to understand why they are critical to a nation and to actively development and deploy them - swiftly and strategically.

Generic and Dual Use Technologies

Very much related to the idea of 'critical technologies' is the idea that certain technologies are 'precompetitive', 'generic' or 'dual use'. 'Pre-competitive research', which Canada has very successfully focused on through such industrial/university organisations as PRECARN, an Ottawa-based pre-competitive research consortium with more than 39 industrial members, refers to a stage of the technology development process that occurs before commercial potential can be assessed. 'Generic' technology refers to technology that has potential for applications in a broad range of products and processes. And 'dual-use' technologies are those technologies with applications in both the military and the commercial sectors.

The wide currency of these ideas reflects an increasingly widespread concern amongst countries with the potential applications of R&D and with new emerging technologies - that is, on the potential payoffs to investment in technology development. The use of these types of terms reflects an attempt to inject a more precise set of distinctions into traditional classifications of R&D and technology development, and thus to provide a more discerning basis for determining the relative roles of the federal government and private sectors.

TECHNOLOGY POLICY AND SECURITY

Technology has been, and will continue to be, an important element in any nation's security response capability. This is clearly the case in Canada. Today's research horizons reveal a multitude of technologies that could revolutionise the meaning of defense. However, the ability of countries, including Canada, to fully capitalise on such advances may well be limited or shaped by political, bureaucratic, economic and technological factors. Throughout the latter half of this century, the militaries of the west have driven, to at least some degree, the development of new technologies for procurement and R&D programs. In Canada, these have ranged from aviation to nuclear energies and integrated circuits and include such examples as the Avro Arrow, CANDU reactor and the Bell Northern switching devices. These technologies have influenced the shape, size, and scope of both military forces and civil economies. But contrary to popular perception, defense related technologies have only been evolving slowly in recent decades. The rate of technological innovation is outstripping the integration of technologies into currently deployed systems. These realities are all being felt and managed by Canada's Department of National Defence (DND). Shaping the nature of this response is a number of factors: for example, (i) the political reality that debt and deficit will continue to downsize overtly defense-related budgets that the geo-political reality will continue to deescalate Cold War tensions; (ii) that the bureaucratic realities associated with developing 'leaner and meaner governance structures'; and (iii) that the economic reality that a well-connected, well distributed, technologically-intensive and competitive industrial sector will increasingly define the new security. Together, these features will deliver new linkages between technology policy and a nation's security. By way of illustration, we can briefly look at Canada's recent experiences and strategy vis à vis avionics and systems integration.

Critical Technology and Canada's Emerging 'Security' Policy

The introduction of Canada's Department of National Defence (DND) to the world of dual use technology and digital integrated avionics systems began with its acquisition of the CP-140 Aurora fleet in the late 1970s. Since then, a wide range of acquisition and update projects has been implemented, introducing integrated avionics systems into the majority of its considerable military aircraft fleets. This trend will continue as downward budgetary pressures continue. As a result of the 1995 budget, DND the lose nearly $2 billion from its roughly $12 billion annual budget in the next few years. This will mean that DND will need to seek cost savings through a commitment to fleet upgrades over fleet replacements; to a maximum use of off-the-shelf equipment and technology that are produced to commercial open standards; an increasing reliance on ever more integrated systems; and the development of technology security solutions in Canada wherever possible. It will also mean that DND will have to shift its mandate and activities increasingly towards private sector needs and involvement.

Canada has long had a somewhat unique 'security' function. It has the world's longest undefended borders, shares security functions (including 'search and rescue') with the US Coast Guard and Armed Forces, has been a member of NATO and the UN (to mention but two), and has been taking a leading role in the move of the UN Security Council towards 'peace-making' and away from 'peace keeping'. Out of a $12 billion budget, DND spent roughly $250 million on S&T activities in 1994 - 55% of which was intramural. Almost all of this (99%) was on R&D (not 'related scientific activities' - RSA).

In response to these trends, many policy initiatives are underway. On the one hand, Canada's geopolitical concerns continue to mirror those of the US Security Council and there is a renewed commitment to fulfilling Canada's defense-related obligations. In order meet these requirements whilst building upon Canadian capabilities to support DND requirements to upgrade existing fleets and acquire new aircraft types, the Chief of Research and Development (CRAD) is currently developing a strategy to establish a sustainable avionics systems integration technology base capability in Canada. On the other hand, DND has recognised that the nature of Canada's defense requirements are different from, say, the US, Germany or Sweden. Its capabilities are far more modest, are less well defined in terms of 'hardened', military-specific, applications. These two facts have helped to move parts of the DND's management towards a strategy of 'dual-use' policy. In an important case, they have chosen to focus on avionics and systems integration. They have chosen one - avionics - largely because military procurement policy can exert a powerful influence on Canadian academic research agenda and Canadian industrial development. They have chosen the second - systems integration - because there are tremendous costs involved in developing and deploying 'one-off' systems: that is, systems that can only 'fly' in a specific platform or environment. Clearly, if a robust 'black-box' can be migrated from a Hercules transport plane to a CF-18 fighter jet to a Chinook helicopter then the costs and design specifications improve dramatically. Together these create what amounts to Canada's dual-use techno-economic policy.

AVIONICS

'Avionics' has been defined by the DND as 'electronics that are applied to aviation'. 'Avionics systems integration' has been defined as 'a process that begins at the successful testing of the production-ready integrated system. The total process of systems integration can be discerned at 7 levels: physical data, data link, data networking, data transport, session testing, presentation (including visual display), and application.' Avionics systems are present in every airborne craft.

Over the last two decades, microelectronics capability has doubled (some say quadrupled) every two years, a trend that is expected to continue for the foreseeable future. The impact of this explosion in capability on digital avionics products has been stunning, enabling the industry to implement impressive and new functionalities and at the same time reduce avionic systems weight and costs of increase in complexity, particularly with respect to the software. Moreover, our ability to successfully integrate complex avionics components on time and on budget has failed to keep pace. As the Canadian military has required more and more functionality in its systems, and as the technology to enable it to do so increases in sophistication, the complexity of the products and processes used to create the system and coordinate the added effort has grown at a non-linear rate.

The development and maintenance of an avionics systems integration technology base requires that basic and applied research organisations develop and maintain sufficient knowledge of product and process technologies (either through research of professional exchange) and make that knowledge readily available to development and production organisations. It also requires that development and production organisations acquire knowledge of technology (from the research organisations, as well as other sources) and develop and maintain the know-how to efficiently apply technology to produce effective integrated avionics systems.

The Avionics Industry

Avionics is widely considered to be a key activity in both technological and economic terms. This is true because avionics as an area of activity underpins a wide range of industries - particularly those in aerospace and defence electronics. Indeed, it is fair to say that in many ways, the future of these industries - their economic viability, the character of their products and processes - will depend on avionics activities. Avionics represents only about 10% of total aerospace industry employment but roughly 30% of total industry output value. Thus, in terms of economic impact, the 'avionics sector' carries a disproportionate economic weight.

Over the past decade, there has been a significant decline in the world avionics industry. In 1985, global avionics R&D and procurement was a $20 billion plus business. In 1994, it is expected that the total avionics R&D and procurement will be about $9 billion and will remain at this level out to 2003. In this environment, there will be fewer new research programs, but opportunities will arise with upgrades of older platforms (Adams, 1994, p.33). Although there will be a continued decline in new platforms there will be increased requirements for modelling and simulation capabilities applicable not only to simulation and training but to weapons design, test and evaluation. This area is forecast to grow from less than $3.5 billion in 1994 to $5 billion in 2003. Part of this increased demand in synthetic environments appears to be the need for a reduction in concept to product time. For electronics, most companies believe that this time, in the foreseeable future, must be reduced by 40% to remain competitive (Stahlschmidt, 1993).

As a result of this significant budgetary contraction and the globalisation of industry, most of the large companies have been laying off workers and mergers and acquisitions have become common to enable companies to remain competitive and profitable. This type of reorganisation is occurring throughout the industrialised areas of the world, including the United States, where some observers consider that within four years there will be just two major avionics manufacturers in name. Nevertheless, in the case of avionics and electronics, 'it has to be said, at the risk of upsetting some people, that much of the pace-setting is still in the United States.' (Parry, 1994, p.29) Currently, in the military arena, that pace setting has been tied to the F-22 Advanced Tactical Fighter and the RAH-66 Comanche helicopter projects with their integrated architectures.

Competition is indeed fierce. 'While the trend toward mergers and acquisitions is already well established among large companies, almost unnoticed are small companies, typically those with fewer than 30 employees, which have been growing. These small companies are well represented in the avionics industry and tend to be high-tech, highly specialised, strongly entrepreneurial, and willing to take risks to develop product lines that the market needs. Significantly, many of them supply the larger companies, who cannot match the delivery times and costs that these smaller enterprises can achieve while demonstrating an ability to be flexible, adaptable, and open to new ideas.' (Parry, 1994, p.29)

In Canada, the aerospace industry offers specialised capabilities for research, development, manufacture, marketing, and support of complete aircraft, propulsion related systems and components, as well as space equipment, navigational and defence electronics, and defence systems. The industry's markets include transport and general aviation aircraft manufacturers, regional airlines, business aircraft users, as well as major civil and defence aerospace contractors and government agencies. Avionics is a key part of this industry.

The structure of the aerospace industry can be thought of as comprising three tiers. On the first broad tier - the base - one can find aircraft manufacturers which have a full range of systems integration capability. This tier accounts for some 45% of the industry's annual output and consists of the largest sector firms (over 2,000 workers). Examples include Pratt and Whitney, Boeing Aircraft Canada, de Havilland, Canadair and Spar Aerospace.

On the second tier, one can find firms which produce integrated systems (including avionics systems, propulsion systems, and sub-systems/sub-assemblies - e.g., antennae). This tier is composed of about 40 medium-sised companies which collectively account for about 45% of the industry output. These companies are primarily suppliers of proprietary products and build-to-print components, most of which are sold to foreign aerospace manufacturers. The main products of the second-tier firms include aircraft navigational and defence electronics systems, aircraft simulators, anti-aircraft defence systems and major sub-assemblies.

Third-tier firms manufacture components and provide support services. This tier is composed of more than 100 (mostly) small firms with annual aerospace output worth under $20 million. Collectively, these firms account for the remaining 10% of total output.

In 1993, output in the aerospace industries in the world's 8 largest aerospace manufacturing countries (France, the US, Germany, UK, Japan, Canada, Australia and Saudi Arabia) totalled $260 billion. Canada's output is estimated to be steady at about 3.7% of the total world output - or about $9.6 billion. Roughly 72% of its industrial output is exported.

At this level, Canada's aerospace industry is a major contributor to the country's trade balance. This 3.7% share of total output has roughly remained constant since the 1960s and 1970s. However, the expansion of the industry that resulted from the increase in the US defence spending benefited Canada's industry. Canada's defence acquisitions, such as that of the CF-18 program, coupled with the government's divestiture of de Havilland and Canadair, assisted in this growth. Similarly, the introduction by Pratt & Whitney of its PW100 series of regional aircraft engines improved its performance by allowing it to become less dependent on a declining general aviation market.

During the decade ending in 1988, the industry achieved an annual sales growth of approximately 9% in constant terms. This compares with zero growth in the previous decade. The airframe sub-sector led the industry with an average growth rate of 13%, followed closely by avionics and the propulsion sectors with 12% and 8% respectively. Overall, Canada's aerospace output since the 1970s has outpaced the other major aerospace nations. Comparative current dollar data for the period 1984 to 1988 suggests that whereas sales in the American and British aerospace sectors grew by 37% and 50% respectively, Canada's industry grew by 84%. This, in part, was brought about by the addition of Bell Helicopter Canada as well as to the industry's focus on civilian markets which tended to fare better than defence markets. As the president of AIAC William Weston recently remarked: 'Canada has been converting its aerospace industry from defence to civilian markets since the demise of the Avro Arrow in the late 1950s' (Jones, 1994, p.60). Thus, the loss of employment and the impact of restructuring has been less severe here than in the United States. Indeed, of its sales in 1992, 69% were focused on civilian markets whereas most international competitors depend on military markets for between 50-70% of sales.

In terms of world aerospace, Canada ranks 6th in terms of importers (behind France, US, Germany, UK and Japan) and 5th in terms of exporters (behind the US, UK, France and Germany). In 1994, the United States remains Canada's principal export market, accounting for nearly 39% of sales. Other countries collectively account for 35% and domestic sales account for 26%. US manufacturers and the US government collectively accounted for 42% and 10% respectively of direct American sales. Of the foreign direct sales, manufacturers and governments accounted for 21% and 26% respectively. Nationally, Canada imports about $2.6 billion worth of aerospace products annually providing a substantial net surplus.

The breakdown of net sales by sub-sector reveals that the recent recession impacted most heavily in the airframe, propulsion systems, and avionics sub-sectors. In 1993, avionics accounted for roughly 16%. This is a stable representation with the sector. The industry is heavily concentrated, with Quebec and Ontario accounting for fully 89% of the total industry value. The three largest firms - Canadair, de Havilland and Pratt & Whitney - accounted for 37% of the value of production in Canada.

Canada at present has a sophisticated high technology industry which, in general terms, has a wide and varied capability in the avionics area. The component of the industry which is oriented towards the avionics area has the capability of providing a full range of services. This includes the capability to design, develop, integrate, produce and support state-of-the-art avionics systems to both commercial and military standards (Bennett, 1991).

From a statistical point-of-view, 'avionics' are defined as being 'aviation electronics': that is, as one Industry Canada analyst put it, 'those systems that help aircraft fly'. But in specifying the area in this way, it is difficult to delineate the activity in clear statistical terms (output, value, employment, etc.). In an important way, avionics - the technologies and activities that it represents - do not always manifest themselves in physical, final product form. They are thus considered to be embedded activities. For analytical purposes, this causes definitional problems. (For example, radar that Canadian Marconi manufactures and which is installed on ships is counted as an avionics system by that firm, because of where in-house the product is developed and accounted for.) Thus, any attempt to clearly discuss an 'avionics sector' is necessarily an exaggeration. To be sure, there <u>are</u> firms that specialise in aspects of avionics, but the majority of these activities represent <u>aspects</u> of a firm's total activity.

Avionics forms an important aspect in all three tiers. Industry estimates suggest that the value added of avionics ranges from 30-35% at the high technology/market end to 20-25% of the low-technology/market end. Thus, the direct economic value of avionics is estimated at being upwards of $3 billion with approximately 6,000 people directly responsible for this output.

Thus, Avionics Systems Integration has a very high value-added industrial benefit. In the future, the aging of aircraft fleets of all types and the need to upgrade avionics to remain competitive will create a large market segment. Therefore, a strong avionics integration capability will have a large industrial benefit, positively impact Canadian society and enhance technological expertise and competitiveness within the global marketplace.

The avionics component of the industry supports a wide and varied customer base in Canada. This base includes the Federal Government, provincial and municipal levels of government, major aerospace industry, airlines, and private carriers and to a lesser degree general aviation. The avionics industry also vigorously markets offshore and a considerable portion of the business base is outside Canada (Bennett, 1991). However, in Canada, the Federal Government is one of the largest single customers of the Canadian avionics industry. Within the Federal arena, the Department of National Defence is by far the largest customer of the industry.

Unlike most industries, there is a surprisingly low degree of direct, 'head to head', competition in the avionics sector in Canada. Indeed, one could almost say that the sector has undergone an intelligent shakeout. Firms involved in avionics have evolved along highly specialised niche areas and tend to define themselves, or their activities, according to these niches. There appear to be 3 major axes along which firms find their competitive markets. These are technological (high end versus low end), product-based (type of airframe such as fixed wing or helicopter), and market-based (military versus civilian). The market-based axis can be thought of as the environment in which the equipment is intended to operate. This is a very important distinction with respect to the niche because much of the development and performance requirements of avionics are driven by the environmental constraints. In addition, there are unique requirements associated with the military use of these systems. For example, an intercommunication system that is acceptable in a commercial helicopter may not be acceptable in a military helicopter because of security reasons even though the technological sophistication, the platform and the environment are similar. Thus, in differentiating between military and civil markets, it is often assumed that the key factor is the 'technological hardness' of the system. Examples abound. For instance, Canadian Marconi and CAL both manufacture satcom antennas, but they do not compete directly since Marconi installs its product in the European Airbus while CAL installs its antennas in executive jets such as those made by Lear. Similarly, Marconi is involved, as is Allied Signal, in electro-optics and thermo-imaging. But Marconi finds its application in the high-end (i.e., space) whereas Allied Signal occupies the low-end applications niche. In communications controllers, Northern Airborne Technologies services police, ambulances and air rescue, and thus avoids competing with Marconi in the same technologies since they, again, concentrate on the high end. MacDonald Dettwiler and Associates (MDA) of Vancouver has somewhat gone against the grain by moving - not increasingly in commercial markets but, into military applications. Already a leader in remote sensing, avionics, and image analysis, MDA's Avionics Systems and Geo-Information Systems account fro 20% and 60% of the Space and Defence Systems Division revenues of US$73 million. Moreover, they are selling products and systems to such groups as the Canadian Maritime Coastal Defence Vessel project (US$81.7 million).

CONCLUSION

The unique competitive challenge that faces avionics and dual-use policy in Canada will not rely on industry's ability to wholly create new products or even its ability to 'stretch' existing platforms and technologies into 'robust' and innovative frameworks. Instead, and just as avionics is an important upstream and downstream activity (for purposes of economic linkages), the challenge for the avionics sector will be how it manages its way to forging technological linkages: for example, between satcom, geographical positioning systems, data links, flight management systems, and antenna. Industry analysts seem to be uniform in their view that the future of defence electronics, aerospace products and systems, dual use technologies, and the entire way in which we view aerospace operations will depend on the integration of avionics systems. In many middle power countries, where security issues are being very directly framed in terms of economic competition, we will increasingly see such 'technology dual-use' efforts as are currently underway in Canada viz a viz avionics and systems integration. The linkages between the national military establishments, universities and industry will continue to be forged by government policy. And in this way, not only will efficiencies and cost savings be found within government activities, but techno-economic synergies will be developed in support of national industries. Technology policies and the new security will continue to evolve.

---

* An earlier version of this paper was delivered at a NATO Advanced Studies Workshop on Defence Conversion in Budapest in August 1994. The authors would like to acknowledge the generous support of the SSHRC (grant numbers 410-93-0471 and 809-94-0002), as well as the Department of National Defence (DND), the North Atlantic Treaty Organization (NATO), and the European Association for Science and Technology Studies (EASST).

REFERENCES

1. Adams, C. (1994) US Military Avionics: No Surprises Anytime Soon, *Avionics Magazine*, January, p.33.
2. Alic, J., et al. (1992) *Beyond Spin-Off*, Cambridge, MA.:, Harvard Business School Press.
3. Bennett, P. and Associates (1991) *Avionics Systems Master Plan*, Revised August, pp.2-64.
4. Branscomb, L. (ed.) (1993) *Empowering Technology*, Cambridge MA.: MIT Press.
5. Charlton, M., and E. Riddell-Dixon (eds.) (1993) *International Relations in the Post-Cold War Era*, Toronto: Nelson.
6. De la Mothe, J., and P. Dufour (1995) Techno-Globalism and the Challenges of Science and Technology Policy, *Daedalus*, Summer.
7. De la Mothe, J., and G. Paquet (1994) The Technology-Trade Nexus: Liberalization, Warring Blocs or Negotiated Access?, *Technology In Society*, vol.16 , no.1.
8. De la Mothe, J., and G. Paquet (eds.) (1996) *Evolutionary Economics and the New International Political Economy*, London: Pinter (in press).
9. European Commission (1994) *The European Report on Science and Technology Indicators 1994*, Luxembourg.
10. Jones, D. (1994) Caught in the Downdraft, Report on Business, *The Globe and Mail Magazine*, March, p.60.
11. National Science Board (1993) *Science and Engineering Indicators 1993*, Washington: DC, USGPO.
12. Ostry, S., and R. Nelson (1995) *Techno-Globalism and Techno-Nationalism*, Washington, DC., Brookings Institute.
13. Parry, D. (1994) View from Europe: Reading the Runes, *Avionics Magazine*, January, p.29.
14. Roberts, B. (ed.) (1992) *US Foreign Policy After the Cold War*, Cambridge MA.: MIT Press.

15. Roberts, B. (ed.) (1993), *US Security in an Uncertain Era*, Cambridge MA.: MIT Press. Lynn-Jones, S. and S. Miller (eds.) (1993) *The Cold War and After: Prospects for Peace*, Cambridge MA.: MIT Press.
16. Stahlschmidt, R. (1993) International Defence Industry Study, *The Financial Post* Conferences, The Canadian Defence Industry: Making the Most of the Market, Proceedings, November 10.
17. Tolchin, M., and S. (1992) *Selling Our Security*, New York: Penguin.

Beyond the Frontier: The Convergence of Military and Civilian R&D in the United States

HENRY ETZKOWITZ

State University of New York at Purchase
United States of America

INTRODUCTION

The end of the Cold war has inaugurated as significant a change in US science and technology policy as was brought about by the end of World War II. Just as a lack of land closed the frontier in the late nineteenth century, a lack of funds threatens its substitute, the so-called 'endless frontier' of science (Bush, 1970). The scientific frontier, based on an inexhaustible supply of funds for military research, and militarily legitimated basic research, was similarly subject to closure in the late twentieth century. During the early post-war era a nominally independent defence R&D sector emerged after a congressional struggle between scientists and the military over the control of nuclear research (Smith, 1965). A delicate political compromise created a system of scientist-led weapons laboratories, managed by companies and universities under government contract (York, 1970; Kevles 1988). This scientific establishment was tied to the military but separated from civilian life even though it was officially under civilian control (Swomley, 1964; Nieburg, 1966; Melman, 1970; 1974).

The driving forces of current US science policy are the contraction of the military economy and the need to make government supported research contribute more fully to the civilian economy in the context of increased international economic competition. The US has had a dual economy since World War II, with a civilian economy which could, more or less (given the competition-suppressing activities of large oligopolistic corporations), be called a market economy, and a military economy which was essentially government controlled. Ideological prohibitions against breaching laissez faire walls between government and industry have required elaborate subterfuges to make direct intervention possible. During the Cold War, 'national security' was invoked to support measures in such diverse areas as human resources and transportation policy, and state governments maintained their industrial policies on the grounds of traditional responsibilities for supporting local economies. The federal government, however, was expected to desist from such activities save for the exemptions granted by all-out war. It was only military and space competition with the former Soviet Union that provided exceptions to this ideology.

P. Gummett et al. (eds.), Military R&D after the Cold War, 119–135.

Three anomalies have appeared calling into question the 'science policy paradigm' that has been in place since the end of the Second World War (Ruivo, 1994). The first anomaly can be found in the widespread presumption in the literature that the US government, in contrast to that of many European governments, is reluctant to intervene directly to support civilian technological development. However, this statement may no longer be as true as it once was for the US. The logo of the Technology Reinvestment Program (TRP) (the two hands, one military, the other civilian, a circular linked chain going around them) represents the second anomaly (Cronberg, this volume), the emergence of a 'decentralised corporatist planning system' in the operation of the TRP and other federally sponsored technology programmes. The third anomaly is the maintenanance of a high rate of military R&D spending despite the lack of a technologically sophisticated opponent. Emerging convergences within and between military and civilian R&D organisations are the key to explaining these anomalies.

DISJUNCTURES IN THE MILITARY R&D SYSTEM

After World War II the US created a 'dual linear system' for military R&D with two starting points: military needs and fundamental investigation. Mission requirements originated within military strategic planning and were then translated into desired technical capabilities. Subsequent R&D then mostly took place in the specialised industrial subsector that Seymour Melman called 'Pentagon Capitalism,' firms that were tied in to the military and primarily built weapons systems. Sometimes the requirements would come from the government and the firms would then conduct R&D to realise the military's specifications. The firms could also put forth their own ideas for new weapons systems and then get seed funding to develop a concept or build a prototype.

However, the dual system created significant disjunctures between military and civilian innovation. When a firm conducted research the results had to be handed over to government so that the next step of development could be opened to competitive bidding. Naturally much of this competition was a facade and in reality the same firms usually continued on to build the systems they had initiated. Nevertheless, the requirement to turn over all results to the government led some firms to establish separate civilian and military R&D divisions, with a wall between them, to protect their civilian proprietary R&D from inadvertent disclosure. Alternatively, firms concentrated solely on military R&D. The disjunctures built into the system helped produce some of the super expensive equipment that has repeatedly been the object of congressional investigation. Such duplication was costly but not a problem for military innovation so long as civilian R&D was less advanced.

The other linear system started from the opposite direction and moved from basic to applied research. Programme officers in the Office of Naval Research (ONR), and the comparable offices in the other military services, had the discretion to fund what they judged to be the best leading edge research. The airforce, army and navy also had separate technology offices. Recently, the navy has combined its basic research and technology offices. The idea is, of course, to break down some of the barriers within the services. Links across the services are also increasing, through efforts to establish inter-agency committees. Formerly, such groups were largely formal devices. Given declining budgets or expectation of same there is more of a reality to the cooperative arrangements among the different research agencies, including combining related programmes. Even if deep budget cuts should occur, R&D programme officers believe that the same level of R&D can be continued cooperatively, by reducing extensive duplication.

The 'dual linear' model of organising R&D presumes a one way flow from basic to applied research, in one direction, and from mission requirements to technological capabilities, in the other. In the past, gaps in the innovation system have led to the creation of new bridging agencies. For example, in the aftermath of the crisis brought about by the Soviet Sputnik space achievement, an Advanced Research Projects Agency (ARPA) was created in the DOD in 1958 with broad responsibilities to pursue a wide range of far reaching projects spanning R&D spectrum. The more recent Strategic Defense Initiative (SDI) project, founded in 1983, is an instance of a cross-cutting programme within a particular R&D field.

The gap within the defence R&D system was further exacerbated by the widening gap between civilian and military technology. Civilian R&D has become more advanced especially in the electronics technologies which make up an ever increasing proportion of weapons systems (van Opstal, 1993). This reversal of an earlier trend in which defence procurement paved the way for civilian products was a sign of a maturing industry (Utterback and Murray, 1977) Rapid technical advances on the civilian side of the industry were driven by large production runs, expanding markets, and new ideas for products. This brought about the unexpected phenomena of older technology embedded in weapons systems than could be found in local commercial electronics stores.

Segregation of research and production was reinforced as an unintended consequence of the 'laisses faire' policies of the Reagan administration. During this era, the validity of government support for basic research at universities was accepted but there was a strong aversion to support of research in companies. Thus, government-supported cooperative R&D projects among companies or academia and industry were avoided since the Reagan-Bush administrations thought industry an improper partner for government to support. A few exceptions were made under pressure from industry as the result of strongly felt need to meet Japanese competition in semi-conductors and micro-electronics.

Even as the executive branch widened the technology gap, Congress attempted to bridge it. Legislative initatives to encourage closer linkages between universities and companies partially closed the gap, at least in principle. These links were mostly made downstream, after research had been completed, by turning over to universities the intellectual property rights to federally funded research conducted on campus and requiring academic institutions to make an effort to see that they were put to use. This indirect approach to industrial policy avoided some of the ideological objections to establishing direct links between government and industry outside of the defence sector.

REFORM WITHIN THE MILITARY R&D SYSTEM

For a brief period during and just after the Second World War, the military R&D system was organised according to an ad-hoc spiral model with numerous feedback loops among research, development and production. Academic-industry collaboration was the norm in important efforts such as the 'Radiation Lab' for the development of radar, the Manhattan Project and the Distant Early Warning Line. This integrated model of R&D was created by the academic scientists who organised the Office of Scientific Research and Development (OSRD) just before the Second World War. OSRD had broad responsibilities for R&D and the early stages of production across the military services (Etzkowitz, 1993a).

OSRD was disbanded immediately after the war and replaced by individual service R&D (Offices of Naval, Army and Air Force Research) in the Department of Defense, established in 1947. A political struggle between advocates of military vs. civilian control of atomic energy resulted in the Manhattan Project laboratories being moved from the control of the army to a new agency, the Atomic Energy Commission which eventually became the Department of Energy. The system of multiple R&D agencies in the Department of Defense and Department of Energy laboratories with similar missions encouraged competition but also resulted in duplication of effort and increased costs. The result was a loose confederation of the services, with only limited controls available to coordinate them. The considerable responsibility that had been given to OSRD was returned to the individual services after the war.

Since the Second World War, first, defence and then energy activities have been reorganised from special purpose mission agencies (e.g Army and Atomic Energy Commission) into broad departments comprising their predecessor units. While the organisation of R&D has been affected by these bureaucratic revisions, it has also largely continued within the parameters defined by the original agencies. Problems in coordination and gaps in the mission agencies have been resolved by the creation of new subunits rather than through a drastic reconfiguring of the elements of these departments.

The R&D organisation of the Department of Energy, founded in 1977, is an amalgalm of the nuclear weapons laboratories descended from the Manahattan Project and various energy research programmes that it inherited from previously independent agencies such as the Bureau of Coal Research, along with newer responsibilites for conservation and renewable energy. The DOE shares responsibility for development of nuclear weapons with DOD.

In the early 1960s, Robert McNamara, Secretary of Defense during the Kennedy and Johnson administrations, attempted to rationalise this system. Wishing to avoid a political battle that would have ensued if new legislation were sought to increase the influence of the Secretary of Defense, McNamara attempted to achieve the same goal through the imposition of information and planning systems, a measure well within his existing authority. He divided R&D into discrete (budget number) categories: 6.1, basic and applied research; 6.2, exploratory development of the applications of that research, and 6.3A, the construction of prototypes to demonstrate the principle of an application.

These categories were created in the belief that they would increase management control and improve efficiency; responsibility was then given to separate bureaus, in the different services, to administer programmes in each category. Specific system development programmes closely linked to procurement take place in categories 6.3B and 6.4. The former categories are said to represent 'the technology base;' both sets comprise the 'defence technology base' in DOD terminology (OTA, 1988; 1989). A portion of the technology base is nested in the 'defence industrial base', comprising the companies that design and produce weapons as well as conduct R&D themselves.

The defence R&D sector is in a state of flux today. Driven by severe budget constraints in the early 1990s, the military service R&D agencies are increasing their co-ordination to reduce duplication and share the support of projects and programmes. According to a former director of the Livermore Laboratory, in a previous era 'We spent about twice as much money and employed about twice as many people on these development programmes as we should have' (York, 1987, p.102). At present, to eliminate waste informal coordination is being supplemented by formal planning mechanisms and some insiders think that merger of research, development and acquisition functions is a possibility in the future.

Rooted in a military culture, this system has been coordinated vertically, rather than horisontally - to the extent that coordination takes place at all. With the end of the Cold War the normative basis of this system is changing as military requirements are displaced by economic needs. Within the agencies themselves the integration of research and development activities is forced by 'hard budget' constraints. Sharply reduced budgets make duplicative and disjunctive R&D policies, allowable in a period of rising budgets, impossible to sustain. Increased collaboration among research agencies, both military and civilian, is taking place as a result. Individual services, such as the Navy have already merged their science, technology and industrial relations units into a single organisational framework to ensure closer collaboration. A leaner defence R&D system, more fully integrated into the civilian R&D system will be the outcome.

In some ways the restructuring of the military R&D following the path of the reorganisation of government supported civilian R&D during the 1980s. Some of these same technology transfer mechanisms used by the universities are being taken up by federal laboratories. Dual university-industry and government-industry cooperative arrangements are being overlaid by broader arrangements for academic-industry-government collaboration (US Congress, 1991).

Recent developments and current thinking at the Office of Naval Research provide an indicator of future directions. There is an atmosphere of change at ONR. Its director, Dr. Saalfield, believes that with end of the Cold War, 'the world has turned again,' requiring change potentially as significant as that which occurred at the establishment of the current system. He holds that the current issue is, '... how to take a new step and integrate science and technology in a way that gets more out of funds; to replicate what was done in 1946 in a new way' (Saalfeld, 1993).

The final barriers between the parallel R&D systems in the military and civilian economies are falling. Having merged its science and technology programmes into a single unit, ONR also participates in joint committees with army and airforce research agencies to reduce duplication. The agency is seeking to establish ties with relevant civilian research agencies. ONR plans to extend this outreach and '... bring industry more into play.' The director said, 'I'd like to form alliances with universities and industry [using] the agricultural extension services as a model for technical extension services.' The goal is to infuse industry with new technology from ONR supported research, within the bounds of supporting science and technology to meet Navy needs. Nevertheless, in this new regime, given '... a choice between two programs of equal militay merit; the one with commercial fallout would get support' (Ibid).

Since innovations currently take place primarily on the civilian side and can be taken over to the military side as needed, there is little basis for supporting a huge military research system for itself. If such a system is to be maintained on something approaching its present scale, it has to be justified on the basis of its contribution to civilian innovation. Certainly the capabilities are there. ONR programme managers, for example, believe that their agency is more effective in supporting research than NSF, with its reliance on peer review, and some at NSF share this evaluation. ONR believes that government will want to use their demonstrated capabilities for new tasks. Indeed, the way that the Technology Reinvestment Program (TRP - see below) has been organised, with military research funds providing the bulk of its support, is good evidence for the thesis of reorienting military research agencies in support of civilian goals, without removing them from the military context as occurred in Japan for reasons of political survival, just before the end of the Second World War. In the US, political exigencies suggest that it will be easier to support civilian research from within the military rather than risk an ideological controversy by attempting, for example, to civilianise ARPA.

FROM SPINOFF TO FRAUNHOFER MODELS

In addition to defence contractors and university grant recipients, the military R&D system also includes the military's own labs, and labs that companies and universities run for the Defense and Energy departments. Since the end of the Cold War the national laboratories have been revising their mission to include cooperative R&D on civilian technology. There were three stages in their transformation into a support system for industrial R&D. At first, in the 1960s, led by the National Aeronautical and Space Administration (NASA) the spinoff model was inaugurated, If a technology developed for a military purpose had a potential civilian application, then some funding was made available to support that transition. There has been much debate and many studies, from the '60s on, as to whether spinoffs are real or a mirage. Nevertheless, in 1986, Congress made technology transfer a subsidiary mission of the national laboratories, following by several years the assignment of such a mission to the universities. Funds were made available in the laboratory budgets for programmes of cooperative research between national laboratories and firms.

The Cooperative Research And Development Agreements (CRADAs) programmes have grown greatly since their establishment. Since the end of the Cold War, many of the relevant laboratories have lost, or have signficantly reduced their primary military mission. They have to find a new primary mission. The only one available is in the civilian economy or in the closest substitute they can find to military demand, namely, police equipment. There have been reports about laboratories trying to adapt military research to non-lethal police equipment. For example, Sandia labs has demonstrated a sticky substance that will help catch a criminal suspect but then there is the catch that the substance may trap the police officer as well. There certainly is much room for scepticism about whether this system of laboratories can be effectively transformed. But there is some lee way for the transition of the national laboratories.

The national labs have such economic importance, and thus political support, in their local areas that there is very little political pressure as yet to look too closely at the transition effort or to consider closing some of them down. Nevertheless, just as there was a military base closing commission, which actually did close some military bases, so there is also the possibility that not too far dwn the road there will be a laboratory closing or restructuring commission. There would then be a review, followed by serious analysis of the extent which these laboratories have managed to transform themselves. What is clear now is that they know that the old mission is gone. There are always a few people left who think that perhaps the Soviet Union will reappear; the old mission will come back. However, most directors of national laboratories are quite realistic and know that they have to come up with a new mission tied to the civilian economy. Two obvious possibilities for a civilian mission for the laboratories are either spinning off 'startup' firms or supporting existing firms in their R&D and product development. It can be expected that the national labs will increasingly justify themselves on local and national econmomic development grounds. As the laboratories are transformed into an R&D support system for industry, the US will acquire the virtual equivalent of the German Fraunhofer Institute structure for its civilian economy.

DISJUNCTURES IN THE CIVILIAN INNOVATION ENVIRONMENT

From the early post-war era through the 1960s, the prevalent innovation model was one in which a large firm, either in a traditional technology area such as chemicals (Monsanto) or in a newer one such as photocopying (Xerox) relocated its laboratories to a separate location from its production facilities, and then moved its headquarters to still another location. A disconnection between the different parts of the firm was introduced under the guise of functional specialisation and modernisation. During this period, despite predictions of a 'triple revolution' based on automation, companies acted as if change would be relatively slow and that innovations could be phased in gradually to maximise profit. No matter what research came up with, the product line would be in place for a relatively long period of time. Close connections among different parts of the company were considered to be less important than creating an attractive camnpus environment to attract scientists. A headquarters located nearby the CEO's place of residence could prevail over physical contiguity of the firms elements. Each component part of the firm could be located separately. Separation also allowed replication of elements, making possible the multi-national firm with manufacturing and R&D facilities located in different regions and continents (Fusfeld, 1994).

IBM was the quintessential distributed firm, with its world headquarters in suburban New York, Armonk, research laboratories in another part of Westchester, Yorktown and Hawthorn as well as Almaden, California and Zurich, Switzerland; development facilites in Boca Raton, Atlanta; and production facilities in Fishkill, N.Y., Burlington, Vermont and elsewhere in the world. Under the strain of international competition, these disjunctures are breaking down both within large firms and between them.

On one hand, IBM has less resources to put into the basic research as an end in itself. For a long time, IBM maintained research laboratories as a national resource, without expecting them to contribute to innovation within the firm. Many of the technologies that were invented such as the reduced instruction set computing (RISC) were not taken up by IBM for more than a decade. Many of these innovations were brought to market by other companies, typically startup firms that were spun out of universities with support from ARPA (for example SUN and Silicon Graphics workstation companies). During the Cold War, Defense Department support for new firms, whose technology had long term military implications, was the actual industrial policy of the US (Scott, 1993).

RESTRUCTURING THE CIVILIAN INNOVATION ENVIRONMENT

We are moving into a new innovation environment in the civilian economy. Individual companies, even the largest ones, no longer view themselves as self-sufficient. They increasingly rely on alliances with other firms, large and small, in their R&D and product development (Harrison, 1994). Firms also look to universities as a source of technology as well as trained personnel. Local and regional government also view local universities in a new light as a potential source of contributions to the economy through the formation of start-up firms.

STRATEGIC ALLIANCES

Increasing international competition, requiring a faster pace of innovation, has made strategic alliances among firms a common model for organizing innovation. Two or more firms, or segments of large firms, come together and divide up an R&D project, with each firm doing the part that it has special expertise in. This both speeds up the process and reduces the cost. Alliances have become a popular mode of operation and have spread quite broadly from R&D to other aspects of corporate activity, including purchasing and marketing. Now the concept is shifting again from discrete alliances for particular projects to longer term engagements. Firms that have come together for a single project might now jointly develop a series of projects in the same or related fields. This expansion of the concept suggests that alliances are evolving into a new innovation environment including large firms as well as start up firms who may have a particular area of technological expertise but not necessarily the development or marketing capabilities. Such firms would now tie in to these capabilities, without having themselves to develop at an early stage this larger sector. Such ties often develop more fully among firms within the same geographical region (Saxenian, 1994).

Another recent development sees the universities becoming more explicitly part of the innovation system, as university-industry linkages spread across the academic system. Until 15 years ago, relatively few academic institutions such as MIT, Stanford, the land grant universities and a few enigneering schools engaged in the transfer of technology to industry. In response to increased intenational competition and the decline of major sectors of US President Carter, during the late 1970s, proposed to involve government more directly in reviving industry, through a policy of 'reindustrialisation.' The political resistance in Congress to government taking such a direct role at the time was so strong that the executive branch abandoned the project, at least as an overt policy.

Nevertheless, in another guise, an industrial policy, going beyond reliance on military R&D spinoffs was begun in 1980. At the initiation of Congress an indirect industrial policy was instituted in which the universities were used as a mechanism for government to reach industry. Government could not deal directly with the firms to encourage civilian innovation: this was ideologically forbidden territory, not only for President Carter who wished to intervene, but even more so for Presidents Reagan and Bush who were firmly opposed to any such interventionism.

On another, related, issue both proponents and opponents of industrial policy could agree that the enormous amount of potential intellectual property that had accumulated in the universities, arising from federal research grants, should be privatised. Research results with potential commercial utility were in an uncertain legal status as to who really owned them. Officially, of course the federal government owned these rights. However, given the strength of anti-industrial policy feeling, the federal government was hardly going to engage in R&D or commercialisation activities, while firms were not willing to undertake these tasks in the absence of a clear title. If they did produce something successful, another firm could argue that the technology originated from a government sponsored research project, and claim an equal right to it. For this reason, such government-owned intellectual property tended not to be utilised.

The outcome of the late 1970s debate over whether to have a federal civilian industrial policy was that nothing was done directly. Nevertheless a hidden industrial policy, and programmes to carry it out, was set in motion indirectly. It was seemingly established for another purpose, to clarify the ambiguities in federal intellectual property rights by turning them over to the universities, but on condition that universities had to take steps to commercialise this intellectual property. From 1980, the general research university system of academic institutions, managing significant federal research grants, started administrative offices and began to experiment with various models of technology transfer and relations with industry. Most of these formats for academic-industry relations had been developed over the past 60 or 70 years at MIT and then were taken up at Stanford after the Second World War. These practices were generalised throughout the research university system as an outcome of the failed debate on industrial policy.

Thus, schools such as MIT and Stanford which had been anomalies within the US academic system now became the models for other universities to emulate. Schools such as Columbia which previously viewed themselves as playing a policy and srvice role in having faculty members go to Washington to serve temporarily in government now found themselves trying to establish new ties with industry, often in their local region. They typically did this by assigning the task to an attorney who was already a member of the administrative staff or by hiring a scientist from industry as Director of Technology Transfer.

The academic technology transfer office would then focus on areas of research with commercial possibiliites, identifying potential intellectual property for patenting and licensing and making contacts for their sale to industry. Soon, intermediary groups appeared and organised regular meetings and conferences to bring university technology transfer offices together with industry scouts to facilitate the transfer process (Etzkowitz, 1993b). Within 15 years, technology transfer activities became a significant moneymaker for a few universiites that originated significant technologies. Others are still gearing up their offfices or waiting for technologies to receive health and safety approvals, so that the royalty flow to the university and its faculty can begin.

The actual and potential financial worth of academic technology transfer has recently received unfavourable public attention in the media and in Congress as the result of publicity about foreign corporations utilising the new technology transfer procedures to gain access to US technology. The intent of Congress in indirectly encouraging the establishment of an academic technology transfer capacity was to improve the cometitiveness of US industry. Some congress persons were distressed to learn that these very mechanisms were being taken advantage of by overseas competitors. Moreover, some technology transfer deals have been for costly drug products, raising the issue that public funds which paid for the research were producing inflated profits for companies at the expense of the public that had originally funded the research through its tax dollars.

Sufficient of an issue emerged that some members of Congress have called for the federal government to take back some of the intellectual property rights that it gave away in 1980. The feeling was expressed that the universities were earning too much money and that some of these profits should be used to lower drug prices instead. By the time this threat to university technology tranfer had developed, the academic technology transfer profession had developed to a sufficient extent that it had its own professional association, the Association of University Technology Managers (AUTM) with a regular schedule of national and regional conference and training programmes for prospective technology transfer officers as well as special media such as the Technology Access Report Newsletter.

In response to the growing controversy AUTM organised a Congressional hearing, through its own supporters in Congress, demonstrating that the original intent of the legislation establishing academic technology transfer was to gain national beneft from the long term outcomes of technology transfer, and arguing that these processes of technology transfer in the universities should therefore be left alone. The return to government would come from increased taxes in the future and gvernment should not try to interfere and possibly short circuit the process. The political pressure that emerged and then receded in the face of a successful counterattack from the academic technology transfer interest group that has emerged in support of the legal basis on which the profession rests suggests that this mode of innovation has become institutionalised (MacNiece, 1994).

THE CONVERGENCE OF MILITARY AND CIVILIAN R&D

The thesis of 'dual use' technology has been propounded in an attempt to resolve the inefficiencies of a bifurcated R&D system (Branscomb, 1993). Its proponents suggest using defence R&D resources to stimulate civilian technologies on the grounds that they can be simulataneously used by the military and transferred into the civilian economy. A clear military use remains a requirement of the dual use R&D strategy; it stops short of industrial R&D policy, that is, openly providing government support for advance of purely civilian technologies.

An expanded role has been proposed for ARPA in industrial development. A report commissioned by the Carnegie Commission on Science, Technology and Government (1992), a private group comprising distinguished scientists, community leaders and former government officials contains a variety of prescriptions for improving US economic performance. The most controversial proposal concerns the interplay between military and commercial R&D. Resting on the assumption that the US has two technology bases (defence and commerical), the Commission recommended that ARPA, which funds research into advanced technology with potential military applications, be transformed into the National Research Projects Agency (NARPA) The renamed agency would step beyond its existing mission to fund research on advanced civilian technologies with military implications at the request of other agencies than the defence department. Thus, ARPA or NARPA would become a government wide agency in its ability to undertake tasks for non-military departments but would still be restricted in its actions by the requirement that these tasks have military implications. Indeed, according to Lewis Branscomb (professor at Harvard University's Kennedy School of Public Policy and former IBM technology chief) the suggestion for an ARPA to NARPA transformation has much more to do with assuring that the Defense Department has access to the best technology, whatever its source, than to using the agency to improve US economic competitiveness. It is believed that through partnerships in developing dual use technologies that defence has the best chance to gain access to leading edge commercial technologies as they are created rather than after they are manufactured. The reorganisation of defence R&D is part of a broader shift in US industrial policy.

During the Bush administration, Craig Fields, then a DARPA official, attempted to broaden the definition of national security to include economic security. Under this umbrella, he planned to support RD in civilian technologies that were an underpinning for military technologies. This approach was rejected at the time by the administration as representing an unaccepable venture into 'industrial policy' which the Bush adminstration viewed as an unacceptable and misguided attempt on the part of government to 'pick winners and losers' in the civilian economy. Fields soon left DARPA to become head of MCC, a government supported corporation designed to do for the computer sector of US industry what he had just been forbidden to institute for a broader range of industries.

This event illustrates the episodic and often contradictory thrust of US science and technology policy in the recent past. It moved in fits and starts, in part because it could only be accomplished as an upstream movement against a strong tide of resistance from believers in a laissez faire ideology of governmental non-intervention in the economy. Nevertheless, even the strongest adherents of this set of beliefs will stand aside if there are strong pragmatic reasons for doing so. For example, under pressure from the semi-conductor industry, the Reagan administration agreed to use government funds to support the creation of SEMATECH, a government-industry research programme to speed innovation in that industry.

SEMATECH, a consortium of semi-conductor manufacturers, founded in 1987 with DOD and industry funding, is currently viewed as a model for other industries (Hafner, 1993). Although supported by government, the consortium is led by its industry members. An analysis of the industry's competitive problems with Japan revealed deficiencies in manufacturing; these were to be remedied by, among other means, establishment of an engineering research center staffed by researchers drawn from individual member companies. SEMATECH's research facility was located in close proximity to the University of Texas, Austin. An important reason for choosing this location was a commitment by the state of Texas to expand university research in this field, thereby making a larger group of academic researchers available to collaborate with their counterparts at SEMATECH. In this model, DOD is a largely silent partner, with academia a subsidiary element, of an industry led pre-competitive R&D scheme. SEMATECH has recently announced that it will no longer need government funds; henceforth it will be based so on industry support.

THE EMERGENCE OF A 'PLANNING SYSTEM' IN THE US

The impetus for convergence between the military and civilian spheres is largely an outgrowth of the end of the Cold War. The demise of military competition between the US and the former USSR brings to the fore the issue of the continued high level of military R&D budgets (Gummett, 1994). A credible military R&D threat to the US no longer exists. Defence policy is now based, however, on the assessment that the US might have to fight two regional wars simultaneously. Yet even at that level of force, given the type of conflicts expected and capabilities of the prospective opponent, it is hard to see a justification for R&D expenditures at Cold War levels. Nor is there any country on the horizon with the sophisticated scientific and technical resources of the former Soviet Union, that could conceivably engage in a military R&D race with the US. Nevertheless, since high research budgets persist we must seek an explanation of them. In order to do so, let us examine some of the recent innovations in the military budget, namely, the Technology Reinvestment Program (TRP), which is led by ARPA; the Small Business Innovation Research Program (SBIR); and the Advanced Technology Program (ATP) which is aimed at civilian technology more generally.

How do the ATP, TRP and SBIR spend their funds? Although there is an open call for proposals in any relevant area of comercialisable science and technology, these programmes increasingly rely on a more focused approach based upon the critical technologies list. Within the broad guidelines of the list, government R&D programme managers and companies suggest specific technologies for special attention, and a conference is organised to bring together TRP programme managers with representatives from interested companies, both large and small, and academics.

The meetings are held in workshop settings in which the discussion focuses on the area of blockage that needs to be addressed to move the particular technology forward. Once a consensus is reached, there is a competition for the funds in which both technical and business reviews are carried out. In the ATP and TRP programmes companies also have to commit matching funds.

These technology blockage brainstorming sessions, and the decision that results to mount a competition for funds in the area of blockage identified, constitute an informal, corporatist, bottom up planning system. Out of these discussions, the Request for Proposals (RFP'S) are made much more specific. Instead of being directed toward a general critical technology, which is typically so broad a category as be almost meaningless, the planning process reduces the general category to a particular point, at which the people who are closest to the technology agree that a blockage exists. Industry, government and academia together target what the historian Thomas P. Hughes (1983) has called 'reverse salients', technical problems which, if successfully addressed, open up new technological and economic vistas.

Congress began the ATP and TRP programmes on a very small scale during the Bush administration; SBIR is an even earlier initiative. The new element in the Clinton administration is that the ATP and TRP have been scaled up dramatically. A quantitative shift in funding is creating a qualitative change in government policy. What was a $20 million programme in the previous administration is now $250 million and is moving rapidly to $750 million (Good, 1994).

What emerges from this analysis is that a major structural and ideological change in US science and technology policy is underway, even though no new laws have been passed. A shift in funds and a transformation of programme management procedures is bringing about a new relationship between government, industry and academia. The discussion processes built into the ATP, TRP and SBIR are creating a corporatist environment in which sectors that formerly acted separately are working together. To get access to funds from the TRP or ATP it is often necessary to create a consortium of large and small firms with complementary R&D skills, with perhaps a university reseach centre brought in also. Thus, the model of strategic alliances is being extended from industry to academic-industry relations, from the civilian into the military environment, and across the two.

The innovation environment currently being created in the US combines elements of a planning system with elements of a corporatist system at the federal level. It also includes the various state programmes that grew up during the 1980s when the federal govenrment removed itself from supporting near market technological development. The federal government currently supplies money to the states to expand their outreach programmes to improve manufacturing in firms. At the local level innovation systems are emerging based upon strategic alliances connecting companies and the national laboratories, drawing upon industry, state and federal funds for joint projects. Following Japan and Western Europe, the US is developing a national innovation policy from these programmes and alliances.

CORPORATISM AMERICAN STYLE

Corporatism, the European doctrine of cooperation between government, industry and labour, is being Americanised (Streeck, 1993). American corporatism is characterised by the emergence of an interventionist state, in science and technology policy, at the federal and state levels. Government plays an increasingly open role in setting industrial policy in cooperation with industry and academia. American corporatism is developing within the technology programmes originated during the Bush administration at the instance of Congress and greatly expanded by the Clinton administration.

Until the Clinton Administration, only a 'hidden' industrial policy was politically acceptable at the national level (Etzkowitz, 1991). Ideological prohibitions against breaching 'laissez faire' walls between government and industry required elaborate subterfuge to make intervention possible. During the Cold War national security was invoked to support measures in such diverse areas as human resources and transportation policy. State governments maintained their industrial policies on the grounds of traditional responsibilities for supporting local economies (Eisinger, 1988; Graham, 1992; Dougherty and Etzkowitz, 1993). The federal government, after the abortive attempt of the National Industrial Recovery Act (NIRA) programmes of the 1930s depression, was expected to desist from such activities save for the exemption granted by all-out war.

Lacking ideological blinders the current administration is actively seeking to implement an industrial policy. Unable to obtain new resources from Congress, it is attempting to redirect existing resources to support its goals of job creation, formation of new firms and reviving the technlogies of existing firms. Not since the Japanese agency responsible for military R&D moved itself from the War department to the Commerce department in the closing days of the second World War, recreating itself as MITI (Johnson, 1982; Patrick, 1986), has such an important transition been at hand. The US Departments of Defense and Energy are restructuring themselves and their relationships with industry and universities. As they expand their mission from contracting for R&D to supporting technology transfer, they are carving out a new role for themselves in US industrial policy during the post-Cold War era.

CONCLUSION: US INDUSTRIAL POLICY: COMING OR GOING?

The 1994 mid-term Congressional election results appear to presage a gloomy future, and brief past, for activist science, technology and industrial policy. During the Reagan and Bush administrations, conservative academics and politicians enforced a hands-off approach to civilian industrial policy, preferring to rely on (mythical) free markets and government intervention through the military economy. Throughout the rest of the world, governments and groups of companies joined together to gain a competitive edge. In the US, only the strongest lobbying efforts of a united semiconductor industry (with the support of the military) were able to overcome ideology to create Sematech.

More quietly, lifting the (liberal) threat of anti-trust litigation sparked the creation of hundreds of research consortia during the 1980s.

While critics still question Sematech's role in the revival of the US semiconductor industry (Noll and Cohen, 1994), skeptical pragmatists still may properly ask, can the US government play a legitimate role in fostering industrial competitiveness; do federal agencies have the intelligence and capabilities to accomplish this purpose? The optimistic answer lies in the innovative approach that the administration has taken to organising the ATP, TRP and SBIR programmes, encouraging participation by firms large and small, local and state governments and academia.

The Clinton administration's decentralised planning system for identifying and overcoming technical barriers has created a series of industry-government-academic R&D consortia in both old industries (eg, lasers for customised clothing design) and emerging industries (eg, new thin film processes for photovoltaics production). The conferences held across the country, bringing together representatives from industry, academia and government, to discuss problems in specific technologies, constitute a new form of bottom-up R&D planning. These efforts promise to reduce duplication of effort and bring academic, corporate and governmental skills to bear on R&D bottlenecks in a concentrated fashion. Such programmes, even in a lower key civilian format, have not been seen in the US since the Office of Scientific Research and Development (OSRD) efforts of the Second World War on radar, the proximity fuse and the atomic bomb.

It must now be asked whether the Clinton administration's innovative approach to civilian R&D be abandoned before it has a chance to bear fruit? Have these new programmes created sufficient constituencies who find them worthwhile, and can demonstrate their worth, against attacks upon corporate welfare? Some Republicans wish to return to a military-dominated economy. With the end of the Cold War and the lack of any credible technologically advanced opponent; such expenditures would be a sad, wasteful and exceedingly indirect way of subsidising targeted industries. In the 1930s a Democratic president saved business against its own protestations; in the 1990s it is one of the ironies of the current political situation that a president who has done more for business than any recent president has failed to keep the support of business.

Some academics say they would prefer to return to the old days before extensive federal research funding was available, arguing that with less resources the universities would be better able to concentrate on their 'core' tasks of basic research and teaching. Similarly, many people in the technology transfer community say they preferred the old days of minuscule resources and no public awareness to the current state of merely inadequate resources, soaring expectations and intense public scrutiny. Those days are gone. The Clinton administration's knowledge-based industrial policy is technology transfer writ large and with an open, bold face; no longer hidden behind a research agenda as an afterthought.

In his letter of charge to OSRD toward the end of World War II, President Roosevelt praised the scientific community for successfully aplplying its skills to the prosecution of the war effort. He called upon the leaders of that community assembled in a committee to consider the future of government support for R&D and asked them to devise a scientific and technological effort commensurate with the need to solve imminent peactime problems of housing and employment. For more than four decades Roosevelt's plea for peacetime R&D was submerged under the Cold War competition with the former Soviet Union. His call for what we now call 'strategic' civilian research has been misinterpreted as a legitimation for fundamental research conducted in an isolated fashion. The scientific and technological community is now at a turning point: it can attempt to recreate the recent past and suport retention of a militarily based industrial policy (the Republicans offer that opening) or it can take a step into the future and attempt to realise Roosevelt's vision of a government supported civilian R&D policy that his OSRD committee failed to specify at the time.

Since 1992, the Clinton administration, both through its own experimentation and its adaptation of ARPA models for military R&D planning, has created the outlines of such a policy and launched dozens of exemplars for its realisation. The scientific and technological community is no longer an isolated powerless, entity, requiring special protection behind special boundaries. Through criticism and opposition, many of its members helped bring about the end of the Vietnam War and a close to nuclear testing. Most members of the scientific and technological community, especially the older generation of academics grounded in an expectation of a succession of renewed research grants, currently uphold the banner of a legitimate role for government solely in support of basic and military research, a throwback to the 'Endless Frontier'(Etzkowitz, 1993a) Some members of a younger generation of academics uncertain of their academic survival in a contricted grants economy and a few academic and industrial scientists who see synergies in simultaneously pursuing theoretical and practical research questions, are open to new modes of research support in which technology transfer is integral to forumulation of the research agenda (Good, 1994). Will industrial sectors that are receiving R&D and product development support form the adminstrations's programmes attest to their validity? Will related concepts of autonomous markets and scientific autonomy override material conditions of the necessity for government, corporate and academic institutions to cooperate more closely in an area of increased economic competition in which the US is not the clear leader that it was during the early post-war era? The successful institutionalisation, or the demise, of the Clinton Administration's nascent industrial policies will be affected by the outcome of this debate over the future of science policy.

REFERENCES

1. Branscomb, L. (1993) *Empowering Technology: Implementing a US Strategy,*: MIT Press, Cambridge.
2. Bush, V. (1970) *Pieces of the Action*, Morrow, New York.
3. Carnegie Commission on Science, Technology and Government (1992) *A Science and Technology Agenda for the Nation: Recommendations for the President and Congress*, The Carnegie Commission, New York.
4. Dougherty, K. and H. Etzkowitz (1993) The States and Science: Industrial Policy at the State Level. American Sociological Association Annual Meetings, August.
5. Eisinger, P. (1988) *The Rise of the Entrepreneurial State: State and Local Economic Development Policy in the United States*. Madison: University of Wisconsin Press.
6. Etzkowitz, H. (1991) Regional Industrial and Science Policy in the United States, *Science and Technology Policy*. April 4(2) pp.10-15.

7. _____ (1993a) The National Science Foundation and United States Industrial and Science Policy, *Science and Technology Policy*. Feb. 6(1)pp. 10-15.
8. _____ (1993b) Technology Transfer: The Second Academic Revolution, *Technology Access Report*, June.
9. Good, M. (1994) Address to New York State Biotechnology Association, October.
10. Graham, O. (1992) *Losing Ground: The Industrial Policy Debate*, Cambridge: Harvard University Press.
11. Hafner, K. (1993) Does Industrial Policy Work? Lessons from Sematech, *New York Times*, Sunday, November 7 F 5.
12. Harrison, B. (1994) *Lean and mean: The Changing landscape of Corporate Power*, New York: Basic Books.
13. Hughes, T. (1983) *Networks of Power: Electrification in Western Society, 1890-1930*, Baltimore: Johns Hopkins University Press.
14. Johnson, C. (1982) *MITI and the Japanese Miracle: The Growth of Industrial Policy, 1925-1975*, Stanford: Stanford University Press.
15. Kevles, D. (1987), R&D and the Arms Race: An Analytical Look' in Mendelsohn, Everett and M.R. Smith and Peter Weingart. 1988. eds. *Science and the Military*. Dordrecht: Reidel.
16. Kundert, T. (1993) *Air Force Implementation of Cooperative Research and Development Agreements (CRADA's) Under the Federal Technology Transfer Act*, Air Force Legal Services Agency.
17. Melman, S. (1970) *Pentagon Capitalism*. New York: McGraw Hill.
18. _____ (1974) *The Permanent War Economy*. New York: Simon and Schuster.
19. National Science Foundation (1993) Selected data on Federal Funds for Research and Development: Fiscal Years 1991, 1992, and 1993 National Science Foundation, Science and Engineering Activities Program, Division of Science Resource Studies.
20. Nieburg, H. (1966) *In the Name of Science*. New York: Quadrangle Press.
21. Office of Technology Assessment (1988) *The Defense Technology Base: Introduction and Overview*, Washington D.C: US Government Printing Office.
22. _____ (1989) *Holding the Edge: Maintaining the Defense Technology Base*, Washington D.C: US Government Printing Office.
23. Patrick, H. (1986) *Japan's High Technology Industries: Lessons and Limitations of Industrial Policy*, Seattle: University of Washington Press.
24. Ruivo, B. (1994) Paradigm for Science Policy, *Science and Public Policy*.
25. Saxenian, A. (1990) Regional Networks and the Resurgence of Silicon Valley, *California Management Review*, Fall.
26. Scott, A. (1988) *New Industrial Spaces*, London: Pion.
27. Smith, A. K. (1965) *A Peril and a Hope: The Scientists Movement in America, 1945-1947*, Cambridge: MIT Press.
28. Swomley, J. (1964) *The Military Establishment*, Boston: Beacon Press.
29. US Congress (1991) Department of Energy Science and Technology Partnership Act. 102nd Congress.
30. van Opstal, D. (1993) *Integrating Civilian and Military Technologies: An Industry Survey*, Washington D.C.: Center for Strategic International Studies.
31. Utterback, J. and A. Murray (1977) *The Influence of Defense Procurement and Sponsorship of Research and Development on the Development of the Civilian Electronics Industry*, Cambridge: MIT Center for Policy Alternatives.
32. York, H. (1970) *Race to Oblivion: A Participant's View of the Arms Race.*, New York: Simon and Schuster.

7 —— (1993a) The National Science Foundation and United States Industrial and Science Policy, *Science and Technology Policy* Feb. of Jap., 10-15.

8 —— (1993b) Technology Transfer: The Second Academic Revolution, *Technology Access Report*, June.

[illegible]

Procurement Policies and Military R&D in the Nordic Countries

HANS SKOIE

Institute for Studies in Research and Higher Education
Oslo
Norway

INTRODUCTION

The four Nordic countries Denmark, Finland, Norway and Sweden have pursued very different security and defence policies in the postwar period. 'Five Roads to Nordic Security' was the entirely apt title of a book on the subject some years ago (Holst, 1973). The consequences for defence procurement and military R&D have been very significant. Today, however, the end of the Cold War may now, in different ways, change this picture.

In this chapter I briefly consider the Cold War period from this point of view, and discuss possible long term consequences for the four countries in the area of procurement and military R&D now that the Cold War is over. The possibility of establishing closer co-operation among the four countries in defence matters will also be looked at.

THE COLD WAR PERIOD

The general picture

The four Nordic countries are different in terms of geographical location. Denmark's closeness to the Continent, Finland's eastern location with a long common border with Russia, Norway's long seafront to the west - including a continental shelf rich in oil and gas - and joint border with Russia in the north east, and Sweden's middle position and closeness to the Baltic Sea, are important in this respect.

Experiences during World War II were also very different for these countries: Denmark and Norway were both occupied by German forces, Sweden remained neutral, and Finland was heavily engaged in two wars with Russia.

These facts are at the root of the different security arrangements which these countries soon developed in the postwar period.

P. Gummett et al. (eds.), Military R&D after the Cold War, 137–145.

It should be pointed out, however, that in the early postwar years, the so-called Scandinavian Defence Negotiations took place in 1948-49 at the highest political level with the aim of establishing Nordic cooperation in security and military affairs (Swedish Commission on Neutrality Policy, 1994). They failed, and Denmark and Norway joined NATO from the very outset in 1949. The guarantee by NATO, and particularly by the United States, of supplies of modern defence weapons and equipment was one important factor in the Norwegian decision to turn down a Nordic solution. Sweden continued to pursue its long-time neutrality, while Finland remained neutral with a very special relationship with the Soviet Union. The delicacy of this relationship was obvious and has been analysed in many books (eg, Volyantes, 1975; Maude, 1976). Table 1 summarises some important facts about the four countries.

Table 1 The Nordic countries - size and alliances.

	Inhabitants millions	Area 1000 km^2	Alliance status
Denmark	5.1	43	NATO
Finland	5.0	338	NONE*
Norway	4.2	387	NATO
Sweden	8.6	450	NONE
Total	22.9	1218	-

* Friendship agreement with the Soviet Union/Russia.

Implications for procurement policies and military R&D

Sweden opted for a position of non-alignment including keeping and developing a significant production of defence equipment nationally - fighter aircraft, submarines and tanks, etc. (Dorfer, 1973; Agrell, 1989). A secret atomic bomb project was also pursued for some years (Agrell, 1990). This represented to a great extent a continuation of major efforts in weapon production initiated and developed during World War II. Prior to the War defence production was very limited in Sweden.

Finland did not develop a similar capability, but chose to seek 'balanced buying' from East and West. Also Denmark and Norway chose to import the major share of the defence equipment which their armed forces required; chiefly from NATO countries and the US in particular. In Norway, a policy of developing national defence production on a more significant scale was advocated by some in the 1950s, however (Wicken, 1983; 1984). This option was not pursued and only a rather limited military production developed. Despite this policy, the country was able to produce and sell some sophisticated equipment abroad, including the Penguin missile system, which the US Navy bought.

Obviously, the home markets in all the four countries are too small to bear the development costs of major parts of modern arms production. The consequent need for export markets has in practice often caused considerable political and public concern and controversies. The fact that Sweden has not been a NATO member has made it particularly problematic for them to sell major weapon systems such as fighter planes to NATO countries (e.g. the Viggen plane in the 1980s - see Dorfer, 1983).

Most important are the self-imposed regulations and limitations in all four countries on what are regarded as politically acceptable products for export and 'receiving countries'. This has been a very sensitive area politically in all of them, and several controversies or scandals have occurred over the years. The Nordic countries can nevertheless be said to have set clear limits on their exports of defence material.

Military R&D resources and organisation

All four countries have in the postwar period been pursuing active policies in order to direct considerable public R&D funds toward a variety of national goals and objectives. This essentially sectoral approach has also included an active government role in developing industrial policies - not least through public R&D funding and development contracts.

Table 2 shows some key statistics for overall R&D spending in the Nordic countries. The figures are based on OECD data collected according to the so-called 'Frascati Manual'. We notice that Sweden spent significantly more on R&D per inhabitant than the other three countries. The high R&D expenditure by industry contributes much to Sweden's strong overall position.

Table 2. Key R&D statistics for the Nordic countries in 1991.

Country	Total R&D expenditure		Publicly funded R&D as % of total R&D	Defence R&D as % of total publicly funded R&D
	NOK * per inhabitant	As % of GDP		
Denmark	2,900	1.7	39.7	0.6
Finland	3,100	2.1	40.9	1.3
Norway	3,000	1,8	49,5	5,7
Sweden	4,600	2.9	35.3	27.0

* NOK= Norwegian Kroner. Source: OECD.

Table 3 gives public R&D expenditures according to the following three major objectives: advancement of knowledge, other civil objectives, and defence. The domestic manufacturing of significant parts of Sweden's own military equipment accounts clearly for the major difference in this Table - the defence R&D expenditures.

Table 3. Total public expenditure on R&D in 1993 by three major objectives. Billion Swedish Kronor (SEK)*

Objective	Denmark	Finland	Norway	Sweden
Advancement of knowledge	4.4	3.0	4.3	8.9
Other civil objectives	2.8	5.4	4.6	5.0
Defence	0	0.1	0.5	4.5
Total	7.2	8.5	9.4	18.5

SEK = Swedish Kronor

Source: OECD.

Tables 2 and 3 clearly show that Sweden spent much more on R&D, both in absolute and relative terms, than the other three Nordic countries. Defence spending accounts for a major part of this difference. In Denmark and Finland only around one per cent of the total public R&D expenditure was spent on defence R&D, while the comparable figure for Norway is around 5 per cent. In Sweden the percentage was 27 in 1991. This picture of defence R&D spending in these countries has been fairly stable in the postwar period. Table 4 below gives the figures for total R&D spending as well as for the defence part (percentage) for the four countries in the period 1983-93.

Table 4. Government R&D budget appropriations in the Nordic countries 1983-93 - Total, and Defence. (Millions Swedish Kronor).

Year	Denmark		Finland		Norway		Sweden	
	Total	Defence (%)	Total	Defence (%)	Total	Defence (%).	Total	Defence (%)
1983	2 059	0.2	2 241	2.0	3 233	9.6	9 241	21.8
1985	2 733	0.7	2 940	1.9	3 775	10.1	10 450	22.4
1987	4 182	0.4	4 081	1.7	4 593	7.5	11 350	25.9
1989	5 419	0.4	5 284	1.6	5 993	6.8	13 674	24.1
1991	5 749	0.4	7 873	1.3	6 935	5.8	16 413	23.6
1993	7 202	0.6	8 473	1.2	9 420	5.0	18 464	24.3

In Norway and Sweden we find major centres for defence research organised as separate defence research establishments with fairly general capabilities, and linked to the respective defence ministries. In Denmark and Finland such activities are smaller and integrated into various procurement agencies for defence material. At the same time, the Defence Ministries in the four countries spend very little on grants and contracts at universities and civilian research laboratories.

The Swedish Defence Research Establishment, FOA, was founded in 1944, and for many years had a staff of about 1500. The Norwegian counterpart, FFI, was established in 1946 as a result of a considerable build-up of technical expertise and research capability by the Defence Ministry of the Norwegian Government in exile in London during World War II. The FFI has had a fairly stable staff size of around 500 in recent years.

The R&D networks and contacts in general in all four countries have been strongly oriented towards the West - particularly Great Britain and the US - in the postwar period. It has also been shown that key personnel in the defence R&D community in Norway were strongly linked to American universities and research in the early part of the Cold War period (Wicken, 1985).. Recently it has also been shown that the Swedish defence research elite and military production establishment have been in fairly regular contact with the military-industrial complex in the West in the postwar period - particularly the NATO countries: Norway, UK and the US (Swedish Commission on Neutrality, 1994).

International co-operation in the S&T area has increasingly been recognised as important in all the Nordic countries. From the latter part of the 1980s the emphasis on internationalisation has been particularly strong. The importance of a close relationship with the European Union and the Framework Programme has been distinctly highlighted.

Arms production and export/import of military equipment

There is a long tradition in all four countries of some degree of arms production. However, we do not have comparable data for the degree of self-sufficiency over the years for all four countries. Naturally, as a consequence of the non-alliance policy, this percentage has been highest in Sweden where it has been estimated at around 70 in recent years (NOU, 1992:31, p.60).

In the NATO countries, Denmark and Norway, co-production and offset agreements have increasingly emerged as part and parcel of the production and supply of defence equipment - particularly within a NATO framework.

Both countries participated in the 'arms deal of the century', the joint purchase with Belgium and the Netherlands of fighter aircraft in the mid-1970s. In return for the purchase of the F-16 aircraft, Norway was, for example, offered a share of the production calculated to generate 4-5,000 full time jobs. To generate jobs nationally has been an increasingly important purpose of similar deals.

The F-16 deal was criticised within the establishment in Norway. Finn Lied, the Director of the Defence Research Establishment (FFI) at the time, argued that such co-production does not give sufficient technical know-how to the small partners - they are not really in on the development act (*Aftenposten,* 25 January 1978). In Lied's view the NATO countries should co-operate on weapons production through standardisation and a real division of labour.

Table 5 gives import and export figures for defence equipment for the Nordic countries for the period 1981-91 as they appear in the US Arms Control and

Disarmament Agency (ACDA) annual statistics (USACDA, 1994). It should be emphasised that such statistics are not necessarily entirely consistent and reliable, though the ACDA data are generally recognised as among the best.

In total the Nordic countries import more defence equipment than they export, with the major exception of Sweden.

Table 5. Estimates of imports and exports of defence equipment for the Nordic countries in the period 1981-1991. Constant US$ millions, in 1991.

	Denmark	Finland	Norway	Sweden	Total
Import	1697	1294	3637	1375	8003
Export	456	919	572	4221	6168

Source: ACDA, Washington D.C., 1994.

The fading of the Cold War has already led to noticeable consequences for security and foreign policy in the Nordic countries. Finnish and Swedish membership of the European Union from January 1995 is also very significant in this respect. Future membership of the Western European Union and NATO are of course also possible options for these two countries. However, the importance of being able to point to a non-aligned position is still great politically, and the matter is very sensitive on the home front in both countries (Agrell, 1994). What happens in the European Union and the Western European Union in the area of foreign policy with regard to real integration and defence co-operation and in establishing of joint capabilities, are of course also of great importance.

The present Norwegian Government is eager to pursue an active European policy despite the outcome of the referendum in November 1994. The significance of NATO membership, an associated status in WEU, and membership of the Economic Area (EEA) are deliberately stressed in this connection. Table 6 shows an overview of Nordic membership in organisations and European R&D co-operation.

Will this increased co-operation with Europe lead to less contact and co-operation with the US in general, and in the defence R&D and procurement area in particular, we may ask?

In addition to modifications in security links and alliances, the fading of the Cold War has also led to some 'downsizing' of the general military apparatus and armed forces in the Nordic countries. At the same time the need for 'high technology defence' has been stressed. Ambitious procurement plans have been worked out despite the fact that the economy in general is in some difficulties. The public sector needs to be restrained and streamlined through efficiency and other measures. At present this applies particularly to Sweden.

Table 6. The Nordic countries and membership in international organisations and European R&D co-operation schemes.

	Organisations			R&D co-operation		
	NATO	WEU	EU	EU R&D	Eureka	Euclid
Denmark	Yes	Assoc.	1973	Yes	Yes	Yes
Finland	No	No	1995	Yes	Yes	No
Norway	Yes	Assoc.	No*	Yes**	Yes	Yes
Sweden	No	No	1995	Yes	Yes	No

* EEA. ** Through EEA membership.

At the same time the limited export market for defence equipment has been shrinking due to 'downsizing' in most countries in the Western world. Another difficulty for defence production in these small countries is of course increasing unit costs due to technical sophistication. The factors of the inevitably limited technical capability in a small country, cost and the constraints on export markets in particular raise the question of whether Sweden will be able to develop and build another fighter aircraft beyond the present JAS-39 Gripen. The Gripen project has in any case met severe technical difficulties and considerable cost overrun has followed. The answer is obviously that Sweden cannot 'go it alone' in this field any more. A consequence is that Sweden is facing a significant 'conversion problem'. This may also happen in other areas in the Swedish defence sector.

Recently, the Under Secretary of State, Mr. Peter Lagerblad, publicly stressed that the Swedish Government could not guarantee regular development contracts to the Swedish defence industry as the Government used to do (*Svenska Dabladet*, 31 January 1995). The issue of the future of the defence industries will be dealt with in the new Government Defence Commissions headed by the same Under Secretary mentioned above. Also the research staff at FOA has been somewhat scaled down in the last few years. As part of the process of restructuring and adjustment to the new situation, Sweden is already looking for new partners abroad. For example, co-operation between SAAB-Scania and British Aerospace over the production and marketing of the Gripen has already been established.

A NORDIC SOLUTION?

In the foreseeable future, all four countries will most likely keep viable defences. The search for good bargains for defence equipment will probably play a greater role in the future in all four countries. The need for self-sufficiency will probably lessen in importance from a security point of view. However, employment arguments for keeping up national military production directly or through co-production and different other arrangements (for example consortia) may become stronger.

If the four countries all end up in NATO or EU/WEU, the possibility for close co-operation in security and defence matters will of course be dramatically improved. An extensive division of labour might even be worked out. Indeed, a joint Nordic army, air and navy under a NATO command and control system has been envisaged in the press.

This is obviously too far-fetched for the time being. We have lately, however, experienced an interesting move by the four Defence Ministers. In 1992, they embarked upon an initiative to establish cooperation in the area of supply of defence equipment and material, setting their officials to develop the details. In the fall of 1994, this resulted in the four Defence Ministers signing an agreement on such co-operation, with a view to moving towards a Nordic arms market. Intentions and procedures seem to give some significance to the document (Nordisk Framtida Försvarsmaterial, 1994).

The group of civil servants has identified several areas in which the possibility exists for three or four of the Nordic countries to work together in the future. Preparatory work discussing and exploring several new concepts in the defence area - including a new submarine generation - is included in the document. Development, procurement and maintainence of material are also mentioned. Equipment for the relatively large UN forces which the Nordic countries establish and send to various parts of the world is also highlighted in the document.

This agreement may be seen as a significant sign of the political intention to increase co-operation among the defence ministries and military headquarters as well as the defence industries in the Nordic countries. However, what it will amount to in practice is fairly open and may be questioned.

The Danish and, above all, the Norwegian attitude may still be strongly in favour of NATO and American 'solutions'. Norway is obviously particularly eager to keep a US presence in Europe, including maintaining some COB-airports and stockpiles of American equipment in Norway. Also, the long-standing collaboration with the US in terms of R&D, defence planning, supply of equipment, training of pilots and other groups of key military personnel, probably still represent considerable reasons and inertia for not going too far or too fast into 'Nordic or European solutions'. Indeed, the Norwegian Defence Minister recently pointed out that Norway might opt to buy American defence material in order to encourage continuous American interest and commitment to Norway (Kosmo, 1995). But the fading of the Cold War may change important things also in the Nordic countries - particularly in the long run.

REFERENCES

1. Agrell, W. (1989) *Vetenskapen i forsvarets tjänst*, (Science in the Service of Defence), Lund: Lund University Press.
2. Agrell, W. (1990) The Bomb That Never Was: The Rise and Fall of the Swedish Nuclear Weapons Programme, in Gleditsch and Njølstad (eds.): *Arms Races. Technological and Political Dynamics*, London: SAGE Publications.
3. Agrell, W. (1994) Alliansfri - tills vidare. Ett svenskt säkerhetsdilemma (Neutrality until further notice. A Swedish security dilemma), *Natur och Kultur.*

4. Dörfer, I. (1973) System 37. Arms, Technology and the Dominification of Glory, Oslo: Universitetsforlaget.
5. Dörfer, I. (1983) *Arms Deal: The selling of the F-16,* Praeger: New York.
6. Holst, Johan Jørgen (ed) (1973) *Five Roads to Nordic Security,* Oslo: Universitetsforlaget.
7. Swedish Commission on Neutrality Policy (1994) *Had there been a war .... Preparations for the reception of military assistance 1949-1969,* Stockholm: SOU.
8. Kosmo, J. (1995) Speech by the Defence Minister, Jørgen Kosmo, as reported by Norwegian Radio, and the Press Agency NTB, 7 February.
9. Maude. G. (1976) *The Finnish Dilemma. Neutrality in the Shadow of Power,* London: Oxford University Press.
10. Nordisk framtida försvarsmaterial (1994) *Rapport 2 avsende Nordisk framtida försvarsmaterial-samarbete* (Report on future procurement of defence equipment, issued by Working Party of the Nordic Defence Ministers), Stockholm, 12 April.
11. USACDA (Arms Control and Disarmament Agency) (1994) *World Military Expenditures and Arms Transfer 1991-1992,* USACDA, Washington, DC.
12. Volyantes, J.P. (1975) *Silk Glove Hegemony. Finnish-Soviet Relations 1944-1974,* Kent, Ohio: Kent University Press.
13. Wicken, O. (1983) Vekst og våpen. Norsk militærproduksjon som industripolitisk virkemiddel i 1960-årene (Growth and Weapons. Norwegian Military Production as an Industrial Policy Measure during the 1960s), Oslo: Forsvarshistorisk forskningssenter.
14. Wicken, O. (1984) *Våpenimport eller egenproduksjon? Hvorfor Norge ikke bygde ut militær industri 1945-50* (Weapons Import or Self-production. Why Norway did not expand its military industry), Oslo: Forsvarshistorisk forskningssenter.
15. Wicken, O. (1985) *Militærforskere i Vestveg. FFI-forskere på utenlandske universiteter 1945-1970* (Military Research in the West. Researchers from the Norwegian Defence Research Establishment at Foreign Universities 1945-1970), Oslo: Forsvarshistorisk forskningssenter.

Transfer of technology and managerial skills: the possible role of foreign direct investment in the development of the East

JEAN-ALAIN HÉRAUD

BETA (Bureau d'Economie Théorique et Appliquée), CNRS and Université Louis Pasteur, Strasbourg France

Some years ago, when Soviet power still ruled over central and eastern Europe, the isolationist position towards the rest of the world was, in the official ideology, justified by the need to protect the so-called socialist countries against western capitalism. Even in the dying days of the Soviet era, when serious (but not official) consideration was given in Moscow to introducing some ingredients of western institutions (such as, for example, a new role for banks, or possible legislation on bankruptcy), a massive inflow of foreign capital was never desired. Then, after the sudden breakdown of the communist regime, western capital was no longer regarded as a demon: indeed, it seemed to become a highly appreciated factor of economic development and restructurating. However, as usual, reality falls short of our preconceptions: we observe that western capitalists have no intention to invade the East; nor would the new democracies accept a massive takeover of their national industry and service infrastructure. Nevertheless, western support is needed, sometimes urgently, in order to reduce economic difficulties, and perhaps also political unrest that could be linked to the present state of social and economic confusion.

A particular aspect of the post-Soviet transition is the need to fulfil privatisation processes under the constraint of limited domestic sources of capital. The conversion of the military industrial complex is also an urgent and difficult task, and one which displays all the difficulties of the transition. From the national (if not nationalistic) point of view of the administration, there will always be a reluctance to dismantle the complex and auction off its best parts. On the other side, as we know from recent western experience, converting to market oriented activities firms or departments accustomed to military techniques and public procurements, is a risky business. The concept of dual-use technology is a wonderful idea *a priori*, but one that proves hard to apply in reality, because of the specificity of technological assets. The human resource

P. Gummett et al. (eds.), Military R&D after the Cold War, 147–151.

is also rather inflexible in terms of attitudes: converting teams used to high-tech custom manufacture to the constraints of ordinary industry is no easier than transferring very specific technologies to new fields.

In practice, defence conversion is probably the closest parallel we have in the West to the problems the East is confronted with. The core of the problem of conversion, as of economic transition more generally, lies in the acquisition of managerial competences and the learning of market mechanisms, rather than simply in the transfer of technology.

In the post-Soviet context, however, the question arises, can foreign direct investment (FDI) by western firms play a particular role, among all the possible forms of support to the East ? In this short contribution[1], we focus on this question. Even if the attitudes of Eastern governments, as well as the actual flow of direct investment from the West, strongly vary from one country to another, FDI is *a priori* in every case an important potential factor of development, with specific virtues. We will first concentrate on these specificities, and then point out some restrictive or negative aspects of FDI.

FDI AND OTHER EXTERNAL CONTRIBUTIONS TO DEVELOPMENT

Basically, there are four possible types of contribution from the West to the process of restructurating and development of the East :

- financial transfers ;
- technical assistance;
- more liberal access to the western markets;
- direct investment.

If the first type of support were extended to a high degree, it could work as a new 'Marshall Plan' for central and eastern Europe. The question is, would it be as fruitful as it was for western Europe just after World War II, or would its results be weaker, as in the case of aid programmes for less developed countries.

The second type, to be very effective, should embody managerial and organisational - as well as purely technological - aspects.

The third type seems to be a serious and generous contribution by the western countries, letting eastern partners take advantage of lower factor prices in the short run. It is true that, if it works and boosts growth, this policy will allow eastern countries to develop economic and technological trajectories of their own and finally meet in the long run the quality standards of the West. But this theoretical view is probably over-optimistic. Not only would the self-interest of western countries prevent

1 In this article, we do not intend to make a complete survey of existing studies nor supply a lot of data, but simply to use some examples and figures to illustrate the point. Besides recent information from the media, the only sources we will cite here are documents published by the Chamber of Commerce of Paris and particularly the results of a seminar held by the C.O.E. (Centre d'Observation Economique, under the scientific direction of Ch. de Boissieu) in Paris (April 1994): 'Perspectives économiques en Europe Centrale et Orientale'.

them from disturbing their own economic balance with imports at what could be considered dumping prices, but also, and more fundamentally, differences in product quality and other standards would not allow a real competitiveness in many cases.

Direct investment by western firms, at first glance, looks superior to the three other types of action, not least because it combines them in a natural way:

- by definition it is a *transfer of capital*, either in building new assets, directly similar to the western models, or in buying privatised companies (in the latter case it is supposed that restructuring to modern standards is possible);
- in building new plants or by take-over of existing ones, the *technical assistance* is performed automatically and consists of a complete bundle of technological know-how *and* management skills; if the firm has sub-contractors or suppliers in the country, it also allows the diffusion of western production standards to further circles of the economy;
- FDI can also be a way to *open western markets*, in so far as the firm (or joint venture) will re-export to the home country and the rest of the world.

Among the success stories of foreign direct investment, the example of Suzuki in Hungary is often cited. The Japanese have been required to use the services of Hungarian suppliers instead of their traditional (Japanese) trade partners. Then, since the Japanese could not accept any reduction in quality and efficiency of supply, they have been forced to transfer technology (and industrial standards, discipline, etc., as well) to a whole set of Hungarian firms or joint-capital 'satellite-firms'. After a period of difficulties and negative reactions of Hungarian manpower, the system has come to work well and has begun to generate strong spillovers.

French firms like Sanofi - in fine chemicals and pharmacy - also have their part in such success stories. But in another case, that the of car-industry, the outcome of French FDI does not correspond with the preceding Japanese model. From as early as the 1980s, Citroen has been investing in Rumania, but it chose to do so on the basis of a car developed for the Romanian market only. In this case, the local economy has been less strongly coupled to the western commercial and technological world, and the learning effect has been considerably reduced.

These examples suggest that, even if in principle FDI leads to dynamic advantages (learning effects), it is by no means certain that it will effectively play such a 'coaching' role in every case - even when it really contributes to the wealth of the country in a more static way.

THE LIMITATIONS OF FDI

Hungary is often cited as a case of relative success in terms of FDI. But the Hungarian situation is exceptional. Since 1989, this small country has received more than US $6 billion of foreign direct investment, i.e., half of the total devoted to the countries of the former Soviet bloc. Thus, it cannot be considered as a model for the other countries - although Poland has similarly begun very recently to win an increasing part of the global flow of FDI - because a proportional effort from the West to the whole Eastern zone could hardly be imagined. We must also observe that this massive flow of western investment in Hungary amounts only to one fourth of the global investment of the country in the last two years. Nevertheless, its impact is, qualitatively, important.

It is, however, worth observing the limitations as well as the potential advantages of FDI in a general context. This leads us to the following comments, starting from the Hungarian experience.

The first remark is that foreign investment in Hungary is highly concentrated. It appears to be focused on only a few sectors, like the food and mechanical engineering industries. In these privileged sectors, sometimes more than the half of Hungarian production depends on foreign capital. In such circumstances, this flow of investment cannot be considered as a balanced factor of development. Furthermore in other countries, with higher initial endowment in heavy industry or military equipment, it is not clear that foreign capital would find it profitable to invest, and thence to support the necessary conversion.

Secondly, although the flow of foreign investment contributes positively to offset some of the balance of payments deficit, it does not have the same effect on the commercial deficit of the country, because these firms sometimes import more than they export. For instance, in the cases of Poland the Czech Republic, contrary to Hungary, the western car industry imports a lot of spare parts from Italy, Germany, etc. In the long run, such practices weaken the impact of FDI on the host economy, because the domestic development triggered by the import of capital is likely to be offset by the external trade constraint.

Finally, one of the most important needs of the post-communist countries is to privatise public (military and non military) firms, and the participation of foreign capital has not been a great success in this domain. It must be stressed that the willingness of western investors is not the only factor to take into account, but also the ambiguous behaviour of the governments on this point. The Czech Republic, for example, is known for its reluctance to open the doors of national firms to foreign capital. Other countries undermine confidence by their behaviour during negotiations, as did the Hungarian government in 1994 when it suddenly interrupted discussions for the sale of certain hotels to an American group. Countries like Romania and Bulgaria have very hesitant policies over privatisation in general, which reduces their attractiveness for foreign investment.

Where FDI has succeeded, it is often because of very specific factors. The case of Eastern Germany is obvious: the only truly massive success of privatisation and capital flow from the West has been based on the solidarity of the Nation-State. A less obvious example reinforces the point: can be cited: Germany's position as the principal investor in Romania (in numbers of joint-ventures) is clearly linked to the German-speaking communities in that country.

In the model story of the Japanese automobile investment in Hungary, we observe a pure economic motivation, but of a very strategic nature: the Japanese firm agreed to invest and transfer all that technology and management competence, but in return gained the opportunity to enter the European continent. Can such a case of FDI be systematically reproduced ?

CONCLUSION

The above arguments and examples show that FDI can bring a precious contribution to the development of a modern market economy in the East, at least in certain cases, but that it does not do so systematically. It should certainly not be considered as a panacea.

Furthermore, FDI is not a policy tool. It does not arise to order, neither from the East, nor from the West. Certain preconditions must be met before western capital is attracted to build or buy industrial assets. In particular, better infrastructures and an adapted (democratic and liberal) institutional framework are needed. Then, the government must set up an intelligent policy towards potential investors in order to optimise the direct impact and the spillovers of the FDI.

The global political attitude for such a programme is, as we see, a well balanced mix of liberalism and regulation. Other countries (typically in the Far East) have succeeded in such a strategy of development. They have rapidly developed their economies without any overwhelming investment from the West, but with selective transfers and, at the same time, a systematic policy of exportation - including the effort to meet the quality standards of the world industrial goods market.

In so far as the flow of foreign capital can be regulated by general policies or by individual negotiation, attention must be focused on the potential *learning effects* that FDI projects could generate in the country, and not on their static direct impact on the economic activity.

The European Union's Contribution to the R&TD Capacities of the Countries of Central and Eastern Europe and the Former Soviet Union

GORDON LAKE

Secretariat, Committee on Research,
Technological Development, and Energy
European Parliament, Luxembourg

(The views expressed here are those of the author, and not necessarily those of the European Parliament).

INTRODUCTION

This chapter is an attempt to describe and explain the major elements which the European Union - in particular the European Community - brings to the process of change in Central and Eastern Europe. It is hoped that this will bring to the attention of all the actors potentially concerned the programmes which might be used to aid the transition from a largely defence based industrial sector to a largely civil based system. In addition, one of the major consequences of the changes in these countries since 1989 has been the need to redesign science and technology infrastructures into forms closer to those found in market economies - or at least compatible with those found in market economies.

The European Union believes that collaboration between the countries of western and eastern Europe can play a key role in this process of restructuring. This should help to ensure, *inter alia*: the preservation of scientific and technological capabilities in the countries in question; improved access to Research and Technological Development and Demonstration (R&TD) resources which were previously only available for defence purposes; and the facilitation of defence conversion. The European Union would also be clearly interested in accessing technologies pertinent to Western Europe and envisages encouragement of commercialisation and technology transfer, and the development and enhancement of long term linkages in scientific, technical, industrial and commercial domains. It supposes that there is a mutual

P. Gummett et al. (eds.), Military R&D after the Cold War, 153–161.

interest in the transfer of certain managerial and administrative techniques from west to east, as well as more subtle elements which might best be described as cultural.

The European Community, as it then was, provided 55 million ECU (MECU) of support in 1992, via an initiative known as COPERNICUS, for cooperation in research with many of the countries of Central and Eastern Europe, to be used for conferences, fellowships, network provision, joint projects, and perhaps most significantly, participation in the EC Framework Programme for R&TD, and in COST projects. (COST - Co-operation in Science and Technology - provides funds only for co-ordination and travel costs; the research is funded by the participant states). A similar budget was made available in 1993. Not all Specific Programmes within the Framework Programme have been opened to participation by Central and Eastern European countries - the most important has been the Human Capital and Mobility Programme, which has essentially provided funding for fellowships to enable East European scientists to carry out research in Western Europe, but in addition the Specific Programmes on Environment, Biomedicine and Health, Non-Nuclear Energy, and Nuclear Fission Safety have also been included.

The programme continued in 1993 as PECO, but was renamed COPERNICUS in 1994, when it was re-directed towards applied research, with financial support being made available for participation in the EC's 3rd Framework Programme of Research and Technological Development (29.5 MECU), and for Joint Research Projects (JRPs) and concerted actions (57 MECU). There were no exchange schemes or short mobility grants in this package. Priority areas for JRPs have been: information, communication and telematics technologies; manufacturing, processing and production; materials science and technology; measurement and testing; agricultural and food sector technologies; and biotechnologies.

As a completely separate initiative, INTAS, the International Association for the Promotion of Cooperation with Scientists from the Independent States of the former Soviet Union (FSU), was created under Belgian Law in 1993. It provides support (21 MECU in 1994) for joint research projects between teams from FSU countries, and Western European countries.

PHARE and TACIS are of course the main structural aid and assistance programmes developed by the EU, but do not have major components relating to R&TD Policy, except in the domain of nuclear reactor safety.

THE 4TH FRAMEWORK PROGRAMME FOR RESEARCH, TECHNOLOGICAL DEVELOPMENT, AND DEMONSTRATION.

On 26 April 1994 the European Parliament and the Council of Ministers agreed on their first ever joint Decision pursuant to the new Co-Decision Procedure introduced as article 189(b) of the Treaty on European Union ('the Maastricht Treaty'). This decision concerned the Fourth Framework Programme of European Community Activities in the field of Research and Technological Development and

Demonstration.[1] The Framework Programmes are the central mechanism by which the European Union centrally invests in R&TD activities. (Of course the EU's member states continue to have their own R&TD programmes: indeed these still constitute the major part of total funding in this area.)

The Fourth Framework Programme for 1994 to 1998 consists of four 'Activities'. The First Activity is entitled 'Implementation of research, technological development and demonstration programmes, by promoting co-operation with and between undertakings, research centres and universities', has a budget of 9,432 MECU, and is thus the core of the whole Programme. The Second Activity is 'Promotion of co-operation in the field of Community research, technological development and demonstration with third countries and international organisations', with a budget of 540 MECU, which is obviously the programme of major interest to the countries of central and Eastern Europe, including the former Soviet Union, since it is this Activity which will provide funds to these countries. The Third Activity, with a budget of 330 MECU is entitled 'dissemination and optimisation of the results of activities in Community research, technological development and demonstration'. The Fourth Activity is 'Stimulation of training and mobility of researchers in the Community', with a budget of 744 MECU.

The four Activities are implemented as Specific Programmes, one each in the case of Activities 2, 3, and 4; and thirteen in the case of Activity 1, plus one for the EC's Joint Research Centre. Each Specific Programme requires a formal Council Decision to adopt it, following consultation of the European Parliament. The process of formally adopting all these Specific Programmes, plus the three covered by the Euratom Treaty, was completed by early December 1994.

The indicative breakdown of the funds for the themes and subjects in the First Activity is as follows:

	MECU
A. Information and Communication Technologies	**3 405**
1.Telematics	843
2.Communication technologies	630
3.Information technologies	932
B. Industrial Technologies	**1 995**
4.Industrial and materials technologies	707
5.Measurements and testing	288
C. Environment	**1 080**
6.Environment and climate	852
7.Marine sciences and technologies	228
D. Life Sciences and Technologies	**1 572**
8.Biotechnology	552
9.Biomedicine and health	336
10.Agriculture and fisheries (including	

[1] The full text of the decision is in the *Official Journal of the European Communities*, no. L 126, 18 May 1994 (9 languages).

agro-industries, food technologies, forestry, aquaculture and rural development)	684
E.11. Non-nuclear energy	1 002
F.12. Transport	**240**
G.13. Targeted Socio-economic research	**138**
TOTAL	**9 432**

This list is included to give some idea of the relative importance attached to each subject domain in the context of overall R&TD policy in the EU.

It is, however, the Second Activity, with its funding of 540 MECU, which has particular relevance to attempts to develop new directions for previously defence centred R&TD and production systems in Central and Eastern Europe. The Second Activity is implemented by means of a Specific Programme. The legal basis for this is a Council Decision, following consultation of the European Parliament. The provisions of the Specific Programme are summarised below.[2]

SCIENTIFIC AND TECHNOLOGICAL OBJECTIVES

The activity is the main mechanism for international cooperation on RTD with third countries and international organisations. The main aim is to add value to Community RTD via targeted RTD cooperation and synergy with other Community activities, to improve the Community's scientific and technological base and to support the implementation of other Community policies. It also aims at improving coordination of the S&T cooperation between Member States and third countries in order to avoid duplication and to better define the Community's areas of activity, taking full account of the principle of subsidiarity.

Cooperation shall be based on the principle of mutual benefit, which means not only direct or short–term advantage, as perceived by those involved in a project, but also the long–term or indirect advantage to the Community in terms of its industrial competitiveness and external relations. This is not, therefore, an entirely selfless charitable exercise on the part of the E.U.

The activities involved in cooperation will be accompanied by systematic monitoring and analysis of developments in the policies and in the machinery for implementing R&D in third countries in order to adapt Community cooperation policy and to derive maximum benefit for the Community and its partners - which reinforces the above observation. (The European Parliament had been most concerned during negotiations on the 4th Framework Programme to ensure that programmes benefit from continuous constructive monitoring, rather than just post-hoc evaluations.) The collection of data and information and analyses will be closely coordinated with the corresponding activities to be carried out in the programme on targeted socio–economic research. (The latter is a completely new element in EC R&D policy) Other

---

[2] The full formal text of the decision is published in the *Official Journal of the European Communities*, no. L 334, 22 December 1994.

accompanying measures include activities relating to the dissemination and utilisation of results, training and coordination and the organisation of conferences and seminars, etc.

Non–nuclear cooperation activities and activities developed in the earlier Framework Programmes will be incorporated into this programme. The geographical scope covers all of Europe, including the independent States of the former Soviet Union, the non–European industrialised countries and the developing countries. Moreover, greater opening–up of the specific programmes of the other activities to third countries should provide new opportunities for cooperation.

CONCERNING THE DETAIL OF R&TD ACTIVITIES

Different activities are set out in the Specific Programme for each set of countries with whom cooperation is envisaged. The countries of Central and Eastern Europe, and the former Soviet Union, are covered by the second action within the Programme.

The principal aims of this action are to help safeguard the scientific and technological potential of these countries, to redirect research towards social needs (which presupposes, of course, that these were not the priorities hitherto,) and thus restore their productive capacity, and also improve the quality of life in the societies in question. The Community intends to benefit from cooperation with the East European countries by obtaining access to the sometimes highly advanced results of research in those countries.

In more detail, the aims are:

- To stabilise R&TD potential, which is first of all a question of safeguarding human resources and existing equipment. The current earnings of research workers in the countries are relatively low, and the lack of hard currencies indicates a difficult future leading to isolation of East European researchers whose access to equipment is difficult and who have little contact with their foreign counterparts. One of the inevitable consequences of such factors is that, if the opportunity arises, researchers may well leave this sector to go abroad or take up other professional activities. There is therefore an urgent need to promote scientific and technical cooperation as a catalyst for action on a long-term basis. East European scientists have to be associated with advanced research, as for example in the advanced technologies essential to the creation of the future infrastructure of the countries concerned. Links need to be developed between research and industry, especially via the use of computerised communications networks, in order to promote the integration of these countries into European and world markets.
- To help solve problems specific to the East European countries by means of targeted R&D.
- To widen and deepen cooperation via involvement in specific Community programmes. An attempt will be made to identify R&D areas where these countries are in the forefront at the world level, and to introduce balanced cooperation. Several of the countries concerned have very high quality science, but the potential has not always been used in order to stimulate economic development. Thus a reform of science and technology structures in favour of a more decentralised, flexible and open

approach is urgently required, in order that research and development may play an effective part in the transition of these countries towards a market economy and their integration into the Community environment. In order to better integrate the East European countries into the world market, special attention will have to be paid to their participation in pre–normative activities in industrial areas such as information technology, telecommunications, advanced materials, and energy. It is intended, for example, that use be made of the 'energy centres' set up in these countries under the THERMIE programme). It is also intended that participation will be possible in the dissemination and exploitation activities carried out within the third activity.

The mechanisms by which these activities will be carried out include:

- Specific targeted actions to meet specific problems, such as where resource utilisation and production cycles in the East have caused environmental deterioration which goes beyond national frontiers and continents. There is an urgent need to find a common solution in areas such as the rational use of energy resources, and climate change. It would also seem sensible that the information infrastructure established in the East develops in a compatible fashion to that in the European Union, and that research conducted in this area is complementary and convergent. There will also be efforts to combat environmental and public health problems in the new independent States of the former Soviet Union, in particular as a result of major accidents. (This notion was introduced by the European Parliament. in an attempt to circumnavigate possible difficulties arising from the competing competences of the Euratom Treaty and the EC Treaty in this domain).
- The International Association for the Promotion of Cooperation with Scientists from the New Independent States of the Former Soviet Union (INTAS) will be continued, provided that a new agreement is reached between its members.
- The opening–up of the specific programmes of the Fourth Framework Programme to these countries, notably the associated countries. [3]

Actions will supplement those of the Member States and synergy with the PHARE and TACIS programmes will be ensured. At the same time, this should help to coordinate Member States' activities in this area.

Annex II of the Decision gives the indicative breakdown of the 540 MECU 'amount deemed necessary' by the Framework Programme Co-Decision, as shown below. The breakdown between different areas does not exclude the possibility that projects may come under several areas.

[3] Other Community instruments could help to finance such participation.

		MECU
Area A1	Cooperation with other fora for scientific and technological cooperation in Europe	46
Area A2	Cooperation with the countries of Central and Eastern Europe and the new independent States of the former Soviet Union	232
Area B	Cooperation with non–European industrialised third countries	30
Area C	Cooperation with the developing countries	232
	TOTAL	540 [4] [5]

The detailed rules for the Community's financial contribution are laid down in Annex IV to the Decision on the Fourth Framework Programme, while those for the participation of undertakings, research centres and universities and for the dissemination of results are as laid down in the measures provided for by Article 130j of the Treaty.[6] Nonetheless Annex III of this Specific Programme Decision does provide detailed rules for implementing the Programme, an abridged version of which follows below.

Participation in the programme is open, with financial support from the Community:
a) to all legal entities, established and regularly carrying out RTD activities in the Community, or in a third country associated, wholly or in part, with the implementation of the relevant programme through an agreement concluded between the Community and the said third country; and b) to the Joint Research Centre. Participation is also open, without financial support from the Community, and on condition that their participation is in the interests of Community policies, to legal entities established in a country which has concluded a scientific and technical cooperation agreement with the Community relating to activities covered by the programme, provided the participation accords with the terms of the agreement.

Cooperation with the countries of Central and Eastern Europe, the new independent States of the former Soviet Union and the developing countries in specific areas not covered by the programmes of activities 1, 3 and 4 will normally take the form of shared–cost activities or concerted action. A balance will be ensured between cooperation with the Central and Eastern European countries and the new independent States on the one hand, and with the developing countries on the other. The financial

---

[4] Including 4.6% for staff expenditure and 5.5% for administrative expenditure.

[5] A sum of ECU 4 million will be allocated to the dissemination and utilization of the results of the programme.

[6] *Official Journal of the European Communities*, no. L306, 30 November 1994.

contribution for the partners from the Central and Eastern European countries, the new independent States and the developing countries may exceed 50%.

The pilot phase of the International Association for the Promotion of Cooperation with Scientists from the New Independent States of the Former Soviet Union (INTAS) expired at the end of 1994. The Commission proposed to transmit a proposal to the Council in due course regarding the future of this association and the geographical areas and themes to be covered.

Cooperation with the countries of Central and Eastern Europe, the new independent States of the former Soviet Union and the developing countries will be implemented in close liaison with other Community initiatives such as PHARE and TACIS, or other fora for cooperation such as the Lomé Convention, the new Mediterranean policy and the regulation on financial and technical assistance to, and economic cooperation with, the developing countries in Asia and Latin America, in order to permit cross-fertilisation between the efforts and results of these activities on the one hand, and cooperation in the framework of Community RTD policy on the other.

The programme will be carried out in the form of:

- Financial participation by the Community in RTD activities carried out by third parties or by JRC Institutes in association with third parties, via

  (a) *Shared-cost activities*: either RTD projects carried out by undertakings, research centres and universities, including consortia for integrated projects with a common thematic objective; or support for financing the infrastructure or installations necessary for the implementation of a coordinated action (strengthening of coordination).

  (b) *Concerted activities*, which consist of coordinating, particularly with the aid of concertation networks, RTD projects already funded by public authorities or private bodies. Concerted activities can also include the requisite coordination of thematic networks bringing together manufacturers, users, universities and research centres to work on the same technological or industrial objective under shared-cost RTD activities.

  (c) *Specific measures* such as measures in support of the Community's external policies and measures to provide tools for general use in research centres, universities and undertakings. The Community's contribution covers up to 100% of the costs of the measures.

Preparatory, accompanying and support measures include:

- studies in support of this programme and in preparation for future activities;
- conferences, seminars, workshops or other scientific or technical meetings, including intersectoral or multidisciplinary coordination meetings;
- use of external expertise, including access to scientific databases;
- scientific publications, including the dissemination, promotion, and utilisation of the results (coordinated with the activities conducted under the third activity);
- study and monitoring of the developments in the science and technology policies of the third countries and of the socio–economic conditions of international cooperation;
- training activities related to research covered by this programme;

- recourse to the energy centres set up in certain countries under the Thermie programme;
- concertation and coordination activities, e.g. exchange of information to improve coordination with the Member States;
- independent evaluation (including studies) of programme management and of the implementation of its activities.

This Specific Programme will be implemented according to a Work Programme to be drawn up by a Programme Management Committee, which will define, *inter alia*, the precise modalities of participation in the Specific Programmes of the First Activity. In fact the Work Programme will inevitably use much of the same wording as the Specific Programme decision outlined above, since it is already reasonably detailed.

At the time of writing, it seems likely that the major involvement of the EC will be via specific projects aimed at particular problem areas. These will include efforts to safeguard the R&TD potential, projects concerned with environmental protection and health, and applied research directed towards industry. The latter can be further subdivided into: advanced communications and telematics; information technologies; materials technologies; biotechnology; transport; and possibly also agro-food, energy technologies, and measurement and testing. The timetable for the implementation of this programme is that the first call for proposals for the section concerning cooperation with the countries of Central and Eastern Europe and the former Soviet Union was to be published in the *Official Journal of the European Communities* on 15 March 1995, restricted to 4-5 sectors. A more-far reaching call would be launched at the end of 1995, and a last call for proposals would be issued in 1997. The indicative schedule of expenditure in this area, in MECU, is expected to be approximately as follows: 1995 - 14.64; 1996 - 59.25; 1997 - 68.22; 1998 - 66.87; making a total of 208.98 MECU. This would be distributed approximately along the lines of: stabilisation of R&TD potential - 20 MECU; environment and health - 104 MECU; and applied research directed towards industry - 85 MECU. Clearly 1995 would be a year of transition, during which a dialogue would be developed between the services in the EC Commission responsible for this programme, and the countries concerned.

Since the 4th Framework Programme is the first to be decided upon jointly by the Council of Ministers and the European Parliament, under the new procedures introduced by the Maastricht Treaty, the Parliament will inevitably take a keen interest in monitoring progress with the specific programmes. The Parliament also, inevitably, has a keen interest in the political (and hence socio-economic, environmental etc) development of the countries concerned, and will therefore naturally seek to ensure that the monies provided in the Specific Programme here described are used as effectively as possible.

Conversion in Ukrainian Military R&D at the Beginning of the1990s: Some Results and Problems

IGOR EGOROV

Dobrov STEPS Centre
National Academy of Sciences
Ukraine

INTRODUCTION

Conversion of the military sector in industry and R&D is very important for all post-Communist countries. But for such states as Russia and Ukraine, the significance of this process is extremely high, because the military-industrial complex has comprised the best and the most modern part of the economy. In the Ukrainian case, this sector could be the only instrument capable of leading Ukraine into the world market and occupying some specific niches in it.

Several factors determine Ukrainian conversion policy. The economic situation is very uncertain. The Ukrainian state is on the brink of bankruptcy and can no longer provide the military-industrial complex with the volume of orders that it enjoyed in Soviet times. Nor can those elements of the Soviet military-industrial complex that have now been inherited by Ukraine even meet the structural defensive demands of independent Ukraine.

On the other hand, Ukraine still has one of the biggest armies in Europe and, on paper, third rank among the nations with nuclear weapons. Some Ukrainian politicians, including nationalist groups in the Parliament and army officials,[1] invoke the Russian threat to revitalise military preparations. They are trying to prevent conversion of the military industry and R&D. Bearing in mind the size of the military-industrial complex in Ukraine, conversion could induce a rapid rise in unemployment, which is a serious matter in conditions of deep economic crisis. But the political position of the pro-conversion forces is much stronger now, and after the election of Mr. Kuchma as President in July 1994, relations with Russia have become

---

[1] *Golos Ukrayny*, 21 May 1994.

P. Gummett et al. (eds.), Military R&D after the Cold War, 163–167.

friendlier and more realistic. Hence, very few external *political* barriers remain in the way of conversion, unlike the case with *economic* and *institutional* barriers.

UKRAINE AND RUSSIA[2]

In 1992 the Ukrainian Ministry of Machine-Building, Industry and Conversion comprised 2594 enterprises, which in the former USSR were distributed among seven machine-building and nine All-Union defence ministries. In modern Ukraine, this military-industrial complex has preserved its relative autonomy from the rest of the economy.

As for the S&T sector, according to various estimates, 40-70% of all Ukrainian research institutions and technological bureaux worked on military research projects. S&T programmes connected with defence needs were, therefore, carried out not only in specialised research centres, but also in the Academy of Sciences and research centres of higher educational establishments. Professor Pavlo Kysly, deputy head of the Commission on Science and Higher Education in the Ukrainian Parliament in 1990-1994 and Corresponding member of the Ukrainian Academy of Sciences, estimates that Institutes of the Academy of Sciences received 40-80% of their budget from military orders in 1988-90 (Kysly, 1991).

Under conditions of deep economic crisis Ukraine has to rebuild the structure of its economy and reduce its military-industrial complex: in 1991, 750 major technology bureaus and enterprises were engaged exclusively in military production, their number falling to 267 by mid-1993.

To a considerable extent this process is a result of trends in relations between Ukraine and Russia. Ukraine lacks full production on its territory of the entire production cycle. In 1990, 79% of total final arms products were produced in Russia (Falzman, 1992). Moreover, this applies not only to the final stages of production. For example, the major naval-related S&T centres have traditionally been located in Russia (Lomonosov near St.-Petersburg, Zelenograd near Moscow and so on). The Ukrainian shipbuilding industry therefore will need a long period of time to create its own R&D base. At the same time Ukraine has one of the best aviation design bureau of the former USSR, in which such well-known transport aircraft as the AN-225 'Ruslan' and 'Mrya' have been created.

Meanwhile, having lost their traditional partners in the Baltic region and Ukraine, Russian military enterprises are engaged upon creating their own full production cycles within the military sphere, including R&D. Thus, Russia is filling the gaps that have emerged since the independence of the former Soviet republics, but at the expense of Ukrainian enterprises and S&T institutions with the same or similar specialist capabilities.

Sometimes, however, Russian high-tech military-related companies still use the capabilities of Ukrainian enterprises and research institutes. The Ukrainian currency is

---

[2] In the following paragraphs, information from the database of the Ukrainian Ministry of Statistics has been used. I thank Dr V. Karpov, the Director of the Institute of Statistics, and Ms L. Lapenko for this opportunity.

weak even in comparison with Russian one. Average real salaries in Ukraine were 3-4 times lower than in Russia in 1993-1994. Hence, Ukrainian enterprises are eager to take part in joint projects with Russian partners. Russian space contractors alone provide directly for about 1000 jobs in Ukraine.

Despite formal difficulties connected primarily with the underdeveloped housing market in former Soviet Union, some leading specialists have already left Ukraine. Emigration from the military-industrial complex is not on such a massive scale as from 'pure' science in the Academy of Sciences and the Universities, but Ukraine is losing its best specialists in the most important areas of R&D, possessing knowledge which is now much sought after by the Russian military-industrial complex. A good example is V.Utkin, predecessor of S.Korolev and the heir of M.Yangel in the position of Director of 'Yuzhny mashinostroitelny zavod' (Southern Machine-building Factory) - the biggest missile-building complex of the former USSR. It is known that a number of other prominent Ukrainian specialists have received similar proposals from the Russian authorities.

Although the process of emigration from the military-industrial complex to Russia is not primarily a result of ethnic problems, it is worth adding that the introduction in Ukraine of the Ukrainian language as the only official language may well exacerbate the problem. The language ruling has met with a negative reaction from scientific researchers. Traditionally, the bulk of scientific literature and technical documentation has been published in Russian. Dissertations and papers were also written in Russian.

Bearing in mind the size of the Ukrainian military-industrial complex, an 'internal' brain drain, induced by economic decline, is inevitable. Officially, only about 6000 specialists lost their jobs in 1992-1993 in militarily-related R&D in Ukraine. However, the real figure is much higher, because in many institutes and design bureaus professional activity has stopped thanks to the lack of orders, equipment, spare parts, financial problems and so on.

WAYS AHEAD

The picture has, however, a positive side as well. After years of reliance on state help, the Ukrainian military-industrial complex is now forced to seek its own way out of this crisis. Arms export appear to be one of the possible opportunities, but they face a number of serious obstacles.

First, Ukraine lacks its own stable partners who might be consumers of its military production. Second, the international arms market is already shared between the traditional suppliers, in which respect Russia readily assumes the role of heir of the former USSR. Third, as already discussed, in the short term Ukrainian firms face difficulties over the establishment of full arms production cycles. In consequence, military-industrial complex enterprises exports from Ukraine decreased from US$1.5b in 1990 to US$0.3b in 1992. In 1992-1993 further decline was observed. Reversal of this tendency will demand considerable efforts, including the revival of the bulk of traditional co-operative activities inside the CIS.

Some of enterprises and design bureaus have already changed their priorities and have begun to produce less technologically sophisticated consumer goods. The need for product simplification is also rooted in a deep crisis of payments between CIS countries and in foreign trade restrictions. Thus, in 1992-1993 the Ukrainian electronic industry was unable to acquire the volume of gold (for use in equipment) that it had been able to obtain in Soviet times form traditional sources.

The implementation of the National Space programme can be cited as a specific example of a new direction being taken by the military-industrial complex. It includes the development of Ukraine's own satellites, which will use Ukrainian launchers and the Baykonur space complex as launching point. However, the extent of implementation of this programme is now under question, depending, as it does to a great extent, on the relations between the two biggest CIS countries, which have overlapping space potentials.

The State is trying to provide the biggest R&D institutions with orders. However, these orders are frequently entail work that is below the level of qualification of the researchers. For example, a missile design bureau has received orders to create a new trolley-bus and a new machine gun (the famous Kalashnikov having been left to Russia!).

Thus it would be possible to consider two main types of conversion:

1. conversion into civilian production; and
2. conversion within the military sphere as a result of the need to replace suppliers from the other CIS countries (notably Russia).

Unfortunately, very few successful examples of transformation can be offered, especially of type 1.

The latest data confirm the conclusion of Cohendet and Heraud (see chapter 10 in this volume) that it is very difficult, if not impossible, to disseminate know-how from the military R&D throughout civil sector enterprises. So, in Ukraine in 1993 the main applications of R&D from the military-oriented R&D institutes and design bureaux were in the electronics and computer industries (18.6%), space industry (15%) and shipbuilding (13.5%). In contrast, only 2.6 % of results were channelled to the agricultural sector (2.9% in 1992), 0.3% (0.4% in 1992) to agricultural machinery, and 3.7% (6.5% in 1992) to the production of medical equipment. This confirms that the process of conversion has some common features with the same process in Western countries. But it also means that it cannot automatically help traditional sectors of the economy in solving their problems associated with updating obsolete technologies and producing cheap and good quality consumer goods.

In the near future, the S&T potential of the military-industrial complex will in any case face another crucial change. A decree of the Cabinet of Ministers in March 1993 to reduce by 50% the funds for S&T institutions and technology bureaus supervised by the Defence Ministry and the Ministry of Machine-Building and Conversion, was the starting point of a new wave of changes, compounding the problem that wages in the enterprises and the institutes of the military-industrial complex were already 25-40% below the national average. The March 1993 decision has accelerated the process of 'erosion' of the human potential of the military-industrial complex R&D, which has already suffered more than other sectors of the economy.

Any serious prospect of conversion in high technology industries assumes a wide-scale investment programme, tax reductions, subsidies for fixed periods of time and so on. But in 1991-1993, Ukrainian national-communist authorities used a common approach to all the enterprises in the country coupled with a populist internal policy. This aimed at keeping power, based on searching for relatively simple solutions for the complex problems of social and economic restructuring. That is why the bulk of money, provided to convert military industrial complex enterprises and R&D institutions into civil-oriented ones, was used on social benefits for employees, not for restructuring. In 1993, actual investments amounted to only 4.1% of all expenditure on conversion of military R&D!

CONCLUSION

In the new post Cold War environment, Ukrainian military-oriented R&D institutes and design bureaux still have not been able to find a way to open the opportunity to demonstrate their strengths in highly qualified personnel, and a highly skilled work force. A considerable part of the sector has already been 'eroded', but the opportunity to use some parts of it still exists. Ukraine will not be able to solve its problems without a rise in the volume of exports in the near future[3], for which its best-placed sector is the military-industrial complex.

Progress could be achieved through:

1. promotion of exports of high technology products, principally in the shipbuilding, aviation and space sectors;
2. establishment of the appropriate institutional structures (special legislation, low taxes and so on); and
3. creation of more joint ventures with foreign partners.

Implementation of these measures will involve more than simple closure of existing enterprises, or the dumping on world markets by R&D institutes of such things as stocks of coal and steel which happen to be to hand. Otherwise, in a few years Ukraine could turn into something like the worst examples of a Latin American state, with an economy based on badly organised and ineffective agriculture, on the remote borders of Europe.

REFERENCES

1. Falzman V. (1992) Perspectivy Conversyi v Rossyi (Perspectives on Conversion in Russia), *Rossysky Economichesky Zhurnal*, No.8 , pp. 67-79.
2. Kysly P. (1991) Problemy Finansuvannya Nauki v Ukraini (Problems of Science Budgeting in Ukraine), *Visnyk Academiy Nauk Ukrayny*, No.10, pp. 8-10.

[3] In 1992-94, Ukraine's foreign trade was 10-20% less than the foreign trade of similarly-sized European countries such as the UK, France and Italy. Ukraine also has a persistent negative foreign trade balance.

Study of the Requirements and Experience of Utilisation of Knowledge and Results of Military Researchers: Case Study of the Medical Research Institute in Ukraine

GALINA A. KARAS

Department of Medical Scientific Information
Kiev Otolaryngology Research Institute
Ukraine

INTRODUCTION

The state of development of world integrative processes, and the special attention paid by NATO to scientific cooperation with the countries of the former Soviet Union, Central and Eastern Europe, requires urgent and careful investigation of the progressive scientific achievements of the military-industrial complex (MIC) to draw lessons from our current experience of conversion, and knowledge and technology transfer.

As noted by both Farkas and Gummett (chapters 4 and 2, this volume), one of the paradoxes of MIC development was the production from time to time of highly valuable results for the civil sector. At the same time, as Rassadin (1993) has observed, the result of the privileged state of the MIC was the uneven development of technical progress. Successful development of innovation within the MIC correlates with recession in the civil sphere, which is especially deep in the national economy. These peculiarities have more or less common features in different states.

The very high cost of military research has, however, induced debates about the need for shifting the balance towards expenditures on civil needs (Mervis, 1992). Such changes of profile require comprehensive scientific analysis of the peculiarities of military-civil integration, well-directed methods of conversion, and utilisation of highly scientific knowledge and progressive results. Among the first steps that then arise are the task of development of specific forms and methods of technology transfer between the MIC and civil society, and between military laboratories and industry and other organisations (Marshall, 1991). The experience of military-civilian integration

P. Gummett et al. (eds.), Military R&D after the Cold War, 169–173.

and the increase of returns from the defence industry of the USA attracts special attention (Tolkachev, 1992).

Taking into account the above-mentioned issues, we have studied the informational needs of specialists working in otolaryngology in the utilisation of research and design results of the MIC, and have tried to develop a perspective on the use made of this material in the practical development in otolaryngology. A particular case study was made of the condition of one specialised medical institute - the Kiev Otolaryngology Research Institute.

Information needs were identified through analysis of the directions of research in otolaryngology, and of the needs of information users, and study of the priority directions of research projects and the most significant achievements in military-oriented sciences.

Various approaches within the field of information research, including scientometrics, review methods, study of feedback cards, interviews, direct and indirect observations, and information modelling and forecast were used.

We present our results here as a specific illustrative case study of the potential for transfer of knowledge from MIC laboratories to civilian purposes.

PRIORITIES

The analysis enabled us to identify the following main directions of information needs, knowledge and studies, specific artifacts, and technical devices:

- The organisation of neuron nets, and possible methods of information transfer in the normal and pathologically changed human body.
- Functions of vestibular organs in human beings and animals under gravitational changes.
- Specific features and possibilities of the different physical aspects and drugs utilisation for the increase of auditory perceptions and/or reception of auditory perception.
- Design of different electronic systems of auditory perceptions.
- Up-to-date systems of transformation of phonetic information, image analysis.
- Research and design of biosensors, devices such as an artificial 'dog's nose', based on the utilisation of biological materials.
- Special features of acoustic hydrodynamic systems function, which are similar to the ear function and are successfully used in submarines.
- New drugs, biotechnological and immunobiological preparations, which can be used both for the recovery and the prophylaxis and treatment of LOR-organs.
- Use of high resolution optical systems for microscopic and endoscopic diagnostic and surgical treatment.
- Use of the most up-to-date information technologies and automated computerised complexes for the diagnostic and treatment of LOR-organ diseases.

Among the scientific trends that were identified, a special place was held by the problems of utilisation of progressive designs, forms and methods of organisation in catastrophe medicine and civil defence organisations.

fields as identified by the American Institute of Scientific Information. Further confirmation of the importance of these directions came from the decisions of the US Government during the Cold War over access to such high technology fields as biotechnology, high-speed computers, neurosciences, and acoustics research that can be applied to military fields (Schweitzer, 1992).

LONGER-RANGE POSSIBILITIES

Comprehensive analysis of the information concerning the above-mentioned trends in research allowed us to identify many results achieved while fulfilling military researches or in military institutions, and proposed as conversion goals. This analysis further enabled us to identify for possible longer-range utilisation in otolaryngology such developments as:

- methods of decreasing noise intensity for the defence of personnel and equipment from acoustic loading;
- fluorine-carbonate sorbents prepared by the fluorination of carbohydrate rings that may be used for ecological problem-solving and for research purposes in chromatography;
- sorbents based on natural clinotilolyts for radioactive isotope capturing;
- methods and means of acoustic emission investigation are also of interest in otolaryngology.

CASES OF CONVERSION

The real implementation of advanced scientific achievements from the military sector in the practice of otolaryngology in the Ukraine today takes place as part of an organised conversion programme. Examples of activities inlude:

- An endoscopic device for ultrasound therapy, a universally diagnostic microprocessor complex for investigation of functional activity of the principal systems of human beings.
- The Isium instrument-making plant in Kharkov region is developing diagnostic microscopes with enhanced functional possibilities for ambulance and clinical departments.
- Improvements based on utilisation of the most up-to-date optics that satisfy the needs of enhanced functions for clinical practice.
- The design office 'Luch' (Kiev) is developing up-to-date electronic acoustic systems.
- The 'Radar' plant is working on the production of polyphonators, devices which are used for the rehabilitation of children with low-hearing diagnosis.
- The Lubny calculating machines plant is producing an audio-vocal training device for the treatment of low-hearing and deaf children and adults.
- The Research-Productive Association 'Poisk' (Zhelty Vody) has a project aimed at design and construction of electronic acoustic devices for hearing investigation, together with the associated electronic training device.

- the Institute of Instrument-Making and Technologies (Kharkov), and the Productive Association 'Komunar', have created a vestibulometric device and automated nistagmometer for the investigation and training of vestibular organ.
- the Productive Association 'Monolyt' with the participation of otolaryngologists designed devices for cryo- and cryo-ultrasound therapy, and for the diagnostic device ultrasinus (echosinuscope ESS-01).
- Automatised complexes for cardiovascular system diagnostic and devices for searching and estimation of biologically active points and influencing them by means of electromagnetic radiation, have been created by the industrial plants of Kharkov in collaboration with medical institutions.
- Kiev Productive Association (named after S.P.Korolev) also works on automated medical devices for functional diagnosis, analysis of chemiluminograms using the latest bioluminescent and immunoenzyme methods etc. The neuro-muscle stimulator constructed by this association may also be used in physiotherapy departments and rehabilitation centres, and can be used in otolaryngology for the treatment of laryngeal muscle functions.
- The 'Arsenal' Plant and Research Productive Association 'Quant' are working on laboratory blood analysers needed both in otolaryngology and in other branches of medicine.

CONCLUSION

In all the above-mentioned cases, the utilisation of the most up-to-date technologies and military potential is common, and the project is carried out on a competitive basis, which is essential for the development of the national economy. It is worth emphasising that these events became possible in the Ukraine thanks to the conversion process. Further changes in the technological and economic base, improvements in medical care, increasing availability of more sophisticated and reliable devices are the expected results.

It must also be emphasised that these R&D and production programmes resulted from close cooperation and interaction between the medical research institute, defence industry plants and different research groups.

Our analysis allows us to conclude that medicine is one of the branches of the national economy which needs the application of high technologies and can make good use of military potential in the conversion process. The application of scientific information methods can also stimulate the dissemination of the latest information, thus accelerating the conversion process, the application of the potential of military science, the reconceptualisation of military R&D, and the reinforcement of their social orientation.

A continuous follow-up of conversion processes and results of utilisation of military technologies and researches now forms the basis for collaboration in development with European states and other countries.

REFERENCES

1. Marshall, E. (1991) Weapon labs: After the cold war, *Science*, Vol. 254, No. 5035, pp.1100-03.
2. Mervis, J. (1992) Healy attacks U.S. budgeting system, *Nature*, Vol. 356, No. 6370, p.555.
3. Rassadin, V.N. (1993) Voyenno-promyshlennyi komplex kak sistema, *Problemy prognozirovaniya*, No. 1. pp.54-59.
4. Schweitzer, G.E. (1992) US-Soviet scientific cooperation: The interacademy program, *Technology in Society*, Vol.14, No.2, pp.173-85.
5. Tolkachev, VPK. (1992) Novyye rynky i novaya strategiya, *Ekonomika, politika, ideologiya*, No.5, pp.13-21.

Establishment of a Technology Transfer Centre in Bratislava

HEINZ SEMERAD

Business Creation Europe
Vienna
Austria

BACKGROUND

This chapter presents a case study of the establishment of a technology transfer centre in Bratislava, Slovakia, involving an East-West cooperation between the two organisations, Business Creation Europe (BCE) and Ustav Technologie a Racionalizacie (UTAR).

In many parts of Eastern Europe the International Programme 'Conversion through Enterprise Development' was launched with participation of UNIDO in order to elaborate and implement the novel concept of conversion of military industries and military R&D to civil industries. The programmes were primarily implemented through a bottom-up approach, based on the mobilisation of available local resources and also on the involvement of local authorities in establishing an environment conducive to the facilitation of the process. From the economic viewpoint, the main purpose of the various programmes, including the measures for entrepreneurship and intrapreneurship development, was the creation of conditions for optimal utilisation of local and foreign investments.

Business Creation Europe is a private company which started in 1982 and is active in a number of countries in Europe and North America. Initially its focus was on small business development and on mobility services for large corporations. Over the years BCE branched out into revitalisation of real estate and venture capital. Central to the BCE approach is the recycling of the activities, personnel and fixed assets that are redundant to civil and military companies. New opportunities for the redundant employees are identified, either by attracting other companies to the site, by initiating and implementing spin off companies, by developing outplacement programmes and by assisting promising starting entrepreneurs. The redeployment of the redundant employees is, of course, of vital importance in winning the co-operation of the military establishment, political parties and trade unions in the restructuring and conversion.

P. Gummett et al. (eds.), Military R&D after the Cold War, 175–181.

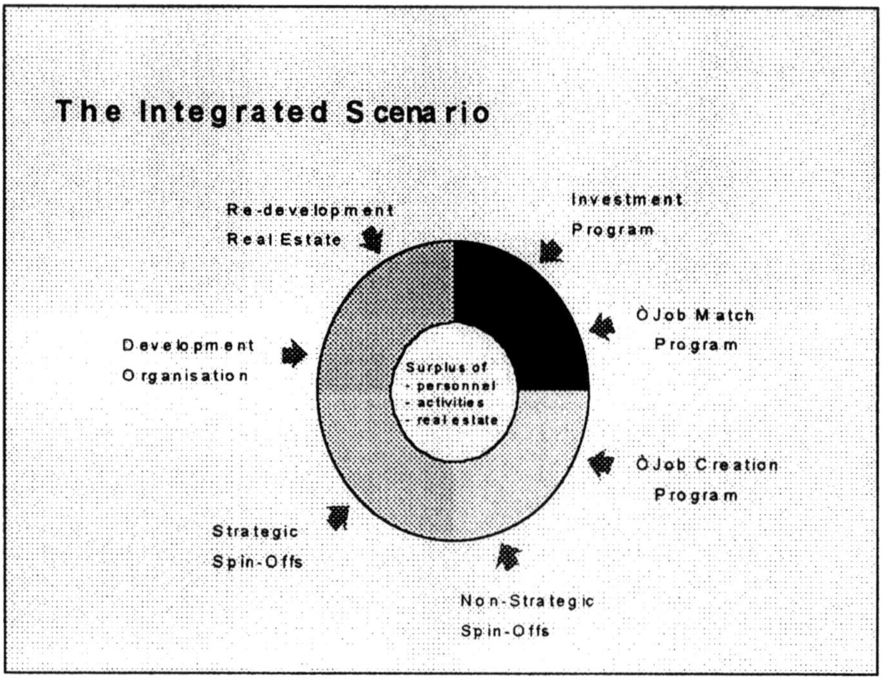

The recycling of the company's real estate is important in the search for new investors, i.e. companies that will absorb real estate and redundant employees. It is also a very effective way to add substantial value to otherwise redundant property. From an organisational point of view, optimal results can only be achieved when the conversion is planned and managed in an integrated manner.

The Austrian subsidiary of Business Creation Europe, Job Creation Betriebsansiedlungen GmbH, was retained by UTAR, a Bratislava-based defence engineering company, to assist with the identification and realisation of new business opportunities in the civil sector. Having agreed the scope and desired focus of the assignment, Job Creation carried out an audit of the client's resources. During the audit work it was found that the UTAR company was not viable and that there was no economic base for its continuation.

The market to which UTAR supplied their engineering knowledge had collapsed, and the management had neither marketing experience nor was it 'western oriented'. A high inflation rate led to high risks for western investors and the production facilities were not competitive. A infrastructure for small and medium sized companies did not exist. Job Creation found a high degree of vertical integration, lack of funds and little opportunity to specialise and develop on existing strengths.

On the other hand, Job Creation found a potential of well-qualified managers and employees, skills in project management, and a real estate which was thought to be convertible. The audit also showed motivated employees, low engineering costs, knowledge of the Eastern European market and a willingness to develop new businesses.

PROJECT STRATEGY

Job Creation decided to develop a project based on conversion through the development of small, mainly technology oriented, businesses, and to present the project to the Slovak government and later to Western investors. The main objective was the establishment of a joint venture company between the Western investors and UTAR. The core of this joint venture project was the development of a Technology Centre.

The project consisted of four sub-projects:

- the conversion of the building to western standards, including the provision of Common Services,
- training of the local management team,
- develop the existing retraining department, create new businesses with the employees of UTAR and
- search for business partners.

The common services consisted of office support comprising physical facilities such as reception area, conference room, canteen and telefax, as well as administrative support such as telephone answering and secretarial services. The common services also included business advice, generally of a first stop and coaching kind, in principle across the whole spectrum of business problems. It was also planned to provide machinery and equipment, with the purpose of enabling the would be entrepreneurs to test out his product ideas and perhaps build a prototype before formally commencing commercial production.

From the outset the newly established Technology Centre started with the creation of 14 small businesses employing 75 people in 1840 m2 of space. As regards the creation of businesses, we will return to it in the next paragraph. The range of businesses include a law firm, an advertising agency, tax consultancy and spin off companies from the old UTAR such as a laser equipment company, a software development company and workshops for small prototype development.

For the retraining centre, UTAR already had one British partner. This team was enlarged by an Austrian retraining expert team. The British company was teaching the use and capabilities of computers about which the local managers had no prior knowledge nor experience. The hands-on courses and tutorials were designed so that many participants could learn for themselves how to operate the hardware and software programmes and the use of sophisticated graphics and animation. The objective of the retraining programmes was to see how information technology could be of value to would-be entrepreneurs and their employees, and to gain sufficient confidence to make use of it in their work. The programmes focused on a wide variety of training needs, ranging from information technology for school leavers to business skills. Together with the local job offices an increasing priority was to establish projects which offer retraining and counselling to workers who faced redundancy in Bratislava. The UTAR retraining centre offers today a broad spectrum of courses from those geared to preparing a competent pool of secretaries, book-keepers, and accountants, to more specialised training needs of companies in Bratislava.

FUTURE PLANS AND BUSINESS CREATION

The enterprises which should be generated and developed can be within regions of a country, and within state or private corporations. The focus in UTAR was upon new technology-based enterprises based on existing skills. The basic ingredients of any business start-up are ideas and people. Opinions differ as to which is the most important, but clearly both are necessary if a successful venture is to be established. However, it is a common mistake to assume that the person with the ideas is the right person to grow the business. Experience shows that this is generally not the case.

A better methodology is to treat the idea and people as two distinct task areas and then bring them together in a joining process in a third area which could be a Technology Centre or Incubator. In order to provide a regular supply of new businesses it is important that these tasks are adequately resourced.

The main difficulty with business ideas is not finding them, but identifying those which will be commercially successful. In Eastern Europe this task should be undertaken by Technology Conversion Units which will require initial external assistance and foreign investment. This will mean, however, that technology conversion programmes will be multi-conditional, including, for example, more than two major partners, or needing additional guarantees and co-ordination before support will be forthcoming. This explains a certain lack of enthusiasm from foreign partners concerning technology conversion programmes as compared to less risky investments. At the same time, if properly arranged, technology conversion may be quite beneficial for all partners due to the unique nature of innovation pools and business ideas in Eastern Europe.

The technology conversion and business ideas should be further developed inside a specialist group which could be termed a Business Ideas Transfer Unit. The next step in the idea evaluation process involves using people who will develop the idea into a business to carry out the evaluation for themselves. This is best done in New Business Courses which bring together the idea and business team which has been developed in special entrepreneur development programmes organised in Entrepreneur Schools.

Experience has shown that the new businesses need the help of western partners which could be found in International Co-operation Exchange Units. The task of such units is to search for potential business partners, select and evaluate them, assist in the business negotiations and team building, and review the business development process after one year.

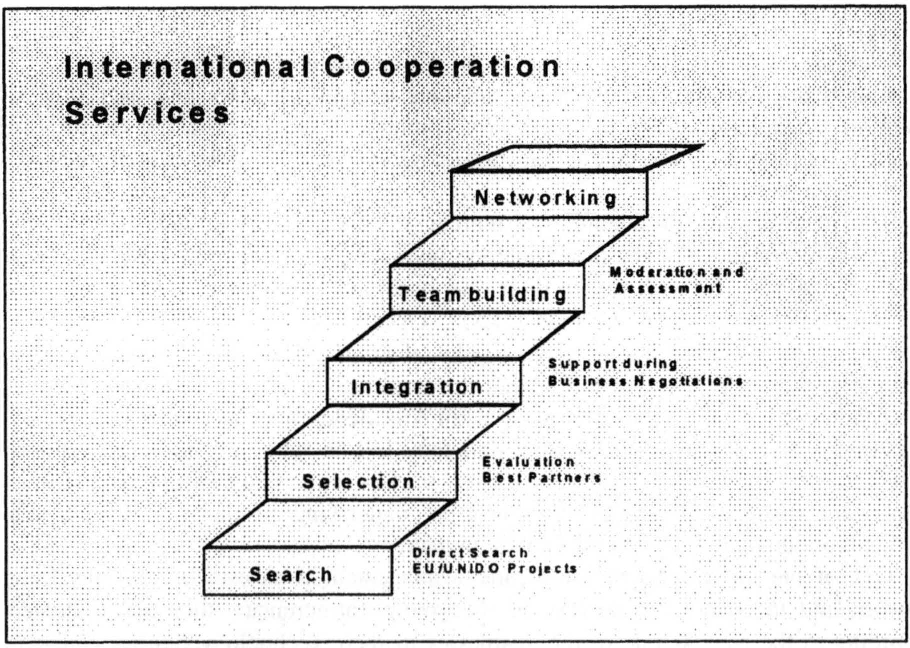

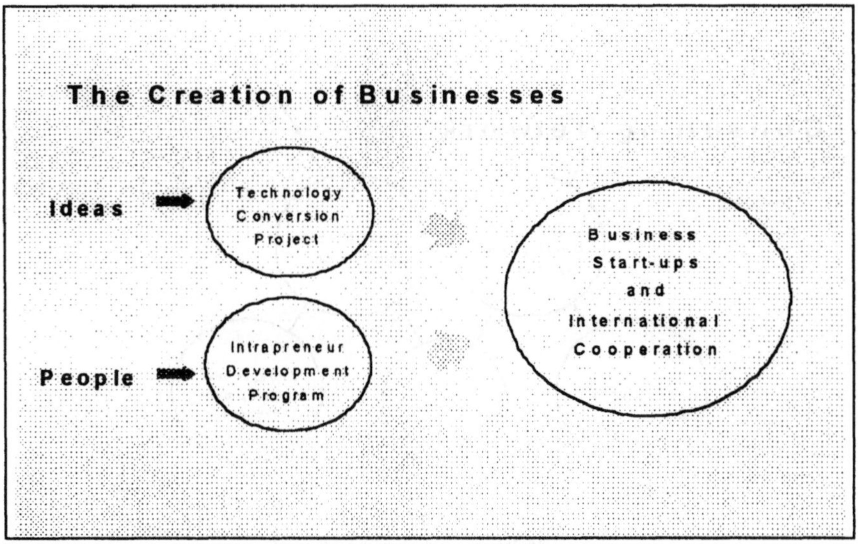

SUCCESS FACTORS FOR A TECHNOLOGY INCUBATOR

The Technology Incubator Centre, TIC, has to be seen as a business which in the medium term should show results and profit, which means that the TICs require result- and profit-oriented leadership. The TIC requires a full-time management which orientates itself to customer demands. The start-up entrepreneur has the right to consider himself as a valuable customer to the management of the Centre.

Experience has shown that a TIC requires a good customer and user mix to guarantee synergy effects and bring about its commercial success. The TIC requires an excellent location within a region, and its strategies have to be coherent with regional development strategies.

The identification of potential entrepreneurs is the most difficult part of the management of the TIC. The direct method involves placing advertisements in local papers for people who wish to run their own business. The indirect method involves programmes at universities and high schools. Once the potential entrepreneurs have been identified, the next step is to ensure that they all possess a level of knowledge which is sufficient for them to start up and run a business.

Today most Centre managers have a fair knowledge of what the ideal primary motives for entrepreneurs are, what action they like to take and on what business activities they should concentrate on. Most start-up entrepreneurs put their future careers and financial security behind the ideas, understand customer orientation and market research, and are prepared to work in teams.

One of the main tasks of the Centre Management is to establish a consulting network and to ensure the success of the young entrepreneur; they are evaluated according to the success rate of the businesses in their Technology Centre, which is normally above 80%.

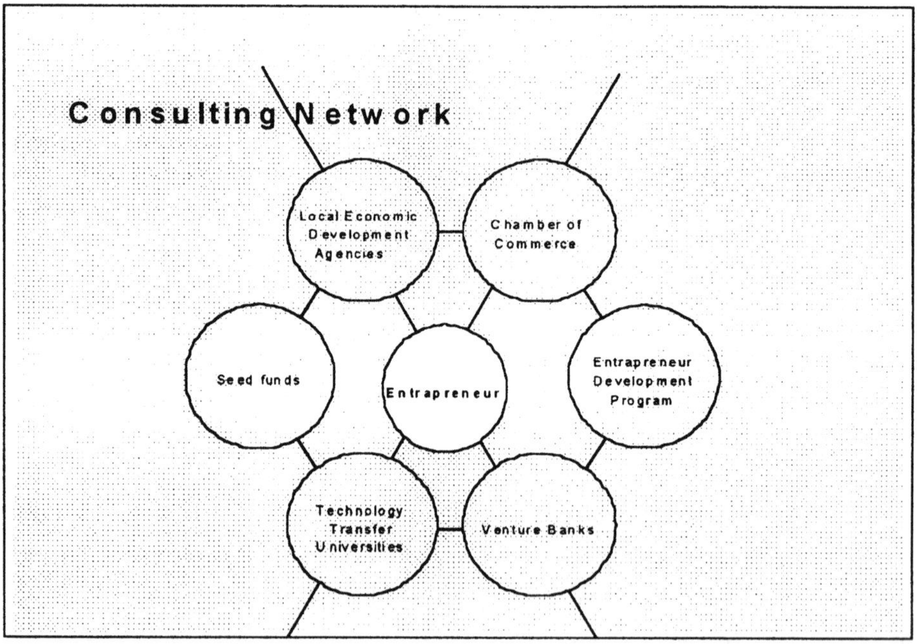

CONCLUSION

Conversion is a 'software' rather than a 'hardware' process, consisting of valuation of assets and personnel, search for potential foreign partners, and upgrading of technology transfer capabilities from east to west and vice versa.

Conversion programmes vary in general and in details depending on their relation to specific industrial sectors and the geographical location of the converted enterprise.

Conversion should be performed mainly by local management, including non-technical groups, guided by international experts.

Technology Centres and Technology Incubator Centres are positive tools for recycling existing assets, consisting of real estate, human resources, business ideas and conversion projects, provided the process is implemented in an integrated manner.

Conversion In Bulgaria: Some Contextual Problems

KOSTADINKA SIMEONOVA

Centre for the Science of Science
Bulgarian Academy of Sciences
Sofia, Bulgaria

Conversion is not a popular subject for study in Bulgaria. This is partly because of the limited experience of it in the country, and partly due to the lack of comprehensive information. This chapter discusses the first steps in developing relevant policies in the post-communist Bulgaria. It deals in particular with: a) initiatives on the level of governmental policy; b) the impact of the economic reforms and transition to the market on conversion; and c) the role of R&D in conversion.

The descriptions and conclusions offered in the paper are based on different sources of information: the analysis of documents and other publications (Government decress, proceedings of meetings, articles in newspapers and journals); interviews with key officials in the Ministry of Industry, the Academy of Sciences, and of scientists and managers; observation of the public reaction to implemented policies (including strike activity in the firms of military industrial complex).

THE HERITAGE

The heritage of the 'Perestroika' period has been favourable for the new orientation towards conversion in several respects.

First, the military industry was subjected to economic analysis, for which purpose the first university chair on 'Economics of the defence industry' at the higher School of Economics was set up in 1986. The aim was to promote research on conversion, including the transfer of knowledge from western countries.

Second, the concern with 'decentralisation' of the military industrial complex led in 1988 to the transformation of the two big state enterprises (METALCHIM and ELECTRON) into 10 smaller firms. This reorganisation guaranteed more flexibility of production, trade and management for the goals of conversion.

Third, although the military industry has always received a large share of national resources (20% of total industrial research potential, and about 20% of the capital

P. Gummett et al. (eds.), Military R&D after the Cold War, 183–189.

investments in all Bulgarian industry), it is important to note that it has been always oriented to civil as well as defence activities. Over 40% of its production was destined for the civil market, including such items as agricultural machinery, medical instrumentation (in particular, laser instruments), a broad range of spare parts for the automobile industry, machine tool construction, manufacturing equipment, textiles machinery, etc. (Andreev, 1990).

The end of Cold War and the radical political and economic changes in Eastern Europe are the milestone in the new policy of conversion.

On the Governmental level, the first attempt to intervene in this field took the form of two Decrees adopted in 1990, the second of which instituted a Programme for Conversion. The most significant change of governmental attitude manifested in the Programme is the introduction of indirect state measures for regulation of conversion, in conformity with the more liberal approach now taken to firms. Most of the measures in question are concerned with tax-regulation and creation of preferential conditions for investment credits. State finance for maintenance of equipment capacity that is only used part-time, is guaranteed. Rather optimistically, the Programme also specified a target of converting 70% of military industrial production within 2-3 years.

The policy adopted in that initial phase has, however, suffered from the inertia of the past, namely:

- A one sided approach has led to the continuation of prevailing political considerations. The argument emphasised more the political and international implications of conversion, while the economic, social and technological analysis were insufficient.
- The short term perspective of the decisions led to a relatively slow dynamic of reforms. Thus, conversion was not based on realistic forecasts of the coming dramatic decrease of industrial production, lost markets, high unemployment rate, etc.
- Conceptually, the prospects for conversion were based on the 'state regulated market economy', presuming stable state support of the firms in the military industrial complex. With the beginning of monetary reforms in 1991, this expectation turned out to be unrealistic, and the state could not afford to stand by the firms in the military industry. In such a situation, the state was not prepared to take effective actions, and the adoption of the Programme was left to the firms.

The Programme for conversion as the expression of the Government's policy was criticised, even before all the shortcomings of the approach became visible (Dimitrov, 1990). In summary, the criticisms were addressed mainly to unsufficient preparatory work on the following subjects: marketing, world trends of development with respec to the products included in the production list of the firms, and the capacities of Bulgaria's technological infrastructure and its possible conversion, and the markets for raw materials. The financial and technological situation of the firms in military industry was also not assessed. Studies of the impact of conversion on demographic and social process in the respective regions were lacking. The participation of scientists in the elaboration of the Programme was merely symbolic (Chekimov, 1990).

As for the implementation of the Programme, the main difficulties arose with coordination between the two Ministries responsible for conversion: the Ministry of Industry, and the Ministry of Defence. According to the latest published statements of the Minister of Industry 'The scheme of hierarchical subordinations in the management of the enterprises in military industrial complex is unclear, that is why all initiatives and analytical developments were forgotten'. He also criticised the activity of the Interministerial commission for the military industrial complex for its misleading decisions, due to the division of interests between the two ministries (*Standart News*, 1994).

When analysing conversion policy at the governmental level one should also remember that in the period 1990-1994 there were five governments, and that the policy has changed according to the prevailing concept - which has been more or less liberal. The dramatic worsening of the financial situation of the firms and the growing volume of strike activity, beginning from early 1993, resulted in more catalytic approach from the state. Its latest outcome has been the decision of the Government to allow the utilisation for commercial purposes by private entrepreneurs of the equipment of the firms in military industry (*Standart News*, 1994).

CONTEXTUAL PROBLEMS OF CONVERSION

Contrary to the expectations of some Bulgarian economists (Dimitrov, 1990), conversion in Eastern Europe is much more difficult to deal with than in Western countries. To the broadly discussed common difficulties (see IEEE 1992), the transition to a market economy adds specific problems. In Bulgaria, the following issues in conversion have emerged from the public debates and views of experts in the field:

a) All countries engaged in conversion have encountered one particular difficulty. It is broadly recognised that military production has as its first consideration performance in combat situations, and not costs, whereas civilian products evolve within severe cost constraints. Integrating these constraints into engineering design may require both a culture shift and retraining, as well as a reorientation of an engineer's knowledge.
b) Until recently, the main concern of firms in the sector lay with technological problems, and not with management in the sense of having to seek contracts, deal with building contractors, marketing, etc., which matters were left to the Government. Production for civilian sector and markets is a new challenge for the managers, who are less well prepared to meet the requirements of the market. Lack of experience and skills are crucial in particular in the situation of lost traditional markets.
c) Different variants of conversion can be identified, including: complete reorientation of production; restructuring of the firm's profile; and diversification of civil production. But each of these variants requires big financial resources. Hence, while it is recognised that conversion can yield economic efficiency in the longer term, in the shorter term the costs of conversion are bigger. Due to the country's economic crisis, the financial situation of the firms in the military industry is difficult: they have huge debts to the banks, coupled with problems of unsold

stocks, incomplete production of certain items, and difficulties over certain raw materials. As analyses have shown, the increase of the share of civil production from 23% in 1988 to 38% in 1990, far from being the outcome of clear conversion, is due rather to a decrease of total industrial production by 25% for the same period.

d) The restructuring of production is combined with institutional reorganisation - unification etc., which has no technological or economic meaning and affects the flexibility of the respective firms and their effectiveness. This process used to be supervised by the Supervision Committee of the Ministry of Economics and Planning, until its abolition in 1991 and subsequent replacement by an Interministerial Commission coordinated by the Ministry of Industry. Both organisation, however, have been criticised for lack of strategy and a haphazard approach to the problems. Suspicions that group interests have influenced the decision-making process are also a matter of public concern.

e) The unique military business culture, with its specialised machinery and skilled work force, faces dramatic change with only limited opportunities for adaptation. The influence of these problems upon the social aspects of conversion is very strong, with unemployment levels among engineers, or salary cuts at a higher rate than those in the civil sector, having had a deteriorating effect on the whole economy of regions in which military industry is concentrated.

f) Enthusiasm for conversion has waned since 1992. Converted or diversified production was hitherto considered to be a possible means for coping with the deficit in consumer goods. The traditional monopoly position of the firms, and their access to the immense Soviet market, had a negative effect on the improvement of quality of production. Today, the economic environment has changed completely, and those firms now lack competitiveness on the open market against imported products of high quality. The hope that civil production could be efficient enough to compensate for reduced weapons production has disappeared. In consequence, the voices of those who seek to retake the old positions in the foreign markets for weapons have become stronger. For example, information in late 1994 from the Interministerial Council on questions of the military industrial complex and mobilisation readiness of the country disclosed that the whole of a special production batch (in particular automatic guns) had been sold due to trade agreements with Russia. Weapons exports for the first six months of 1994 surpassed the total sales in 1993. The stabilisation of the economic situation of the firms in military industry is a desirable precondition for conversion (Popova, 1994).

g) To the economic factors have to be added considerations of national security. They relate particularly to the situation in the Balkans, with the Bosnian conflict. Public opinion is affected by the possible extension of the conflict, which cannot be excluded from possible scenarios of its development. Thus, the issue of re-conversion, that is to combine conversion with maintaining standby industrial capability for possible production surges in periods of crisis, becomes more actual.

SCIENCE AND CONVERSION

Science in firms

One of the causes of the low efficiency of diversified production and of the prevailing approach to orient military firms towards a 'survival strategy' and to maintain production that does not correspond to the high technological capacities of the firms, is inefficient participation of the R&D potential of the firms in conversion. As main shortcomings of the research units, the following are mentioned in particular (Mirchev, 1990):

- the slow progress of research activity, with excessive project lifetimes;
- the lack of motivation to increase the intensity and efficiency of research, as it has no impact on salaries;
- the efficiency of R&D is not sufficient to sustain the R&D personnel, which is why some production units are being integrated with R&D units;
- delay in restructuring R&D units in order to increase personnel motivation according to the quality of results.

Science at the Universities

The economic approach, recognised in the special chair in 'Economics and management of the defence industry', is followed through close relations with firms in the military complex and the army, and through elaboration of the special programme for research about conversion submitted to the Ministry of Education and Science. The priorities in the programme in question are :

- research into the experience of other countries in practical realisation of conversion, its legislation, elaboration of econometric models of conversion in the transition to the market, and organisational and social problems of conversion;
- extension of the research problematic with inclusion of research on international security, economic stability and the environment.

It should be emphasised that in comparison with the 300 peace research institutes around the world, the potential for Bulgaria to deal with this issue is small and insufficient. In particular, Bulgaria lacks the capacity for interdisciplinary research on public opinion, and on the position of different political parties on conversion, disarmament research, the possibilities for political regulation of regional conflicts, and the development of strategies for collective security, etc.

The State Fund for 'Structural and technological policy', Ministry of Industry

As mentioned above, the Ministry of Indusry has special responsibility for coordination of participation by firms in a national competition for applied R&D support. This competition is organised, and the subsidy is distributed through, a special Fund at the Ministry. Since the Ministry is responsible for implementation of the Programme for Conversion, it has the capacity to set priorities that emerge from that programme for the applied R&D competition.

The figures for R&D financed in 1991 show:

Total number of contracted R&D projects:	104
of which:	
- civil industry	57 (55%)
- conversion projects	34 (33%)
- special themes and secret projects (including military)	13 (12%)

As can be seen, the number of conversion projects receiving funding is about three times higher than those related to military-oriented R&D. However, behind these numbers lie some serious problems, including:

- the shortage of candidates and lack of competition between firms;
- the low level of funding, which is reflected in the constantly diminishing number of applications (falling from 1875 in 1991 to 270 in 1993, with projects awarded similarly falling from 300 to 70).
- the short time for submission of proposals;
- the lack of really major projects, with the result that only small and incremental improvements become possible;
- the inertia from the past, with the still continuing atmosphere of secrecy among the departments of the Ministry, resulting in lack of coordination and joint efforts;
- lack of information about the state of the Fund.

In part as a response to this dispersed and chaotic research effort, a new Defence Research Center (DRC) was established in July 1994, on the initiative of 37 founders (firms, banks, universities and others). It will operate as a bridging institution, with a limited staff (now 5, rising eventually to not more 20). Following western practice (its director said that the 'model' was the RAND Corporation), the DRC was set up as an autonomous organisation, with its priorities to be set by a Research Council of 15 eminent scientists. Conversion of high technologies from military to civil industry is among the main priorities. Other fields of activity are: support for innovation by small businesses, development of environmentally friendly technologies, and international cooperation over appropriate projects.

CONCLUSION

Conversion is still a controversal issue in Bulgaria. So far it has not been approached as a complex process: political decisions are not supported by respective economic and social analysis. The context of economic reforms and regional conflicts are making the process even more difficult. The utilisation of the country's research and technological capacities for the completion of the process is inadequate. The lack of a long-run strategy for restructuring the R&D system in general impedes its mobilisation for the conversion of military industry. The emphasis that important national scientific organisations, like the Bulgarian Academy of Sciences, has placed upon fields considered to be 'less fundamental', such as defence technology, has had a deleterious impact on national R&D potential. More political stability and consensus among leading political actors is needed for the elaboration of a consistent and effective national policy for conversion.

REFERENCES

1. Andreev, S. (1990) *Konversiata i naukata* (Conversion and Science), Proceedings of the Fourth Conference on economic of defence and security, Sofia, pp. 65-69.
2. Chekimov, A. (1990) *Niakoi problemi na protcesa na konversia* (Some problems in conversion process), Sofia, pp. 175-83.
3. Dimitrov, D., et al. (eds) (1990) Conversia (Conversion), Higher Institute of Economics, Sofia.
4. Dimitrov, D. (1990) Razvitie I savremeni iziskvania kam konversiata na voenoto proizvodsto (Development and present requirements for conversion of military production), in Dimitrov [3], pp.3-17.
5. *IEEE Spectrum Special Issue* (1992) vol. 29, No. 12.
6. Mirchev, S., Vasmoznosti i perspektivi za issledvane na konversiata (Possibilities and perspectives for research on conversion), in *Konversiata* [1], pp.217-23.
7. Popova, E. (1994) Niama avtomati v voennite zavodi (There are no automatic guns in the military factories), 'DUMA' Newspaper, No. 169, 28 July.
8. *Standart news*, Number 736, 29.09.1994.

Observations On The Socio-Political And Cultural Context Of Military Conversion: A Polish View

LECH W. ZACHER

Department of Political Science
University of Maria Curie-Sklodowska
Lublin, Poland

THE MILITARY AND ECONOMIC CONTEXT

The development and procurement of armaments has been an important motive factor in R&D and technological development, and not only in Eastern and Central Europe. In Poland it was in practice driven not so much by the Cold War directly as by pressure from the former Soviet Union, demanding that Poland contribute its share to the Warsaw Pact and COMECON. The result, however, was that militarily oriented research and production became quite important, and constituted a relatively modern and well organised sector of the economy which, moreover, was a successful exporter.

The collapse of Communism had three consequences in this domain: the destruction of the so-called socialist planned economy; the rupture of military (and other) relations with what became the Commonwealth of Independent States (CIS) and the other East European countries; and the deep economic crisis which ensued, with its associated fall in production, lack of demand, rising unemployment, and rapid downsizing of research. In addition, some new constraints appeared, notably the reduction of arms imposed by the treaty on Conventional Forces in Europe, and also some international restrictions on arms trade (some evidently provoked by Western competitors).

These factors threw into disarray what had previously been one of the biggest armies in Europe, together with its armaments supply system and supporting research, there being no money even for buying spare parts from the CIS, from which the armaments were mostly imported or licensed. In consequence, the size of the Polish army was reduced by almost a half and still remained poor (without money for spare parts, gasoline, training and manoeuvres). Moreover, many high ranking officers (educated as a rule in the Soviet military academies) left the army or retired.

P. Gummett et al. (eds.), Military R&D after the Cold War, 191–198.

It was the economic crisis and the transformations in the political system, rather than deliberate strategies for conversion of military R&D, technology transfer and military production and trade, which were the dominating factors of change. Instead of conversion, Poland simply saw a sharp reduction in national investement in R&D (from 2.5 per cent of GNP in the 1970s to 0.5 per cent in the 1990s), including military R&D. There were no newly emerging research based companies. It was also difficult to make military research and production commercial since the military and civilian sectors were largely isolated from each other. In addition, the links with the former Warsaw Pact partners were broken.

The predominant constraint was lack of investment. Moreover, the neoliberal economic model of economy introduced in 1990 excluded science, technology and industrial policy as ideologically inappropriate for the development of a free market economy. So rational choices and deliberate strategies were not encouraged by this situation. The consequence, therefore, was that Poland experienced liquidation of potential rather than conversion.

In addition, with the changes in the role of the state and its agencies after the abandonment of central planning, and the introduction of new, less direct methods and means of influence, policies for economic stimulation and promotion were not really in evidence. Privatisation took place only slowly and to a limited extent, and the military sector was in any case excluded, being regarded as a 'protected area' important for national security. There were debates, strikes and fear of the possible danger from former Soviet neighbours like Ukraine and Russia which had large armies, nuclear weapons and political instability. Only in 1994 did the final remnants of Soviet troops left Poland (leaving immense environmental devastation of vast areas, which added to the economic challenges). Moreover, questions arose over the need for relocation of Poland's own troops and bases, since previously the Polish units had been oriented towards the Western war theatre. This relocation problem, together with the extremely expensive building of new infrastructure for army units in Eastern Poland, is likely to remain a significant burden for many years.

The Polish military industrial sector consists of 31 firms (26 state-owned). It meets about 90% of the needs of the army, at the same time obviating expensive imports. It is a modern branch of the economy, influencing other branches (e.g. aviation industry, electronics). It is not harmful to the environment. Its products are quite competitive (as to technological level and price) in the international market, although competition is tough, and account has to be taken of UN embargoes on selling weapons to certain countries.

The technological basis of this sector (principally machine guns, tanks etc.) remains production under license from Russia. Restructuring has, however, begun, with the aim of adjusting the size of the productive capacity to the needs implied by the new Polish defence doctrine. It will also set the foundation for the functioning of this industry in the market economy, and will lead to conversion in the two senses of curtailing redundant capacities (built in excess in the 1980s), or converting them for civilian use.

The Government document 'Industrial Policy Objectives' (approved on September 14, 1993) states:

The main objectives of the restructuring of the defence industry sector are:

- implementation of the ownership transformation programme (according to the official decision of the Council of Ministers of 19 May, 1992) into companies 100% owned by the State Treasury or with a majority, controlling interest, while at the same time having the Ministry of Industry and Trade exercise control over the transformations;
- reduction of cooperation ties to a minimum to reduce production costs;
- retooling part of military production to civilian use;
- preservation of production capacity of the industry to maintain the independent status of the country.

('Industrial Policy Objectives', Ministry of Industry and Trade, Warsaw, September 1993, p. 14).

It is also assumed that financial and technological cooperation with foreign defence industries will be developed. Moreover some foreign credits will be used to change the production profile. Rationalisation of employment will be continued. Refunding the losses connected with embargoes of exports to Iraq and former Yugoslavia and due to the changed relationship with the CIS will be assured by the State.

Hence it is clear that there are other goals with at least the same priority as conversion. These include strengthening military research (e.g. in the Military Academy of Technology, the National Defence Academy, or in some industrial or Polish Academy of Sciences units) and industry (several military production factories), and also the arms export trade. In addition, the downsized army is to be better equipped technologically (e.g., computers, telecommunications etc.), and better organised and trained (through more education and more expensive training).

Paradoxically what is expected by the President, the Parliament, the party leaders and publicists is a revitalisation of the military sector. There are constant public rumours that the army is too small and weak (some say: 'it is weak so it should be bigger'). The idea of curtailing the army's size, yet making its technologically and organisationally more advanced and effective, is usually criticised as 'unpatriotic' or 'a surrender'. Some nationalistic political activists (there are more than 265 parties officially functioning in Poland) and publicists (mostly extreme right wing) suggest that Poland should be alert to its historical enemies - its neighbors to the East and West - and so argue that the Polish army should be as strong as possible and oriented against Ukraine, Russia, Belarus; others, however, alluding to the historical record of the past 1000 years, say that it is Germany which has been the greater military problem. In any event, Polish history is dramatically marked by conflicts with the Teutons and Prussia, then the division of Poland by Russia, Prussia and Austria in the 18th century, followed by the Napoleonic wars, then two world wars, and the German occupation, with the Warsaw uprising in 1944 and Auschwitz remaining still very vivid symbols. One should add to this list the Ribbentrop-Molotov Pact, the invasion of the Soviet Union in September 17, 1939, then the installation of the new regime in 1944-45 by the Soviet Army, liberating Poland from the Nazis but staying themselves until 1994. The Yalta Treaty reflected Soviet and Western interests, not Polish ones.

CULTURAL AND HISTORICAL FACTORS

A significant feature of the Polish past and present is the prominent role of the army, politically, socially and culturally. The majority of Poland's historical heroes wore military uniforms, and not only kings and princes. There is a long list to mention, e.g. prince Poniatowski, the Napoleonic marshall; Kosciuszko, also a hero of America (but a Russian czar's general); general Dabrowski, active in the Paris Commune; general Bem fighting for the Hungarian revolution in 1848; marshall Pilsudski (a former Austrian officer), first as the great national hero reconstructing the sovereign Polish state after 1918, then as the dictator dissolving the Parliament in 1926; general Anders, who escaped with the Polish army from the Soviet Union; general Sikorski, head of the Polish government in exile (London); and many others. Some were negative heroes, like commissar Dzierzynski during the October Revolution in Russia; general Swierczewski, Soviet intelligence officer of Polish blood and hero of the Spanish Civil War (described by Hemingway); marshall Rokossowski (partly of Polish origin), an extremely talented strategist; not to mention general Jaruzelski, the author of martial law in 1981; and colonel Kuklinski, his close collaborator who was spying for the CIA at the same time.

Polish history is full of such cases, many ambivalent, not to say negative. In other countries national heroes tend to be philosophers, writers, artists. But Polish literature popularised and built-up the prestige of army, officer, soldier, as well as partisans and rebels. For the gentry class, to be an officer was a normal privilege and an honour, while for the underprivileged, military service was a chance for social upgrading. For the poor there were two ways to advance: the clergy or the army. The patriotic values ('to die for motherland') were always highly appreciated. The image of the army was positive even under Communist rule. President Lech Walesa, the Nobel Peace Prize Winner, likes to show up in battledress during manoeuvres (in contrast to, say, Kohl, Mitterrand or Clinton) and does not accept the idea of a civilian head of the Ministry of Defence.

Poland's dramatic, and even tragic, history shaped the intellectual and political mentality of the people and the elites. Polish society is history-oriented, not future-oriented. Such is its mentality and social consciousness and aspirations, such is Polish education and culture. Polish history has been one of wars and resistance, of marshalls, generals, soldiers - mostly spectacular heroes, often international. So the nation learned down the centuries how to fight, resist, protest, and die for its ideals. It is no accident that this outlook was not accompanied by social striving for work, wealth, excellence, stabilisation, and other constructive, positivistic and 'organic' values which historically have been the motivations underlying the emergence of capitalism in Europe (See Max Weber and his reflections on the role of Protestant ethics). For there was no middle class to fulfill such a social role.

In the face of such traditions, reinforced by the media, there is no political advantage to be gained from reducing the army, diminishing its role, and making it politically neutral. This conclusion gains further strength from an appreciation of the fact that, psychologically speaking, Poles have a betrayal complex: betrayal by Napoleon; betrayal by the Allies during the Warsaw uprising in 1944 and during the Yalta negotiations about borders, compounded by the fact that the Americans knew about Auschwitz and Katyn but said nothing, just as in 1981 they failed to pass on to 'Solidarity' the information that martial law was going to be imposed. All this has made the Poles sceptical about allies. In addition, there other ally of the Second World War, the Soviets, liberated Poland but then stayed there, installing with the help of the Polish Communists a new regime.

Against such a background, Poles are sceptical about their security possibilities. Should they choose Germany and NATO, or Russia, perhaps with Ukraine, or instead neutrality? Historically, there have always been two political orientations - pro-Russian and pro-Western. Hence, Polish scepticism about alliances, and their lack of idealism about international politics is deep-rooted. Perhaps, they say, it is better to have own strong army? There are also some dreams of being a superpower (as in the 16th century), at least on a regional basis. In addition, some (often from military circles) argue that a strong, large and modern army is a conditio sine qua non for joining NATO and having a good position within it.

THE ARMY AND SOCIAL MODERNISATION

The significance of cultural factors that, in the Polish case, are antagonistic to demilitarisation and conversion can be emphasised by noting the important role of the army in social modernisation. It is not fashionable in Poland today to recall that even until the Second World War the country was mostly agricultural (more than 70% of people were in the countryside) with a feudal-peasant system (not independent farmers), big landlords, high unemployment and large-scale illiteracy. That is why, before and after the war, the army was a place, for young village men, of education, culture, social life and discipline, in short, of modernisation. Conscript soldiers learned basic principles of hygiene, good behaviour and cooperation, together with technological skills (driving, operating guns, planes, tanks etc.). The same was also true in other Eastern and Central European Countries (and this pattern is also typical for the Less Developed Countries). The point for current discussion of demilitarisation, however, is that this modernisation role of military structures, training and behaviour remains valid today. It raises the question, how would it be substituted for?

Moreover, the army has long been a place for making a career (albeit on different levels, of course, and including, we should not overlook, the political level), as well as being relatively well paid, abd offering a desirable and comfortable lifestyle for many. Again, then, the question arises of the degree of conformity betweeb such values, aspirations and attitudes with the new set of values that is emerging with the political and economic transformations and their emphasis upon a free market, entrepreneurship and competition, supply-orientation, flexibility, pluralism and democracy, not to mention the disappearance of military enemy.

MOVES TOWARD CIVIL SOCIETY

It is interesting that institutions such as the army and the Catholic Church are so readily accepted in Poland. Defectors from the army are put into prison. And, indeed, there are today strong links between Church and army, the latter having enjoyed an upsurge in Catholic chaplains recently. Generals and high ranking officers have started to go to Church (six former Communist generals have remarried in Church). Recently one general, educated in Moscow, prepared a controversial Catholic catechism (introducing obligatory participation 'by order' in holy mass). The ideas of downsizing the army to, perhaps, 100,000 persons, and making it no longer conscript but fully professional, are criticised as unpatriotic, while discussion of the military budget is almost a taboo, even in political discussion and Parliamentary debates.

Even today, in public opinion polls the army emerges in first place (higher than Church, Parliament, president, etc.) in terms of social standing and prestige. People are proud of the army. During the Warsaw Pact intervention in Czechoslovakia in 1968, many Polish officers and soldiers were proud to be superior over the Czechoslovak army.

George Soros, speaking in 1994 before the US Congress about 'Partnership for Peace', recommended setting up 'Partnership for Security', meaning a new Marshall Plan for Central and Eastern Europe. He argued that the post-Communist societies tend not to strive for the 'open society' (or civil society) idea of democracy, but look instead towards their history for a model of national or ethnical identity. If this is correct, it would seem that the path towards a civil society in Poland, and elsewhere in Eastern and Central Europe, will be long, and not easy. This will not be because of any return to communism, or the mediocrity of the political class, but to a great extent because of the historical societal orientation, which leads naturally towards traditions that are conservative, of peasant origin, politically right-wing, and with a quite fundamentalistic Catholic Church hierarchy.

POLAND AND EUROPE

In public (press, radio, TV) debates, one can notice some scepticism and reluctance over the unification of Europe. This is not only a matter of 'euroscepticism' but also a conviction that internal transformations are the most important one.

Moreover, despite the many western political promises (or political speeches that were interpreted as promises) of aid and cooperation during the fight against Communism, what actually happened in the end was a programme of 'shock therapy' (see the chapter by Redfern, this volume) directed by the World Bank and IMF. This experience has made people afraid of inflowing foreign capital (causing increased unemployment because of competitive superiority). They are also afraid of being 'colonised' (more than half the Polish press having been bought out by foreign owners).

Joining the EU and NATO may mean more competition with much stronger partners. It may damage not only Polish production, but R&D as well, and be harmful for foreign trade. If membership of the NATO requires conforming to NATO equipment standards, it will also entail expensive imports of armaments and spare parts, dependence on suppliers for servicing and research, and acceptance of the EU's and NATO's post-COCOM restrictions on trade with third parties.

Some of these fears are no doubt exaggerated or even unjustified. However, pro-NATO political propaganda makes people suspicious. When Poland signed the association agreement with the EU, it was done without public debate, almost in secrecy. Poles are simply idiosyncratic about foreign domination (for historical and psychological reasons). To overcome these prejudices, the NATO countries' political overtures should be more sensitive, and should be cooperation-oriented, not imperial or colonial. In addition, the 'partnership for peace' could be reinforced by a 'partnership for development'. If not, its advantages will be confined to the political, ideological, strategic, and geopolitical planes, but will not reach the economic, social and cultural levels.

It is desperate and cynical to argue that it is better to be at the periphery of rich Western Europe than at the periphery of poor (and somewhat dangerous because unstable) Eastern Europe. Poles are afraid of the CIS, but they also fear 'cold peace' with nuclear Eastern border neighbours. Strategies ought therefore to be formulated and implemented on the international scale to solve the problems of the post Cold War era.

These include the problems of restructuring military R&D, production and trade, which are shaping the new European and world order. In this process, we may ask whether interests, advantages and chance are equally distributed? Since conversion does not mean total disarmament, there remains a large international arms market in which one may gain a 'peace dividend' by competing successfully for new customers for surplus weapons. So-called peace operations or humanitarian interventions (e.g., Bosnia, Somalia, Haiti, Rwanda) create new markets. Poland not long ago was a serious producer and trader of armaments, but because of the economic crisis and the geographical reorientation of trade, this is no longer the case. Is this advantageous for Poland? Some compensatory mechanisms and means would perhaps be encouraging and helpful to the conversion processes. It is not the case that Poland can easily make a surplus from conversion like richer countries (e.g., Austria, Sweden, USA). The views of the richer and stronger western partners should therefore be resisted, if we are to avoid one-sided partnerships.

CONCLUSION

The obstacles to demilitarisation and defence conversion are not only economic and political, but also historical, psychological, cultural and social. Perhaps they are not all rationally justifiable, but nevertheless they exist. This fact is important for policy making, both internal (e.g. science and technology policy, industrial policy) and external (foreign, especially toward the NATO). NATO policy toward Poland and other Eastern and Central European countries should itself take into account the full range of obstacles identified above.

These obstacles spring from a mentality formed by the historic experience of wars, occupations, uprisings and dependency, with high public acceptance of a large army, strong military industrial sector and extensive weapons trade. They are reinforced by continued misgivings about security and allies, not least the fear of unstable, powerful, nuclear-armed, neighbours to the East. Sovereignty and national security, after all, remain the highest values. Poland has had, in addition, to cope with an unprecedented economic crisis, compounded by the lack of any economic surplus. Even the vast territories, barracks, roads etc., left behind by the departing Soviet troops were not an asset because of the immense environmental damage and deliberate devastation to which they had been subjected.

The modernisation role of the military sector (R&D, industrial base, infrastructure) and the army (education, vocational training, organisation and discipline, technological culture etc.) is still important in a country in which modernisation during the last few centuries has been rather 'shallow'. The transfer of military technologies and export of weapons continues to be desirable on economic grounds (even if sometimes criticised on moral grounds). In Poland, to give up military technological development is viewed as giving up high technology aspirations.

The army and the military industrial sector are job creators. More than this, however, they offer prestigious individual careers and lifestyles, and assure good social and economic status. They are an integral part of Polish society and politics, with all that that implies. Against such a background, the interest of the people lies in political transformations and economic conditions and promises, not in demilitarization and conversion. The army is still perceived as a pillar of the state, and the guardian of order, sovereignty and security.

Index

MIX
Papier aus verantwortungsvollen Quellen
Paper from responsible sources
FSC® C105338
FSC
www.fsc.org

If you have any concerns about our products,
you can contact us on
ProductSafety@springernature.com

In case Publisher is established outside the EU,
the EU authorized representative is:
Springer Nature Customer Service Center GmbH
Europaplatz 3, 69115 Heidelberg, Germany

Printed by Libri Plureos GmbH
in Hamburg, Germany